Writer's Online Marketplace

HOW & WHERE TO GET PUBLISHED ONLINE

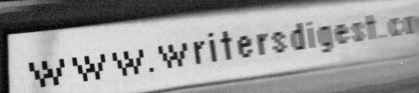

Writer's Online Marketplace

HOW & WHERE TO GET PUBLISHED ONLINE

Debbie Ridpath Ohi

WRITER'S DIGEST BOOKS
CINCINNATI, OHIO
www.writersdigestbooks.com

Writer's Online Marketplace. Copyright © 2001 by Writer's Digest Books. Manufactured in the United States of America. All rights reserved. No part of this book may be reproduced in any form or by any electronic or mechanical means including information storage and retrieval systems without permission in writing from the publisher, except by a reviewer, who may quote brief passages in a review. Published by Writer's Digest Books, an imprint of F&W Publications, Inc., 1507 Dana Avenue, Cincinnati, Ohio 45207. (800) 289-0963. First edition.

Visit our Web site at www.writersdigest.com for information on more resources for writers.

To receive a free weekly E-mail newsletter delivering tips and updates about writing and about Writer's Digest products, send an E-mail with the message "Subscribe Newsletter" in the body of the message to newsletter-request@writersdigest.com, or register directly at our Web site at www.writersdigest.com.

05   04   03   02   01   5   4   3   2   1

Library of Congress Cataloging-in-Publication Data

Ohi, Debbie Ridpath
    Writer's online marketplace / by Debbie Ridpath Ohi.
        p.   cm.
    Includes bibliographical references and index.
    ISBN 1-58297-016-5 (pbk.: alk. paper)
        1. Authorship—Marketing. 2. Electronic publishing. 3. Authorship—Computer network resources. 4. Internet. I. Title.

    PN161.O45   2001
    070.5'2—dc21   00-049423
                                                                                                    CIP

Edited by Dave Borcherding and Michelle Howry
Designed by Sandy Kent
Cover design by Beckmeyer Design
Production coordinated by Mark Griffin

Dedication

This book would not have been possible without the feedback and suggestions from the hundreds of online writers and editors who sent in tips and suggestions in response to my questionnaires in *Inklings* and on Inkspot.

Many thanks also to Angela Adair-Hoy, Moira Allen, Karen Asp, David Borcherding, Leta Nolan-Childers, Marcella Conte, Tracy Cooper-Posey, Jan Edwards, Jamie Engel, John Feldcamp, Amanda Foubister, Doug Gardner, Paula Guran, Jack Heffron, John Hewitt, Brian A. Hopkins, Crawford Kilian, Judy Kirkpatrick, Kathie Meyer, Marilyn Nesbitt, Dana Nourie, Steve Outing, Chris Pirillio, Nancy Price, M.J. Rose, Cathy Rutland, David Saperstein, Kate Saundby, Shane Stacks, Sal Towse, Bev Walton-Porter, Lee Wardlaw, Helen Waters, Pamela Wilfinger, Marcia Yudkin, and those who attended my workshops at the Surrey Writer's Conference for their valuable input and support.

And finally, a very special thanks to my husband Jeff for his technical expertise and personal support during the writing of this book.

Debbie Ridpath Ohi
Inkspot: Resource and Community For Writers
www.inkspot.com

About the Author

Debbie Ridpath Ohi is the founder and editor-in-chief of Inkspot (www.inkspot .com), an award-winning online resource and community for writers since 1995. Debbie spends her time in Toronto, where she lives with her husband Jeff, and Philadelphia, where she works for Xlibris (www.xlibris.com).

She has set up a page with updates about *Writer's Online Marketplace* at www .electricpenguin.com/wom/.

Table of Contents

Introduction

Ten years ago, the Internet was familiar only to the academic world. Today, the Internet is a household word in North America; it's nearly impossible to flip through a magazine or watch television without seeing a Web site address. As the computer industry grows, so does the number of computers in homes and offices. According to a recent study, nearly sixty-five million American adults used the Internet on a regular basis in 1999, and this number is growing rapidly.

The Internet offers a wealth of valuable resources and opportunities for writers. I've been interested in online writing resources since 1995, when I created my Web site, Inkspot (www.inkspot.com). Back then, there was very little on the Web for writers and few paying markets. As the Internet audience grew, however, so did the interest of the commercial sector.

Via Inkspot, I surveyed hundreds of writers and editors about their experiences and opinions writing for the online marketplace. Their professional experience ran from casual e-mail users to those who made a full-time living from their online writing or editing.

What Are Some Advantages Writing for the Online Marketplace?

Lower overhead, saved time. With so many market guidelines available online (and editors who accept queries and submissions by e-mail), the savings on postage, paper, and time wasted in lines at the post office add up. In response to my survey, several writers reported that the first time they made "paper contact" during the online submission process was upon receipt of their checks in the mail.

"Writers who don't have at least e-mail will soon be out of step in the writing/ publishing world," says freelance writer Mary Emma Allen. "This is not to say that print media is a dinosaur . . . but the communications between writer, editor, and publisher is so much easier and faster than the traditional way. Not having e-mail for sending your manuscripts soon will be like sending a handwritten instead of typed manuscript a few years ago."

Less competition. Because the popularity of the Internet is a relatively new phenomenon, there are fewer writers competing for markets. Online publications are also more open to working with new writers. Publishing online can help writers accumulate clips. "The Internet has opened a wide number of markets to me that helped me springboard my career as a beginning writer," says writer Lain Chroust Ehmann. "It allowed me access to a number of smaller markets that gave me experience and exposure."

"Shelf life." If you sell an article to a print publication, its shelf life is usually a few months at most. On the Internet, your article can be online for much longer since publications often keep archives available.

Exposure. Another advantage of publishing online is potential exposure. A regular print publication's circulation is restricted to the number of copies printed, which is limited by the publication's budget. An online publication has a much larger potential audience; anyone around the world with Internet access (and fluency in the publication's language) can theoretically access the content.

"Thousands of people around the world have read interviews with me that have appeared in online newsletters and Web sites," says Lee Wardlaw, a children's author. "This has led to invitations to speak at conferences, workshops, and schools, as well as to write articles for other publications. In addition, I've written articles about the juvenile market that have been published online. Several writer's clubs and organizations, such as regional chapters of the Society of Children's Book Writers and Illustrators (SCBWI), have requested reprint rights for these pieces for conference hand-outs, newsletters, and magazines."

Shorter turnaround time. Many online writers report a shorter response time when making queries and submissions, as well as shorter editorial lead time. Diana Estigarribia says, "Once I have an assignment, I have to get it in the next day. In that way, it's very much like newspaper writing—report the story, write it, file it, it goes up on the site."

No geographic boundaries. Writers working with overseas markets through traditional channels worry about time differences, long-distance phone calls, postage hassles, and slow surface mail. Kristen McQuillin has been working as a freelancer in three different countries and four cities. "The only thing stable in my life is my e-mail address!" says Kristen. "Fortunately, that's usually all I need."

Interaction with readers. "The online market offers much more direct response from readers," says Crawford Kilian, author of *Writing for the Web* (International

Self-Counsel Press). "A magazine article may generate a few letters to the editor a month or two later; an online article may trigger responses within minutes of its appearance. Online writing therefore tends to turn into dialogue."

Are There Disadvantages?

Because it's possible to post a Web page with relatively little effort and cost, almost anyone can get his work into a public forum and be "published." As a result, the quality of the writing online varies greatly. Also, many writers are creating online publications with little or no editing experience.

The main complaint of the online writers I surveyed was about payment. In general, online markets don't pay as well as print publications, though this trend is gradually changing. Ken Jenks, an online publisher, says this is a "chicken and egg" problem. "The reason it doesn't pay as well is because there aren't as many paying customers online. The ad revenue and the paying customers go where the good work is. The good work goes where the money is."

The Internet: A Writer's Gold Mine

As the popularity of the Internet grows, however, so do the number of paying markets and types of opportunities for writers. More well-funded publications and corporate entities are establishing a presence on the Internet, and many need writers to create online content.

This is a new frontier for writers; the parameters and rules are still developing. Surprisingly, many writers make only minimal use of the rich potential of the Internet, using e-mail for some correspondence and the occasional Web surfing.

"I don't have time for learning about the Internet," some of these writers say. "I should be writing instead." And of course they have a point (writers write, after all), but they may not realize that taking a bit of time to become more familiar with the tools, resources, and opportunities available on the Net could help save much time and effort in the long run. The analogy is like buying a top-of-the-line Swiss Army knife and then only using the toothpick. Even if you don't plan on using every attachment, it's always worth *knowing* what's available; chances are good that one of the tools will come in handy eventually.

Web sites move and disappear all the time, so it's possible that some of the URLs mentioned in this book could be inaccessible by the time you read this. If you find a site is no longer at a URL, try using a search engine to track down its new location.

I will also list updates and corrections at my Web site for writers, Inkspot (www.inkspot.com). If you have any comments or suggestions, please send them to me at ohi@inkspot.com.

—Debbie Ridpath Ohi

CHAPTER ONE

The Basics

IN MANY WAYS, the process of writing and submitting to online markets is the same as writing and submitting to regular print markets. Overall, always strive to be as professional in your correspondence and conduct as you would in any interactions with regular print publications.

Before venturing into e-publishing, writers should familiarize themselves with the subtle (and not-so-subtle) differences in working in the online marketplace. This chapter will cover the e-mail and "netiquette" basics, tips on how to query and submit to an online market, and differences in writing style between online and print publications. Crawford Kilian's article, "Chunk It or Archive It?" (page 8), focuses on one of the most important style aspects of writing for the Web.

E-mail Basics

Make sure you are thoroughly familiar with the basics of e-mail etiquette before you begin using it as a means of business communication. Here are some basic guidelines:

Don't type in all uppercase. This is almost an e-mail gaffe cliché now, but I still see it happen on a regular basis. Capitalized words signify "yelling" in e-mail, and editors hate being yelled at.

Use a meaningful subject header. This allows the editor to get an idea of the contents of your message before even opening it. It also helps differentiate your message from junk mail. "Hi" is not a meaningful subject header. Neither is a blank subject header.

Proofread your message before sending it. Check your e-mail for spelling and grammatical mistakes, including the spelling of the editor's name. Many mailing programs come with a built-in spellchecker. This leads to the next important tip—

Learn how to use your e-mail program. Sounds obvious, but many writers learn only the bare minimum necessary to send and receive messages. It's worth investing an hour or two in thoroughly exploring the nooks and crannies of your e-mail program. You may find features and shortcuts that will end up saving you more time in the future.

"Sign" your message. Out of courtesy, include your name at the end of the message as in a regular letter; don't assume that the editor will find it in the header of your e-mail.

Avoid fancy formatting. Unless you're positive that the recipient of your message has a similar mail program, you're better off avoiding the use of special formatting like italicized or bold characters, colors, or different font sizes.

Other Resource:

E-mail Etiquette
www.uwinnipeg.ca/~tss/tss/policy/etiquette.html
By David Harris, Pegasus Mail creator.

Style Basics for Online Writing

The key rule is to be as professional in your online communication as you would in any other business-related interaction.

"Know your craft!" advises online writer Tracy Cooper-Posey. "Just because it's online doesn't mean you can cut corners or get away with less than crisply tailored prose. You must be even more tightly focused and succinct to suit the shorter attention span of Web surfers."

Writing for online publications does demand a different type of writing style than for regular print publications. If you're new to the Internet, I strongly advise you to familiarize yourself with online content before creating your own.

The best way to do this is to find a few online publications that interest you. Read back issues, read the editorial columns and you'll gradually begin to pick up the particular style of the publication, as well as the focus. Some publications also include style guides with their submission guidelines.

A few style issues to consider when writing for the online market:

URLs/Links. Many editors encourage the use of links in text documents. Some prefer the name of the link to be followed by the actual URL in parentheses. Others may want the URL underlined in an MS Word file, with a footnote. Your safest bet is to check the publication's style sheet or submission guidelines.

Pacing. In general, pacing tends to be quicker in an online publication. "An online publication requires a different pacing for your story than print publications do," says Ken Jenks. "It's much more crucial to rivet the reader's attention when the whole Web is just a click away. You can't let interest flag or let the pacing droop for a couple of slow chapters—you'll lose your reader fast."

Length. Pieces tend to be shorter, at least the amount of text appearing on a Web page. Diana Estigarribia suggests, "Write short for the Web. I have to keep things down to 500 words at most, and owing to my audience for scifi.ign.com, I must stick to the lingo of sci-fi fans, so it's a very casual, writer-as-friend tone."

Some online publications, however, may be more likely to buy a lengthy piece than print publications. A Web magazine isn't as likely to be concerned about space as a regular magazine since the e-zine doesn't have to worry about the extra printing and paper costs.

Conversational style. In general, online material tends to be more casual than offline. Avoid flowery prose and overly stiff language. On the other hand, don't go overboard the other way and get sloppy. Again, study the publication carefully to see what type of style it prefers.

Break information up into shorter pieces. Online information is presented in shorter chunks than print publications. Reading text on a computer screen is a different experience than reading printed text. Eyestrain becomes more of a problem, as does comfort while reading. Rather than presenting information in a lengthy block, it's better to insert blank lines to break up paragraphs (instead of just indenting text) and include headings and subheadings. For more tips related to this topic, see Crawford Kilian's article, "Chunk It or Archive It?" below.

Other Resources:

Contentious

www.contentious.com

The Web zine for writers, editors, and others who create content for online media.

Writing for the Web

By Crawford Kilian (International Self-Counsel Press, 2000).

www.capcollege.bc.ca/magic/cmns/crofpers.html

CHUNK IT OR ARCHIVE IT?

by Crawford Kilian

Crawford Kilian is the author of twenty books, most recently *Writing for the Web* (International Self-Counsel Press). He teaches Web writing and other courses at Capilano College in North Vancouver, British Columbia, Canada.

When you write for a Web site, you're not just slapping a poster up on a new kind of wall. The Web is a very different medium from print on paper, and it requires a different kind of writing.

Low-resolution computer monitors slow down reading speed by up to 25 percent. Most Web surfers hate to scroll. Most Web browsers' default font is something unreadable like 12-point Times, and any font, if it fills up the screen without so much as a paragraph indentation, is unreadable.

Web designer Jeffrey Zeldman says we now have three audiences on the Web:

- Viewers, who are looking for visual stimulation, eye candy, and who don't want very much text at all.
- Users, who want to take bits of information from the Web for their own purposes—a report, a term paper, an e-mail.
- Readers, who are actually willing to sit and scroll through very long texts— or even print them out.

Web writers' audiences are obviously the users and the readers. But they need very different kinds of texts.

Let's take the users first. They come to your site looking for specific information, and they don't want to spend too long finding it. Maybe it's a recipe for chicken vindaloo, or the firearms homicide rate for Denmark, or the specs for your company's high-tech snowblower. Ideally, the information should come in a "chunk"—a single screen of text, probably not more than 100 words and maybe much less. The user can read it, copy it if desired, and surf on to another chunk.

The chunk seems to be the basic unit of discourse for a great many Web users. It provides concise information that can stand on its own without reference to other chunks. Maybe it's part of a sequence, like individual biographies of the Seven Dwarfs, but it doesn't have to be. It's just a hundred words or so about a particular subject, preferably broken into two or three short paragraphs for easier skimming.

The archive, by contrast, is really for readers. They will tolerate almost any amount of scrolling (especially if you provide internal links that let them jump around inside a long text). If the scrolling gets dull even for them, they'll print out your whole text and read it on paper—as you originally meant it to be read.

So here you are, with sample chapters from your novel in progress, some 2,000-word articles, your company's annual report, and all kinds of other print documents that you want to put up on your Web site. Which documents should you archive, and which should you break up into chunks?

Most of them probably ought to be archives, but some may actually improve as chunked documents. Here's why. A novel chapter or a print article is probably organized by a narrative or argumentative structure. Narrative describes events in chronological order. Argument makes an assertion, brings in supporting evidence, and comes to a conclusion.

Narrative and argument usually require quite a lot of text to reach their destinations. Any given hundred words isn't likely to make much sense by itself. In my Web writing course I once chopped up one of my own narrative articles into chunks. It worked, sort of, but not well.

A third kind of text structure works far better in chunks: categorical organization. A print text on "Six Must-Visit Places in Mexico" or "Five Habits of Successful Web writers" is a natural for chunking. In your print version you may have listed the six must-visit places in alphabetical order or from north to south; on a Web site you can do the same thing, but your readers can click through in any sequence they choose.

So if you have print text that easily breaks apart into segments or categories, it may work better in chunks than in a scrolling archive.

Whether you're chunking or archiving, remember that this is a medium hostile to users and readers alike. If the monitor slows your readers down by 25 percent, your text should be at least 25 percent shorter than its paper version. Web-usability gurus like Jakob Nielsen argue that cutting by 50 percent is even better, and I ask my Web writing students to do just that—cut their first essay in half and hand in the result as their second essay. They tell me it's a powerful learning experience.

What if you have an archive document that's 2,000 words long? Cut it to 1,000 words, if only to see if it still hangs together at that length. If it does, put the short version up on your site. Even the most patient readers aren't going to live forever, so why demand more of their time than you absolutely need?

When you're writing chunks in first draft, though, write long. Then cut your 175-word chunk to 80, and enjoy the luxury of having 20 more words to give your reader if you like.

Whether you're chunking or archiving, make every word, every phrase fight for its life before you put it up on your site. If nothing else, that will ensure that every word and every phrase really will be alive on the screen.

FROM WRITER TO CONTENT PROVIDER: SKILLS YOU NEED

by Marcia Yudkin

Marcia Yudkin (marcia@yudkin.com) is the author of *Writing Articles About the World Around You* (Writer's Digest Books), *Six Steps to Free Publicity* (Plume/ Penguin), and seven other books, as well as hundreds of magazine articles. She has written for several Web sites and has posted many of her articles on writing and getting published at www.yudkin.com/publish.htm.

"Content provider" represents much more than just a newfangled term for "freelance writer." This phrase, which you'll encounter from cutting-edge Web entrepreneurs, evokes someone who understands exactly how the Internet environment differs from publishing on paper and who has the skills necessary to deliver words in a structure, form, and style that works online.

What's Different About the Net

Reading transpires differently online, and the business context of a Web site may diverge significantly from that of a print magazine. These characteristics have implications for writers.

As the popular term "surfing" implies, hardly anyone settles down in front of the computer for a long, leisurely reading session. Instead, they scan, they skim, they dip in here and there until with another click of the mouse they take their hair-trigger attention spans elsewhere.

Even if they did hope for a long, leisurely read, technology overrides their desire. Reading words on a computer screen takes more effort than reading the same text on paper. People tire faster online. And rarely are they reading online while lounging in a comfortable chair, in bed, on the beach, or in the bath, in contrast to readers of magazines.

You must recognize too that the Net is a fiercely competitive information environment, where new stuff becomes available 24 hours a day, 365 days a year. Web sites where nothing changes for a month are the exception rather than the rule. Because of the premium on speed, you'll encounter fewer layers of editorial oversight than at the typical magazine, faster decision making, and hardly any fact checkers anywhere.

Finally and most importantly, even where an information product is called an "online magazine," experienced editors are not necessarily running the show. "Clueless kids with $9 million in venture capital," one freelancer said to sum up her frustration in writing for a startup Internet company. Those who hire content providers may have more familiarity with business plans and baud rates than with punctuation and paragraphing.

What's Not Different Online

On the other hand, many things about working for traditional magazines hold true on the Net as well. According to some who deal with writers online, freelancers often approach online work too casually.

A feature story for the *Online Journalism Review* contained complaints from online editors that all too many aspiring contributors to Web sites seemed to have mislaid their common sense. Instead of fully developed queries editors were receiving "undercooked story ideas" and "illiterate rants." Even established columnists relaxed their standards, with one implying to an editor that he was interested in unloading his less than top-notch material on the Web.

Despite the apparent informality of e-mail communication and the fast-changing pace of the Web, you'll need to deliver the same level of quality and use the same journalistic ethics you would for print if you want to succeed in the online marketplace.

Skills a Content Provider Needs

Given this background, prospective content providers do best when they demonstrate an understanding of what Web entrepreneurs and online magazine developers value in freelance contributors. Use the following guidelines to determine which skills you need to bone up on for their sake and yours, and how to pitch your strengths to those buying Web site content.

Fast, dependable turnaround

Things move so fast on the Web that the ability to post content quickly often gives sites a solid business advantage. Brag about your reporting and writing speed, if that's so. Being able to put together something in a day that other writers might labor over for a week gives you an edge.

Ability to edit yourself

This skill might not top the list of important qualifications in the Web entrepreneur's head, but once you point it out, he usually understands the benefit—readable, respectable content without having to hire another layer of management.

Understanding of rights issues

As an experienced freelancer, you probably know more about copyright and the dynamics of permissions than the typical entrepreneur. The business owners I've dealt with had a reasonable attitude toward rights and were willing to negotiate something fair to both sides, unlike some online editors who wouldn't budge from demanding all rights. The more knowledgeable you are here, the better deal you might be able to cut for yourself.

Solid business skills

An absolute requirement: knowing how to negotiate an agreement, how to increase your odds of getting paid, and how to dun a slow-paying company. With a Web site that commissioned me to write twelve articles, I requested partial payment in advance and did not deliver any work until I had that first payment in hand.

Ability to locate and negotiate reuse of resources

Being Web-savvy and already knowing lots about what's on the Net may make you valuable to a Web site. Also, explain to the entrepreneur that as a writer, you're better positioned to solicit or negotiate the use of work from other writers than he is.

Web-friendly writing style

Short paragraphs and crisp, relatively short sentences are de rigueur when people read your work on screen. Become a master of clear organization with frequent subheads. Because I believe that Web-friendly style is infiltrating print as well, I now write in shorter paragraphs and pithier sentences for regular magazines, too.

You can use this article as a model of the lean, succinct style necessary for the Net.

Inventory of material

When someone needs content fast, your backlog of previously published, still-interesting work on a Web site's topic may make you mighty attractive for a package deal of new and old material.

Drawing power

If you've been writing regularly and visibly for a particular market, argue that you already have a liked or trusted name within that world. This may enable you to command higher fees or to secure perks like a live link to a Web site where you promote your books and for-hire services.

Voice

One online magazine told me it was looking for "edgy" columnists. This doesn't mean it wants nervous writers, but rather those who have a sharp, opinionated tone. Mere information is everywhere on the Net, but information with an attitude attracts readers and makes you valuable to a site.

Ability to suggest more work for yourself

For your own benefit, learn about the entrepreneur's big plans and suggest additional ways you can contribute. Unlike magazines, Web sites have few space limitations. If a site wants a monthly column, say you could do it weekly or biweekly. If the site requests a one-shot story, suggest a serial, which will encourage repeat traffic.

Remember, Web sites aim at becoming valued, frequent destinations for Internet users in their target markets. The more you can help them reach that goal, the more respect you command and the more monetary rewards you deserve. By presenting yourself as a "content provider" rather than a "writer," you appeal to entrepreneurs prepared to reward you handsomely for writing-related skills.

Get involved early and deep enough and you might even receive stock options from a site that becomes the next Yahoo! or About.com. How's that for a thought?

CHAPTER TWO

Online Queries and Submissions

DO CHECK THE publication's guidelines to make sure it accepts online queries before sending a query by e-mail. Some editors (even those of online publications) prefer traditional methods. "The sheer ease of contacting editors seems to have backfired," Crawford Kilian, author of *Writing for the Web* (International Self-Counsel Press), points out. "Many editors must feel they're being spammed and don't reply to electronic queries. A snail mail query looks more 'serious'; it may not be, but the sheer solidity of a print-on-paper query or article conveys more than the ephemeral e-mail letter."

In many ways, querying an online market is very similar to querying a regular print publication. The regular rules apply:

Do your research. Read the submission guidelines and familiarize yourself with back issues and current material being published. Find out the editor's name and make sure you spell it correctly in your correspondence.

Tailor your query. Because e-mail is such a convenient and inexpensive means of communications, some writers get lazy when sending out queries and write one generic letter, which they send out to many publications at a time. Like editors of print publications, however, online editors will recognize this sort of "shotgun approach" right away.

Don't be too familiar. Although e-mail generally tends to be informal, keep the tone of your correspondence as professional as you would in surface mail queries. Don't use "Hi, Ken!" as a salutation. Instead, use "Dear Ken" or "Dear Mr. Smith." Remember that some editors will be new to the Internet, and they might be traditional in how they prefer to interact with authors in spite of the online medium.

Avoid using emoticons (e.g., "smiley faces"), Net slang, and abbreviations in your business correspondence. Save those for your personal e-mail.

Use a signature. A signature is a small block of text appended to the end of every e-mail message you send. Most e-mail programs allow you to create your own signature. A typical signature would contain basic contact information plus a URL or personal quote. Here is a sample:

> Gomer Glotz, Technical Writer
> E-mail: gomerglotz@hotmail.com
> URL: http://www.gomerglotz.com
> "No matter where you go, there you are."

Always use a signature if you can. It helps identify you and also provides you with a nonintrusive means of promoting yourself. Keep your signature short, maximum seven lines.

Don't use attachments without asking first. Keep the content of your message within the body of your e-mail message unless the submission guidelines specify otherwise. Before sending an attachment containing clips or other information, ask if it's OK. Find out what format the editor prefers—ASCII text? MS Word? RTF (rich text format)?

I recently received an e-mail message from someone who wanted to send me his picture book about castles. Not only did the sender obviously not read my submissions guidelines (I don't publish picture books), but his message was riddled with misspellings and grammatical errors. He said he wanted to send me a 10MB PowerPoint presentation file containing his book. Before I could reply, he sent the file anyway, followed by a 2MB scan of his business card. The file blocked my incoming mail for nearly twenty minutes as it downloaded.

Needless to say, my response was not entirely enthusiastic.

Include context when replying. When replying to an editor's message, include enough context to remind the editor of the original message. Don't assume that the editor will remember; some editors receive hundreds of messages a day. You can include a context reminder by including excerpts from your previous correspondence, or by a brief introductory sentence or two.

Send yourself a copy. Be sure to send yourself a copy of the correspondence by "cc:ing" yourself for your own records and in case the e-mail is lost. Moira Allen, author of *Writing.com* (Allworth Press), advises creating a mailing "nickname" for yourself to save time and typos, or setting your e-mail program to automatically save a copy of all outgoing mail.

Sample Query Letters
KAREN ASP—Health and fitness writer

SAMPLE QUERY LETTER:

Feb. 23, 1999

[Editor name]

Editor

[Publication name]

Dear [Editor name],

You're in the middle of a great workout when you suddenly start coughing. You have a hard time catching your breath. Your chest tightens, and you stop exercising. Dozens of minutes pass before you regain control of your breathing. Did you push yourself too hard today? Maybe. But you're not out of shape; in fact, you're in the best shape of your life. And this isn't the first time it's happened while you were exercising.

If this sounds familiar, then you may be part of the 7 to 15 percent of the population, including top athletes like Dennis Rodman, who experiences exercise-induced asthma (EIA), says William Storms, M.D., an allergist with Asthma and Allergy Associates in Colorado Springs, Colo.

A health and fitness writer who has most recently written for *Shape*, *Walking* and

Oxygen, I'd like to propose an article titled "Exercise and asthma: Is exercising putting your health in jeopardy?" for [Publication name].

In the article, I'll define EIA as an asthma attack that occurs while exercising or immediately after exercising. Symptoms of EIA include chest tightness, wheezing, shortness of breath, and coughing. Although EIA typically occurs in asthma sufferers, it also affects children and adults who suffer from allergies but don't have day-to-day asthma symptoms. It can occur in people of all fitness levels. Irritants that trigger EIA include tobacco or wood smoke, other air pollutants, respiratory viruses, allergens such as pollen, and cold air.

Your readers will also learn how EIA is diagnosed, how EIA is treated, and how EIA can be prevented. Prevention advice includes breathing through the nose rather than the mouth while exercising, warming up thoroughly before exercising, taking short rests between bursts of intense activity, covering the mouth when exercising in cold weather, modifying or postponing exercise programs when sick with colds, and always carrying an inhaler.

My sources will include Dr. Ronald Brown of the University of California-Davis; Dr. Sally Wenzel, a staff physician at National Jewish Medical and Research Center; and Dr. Katherine Storms, an allergist in private practice in Colorado Springs and co-chair of the Olympic Exercise Asthma Conference in 1994.

I have enclosed a copy of my writing background as well as two writing samples.

I look forward to hearing your response. Thank you for considering my idea for [Publication name].

Sincerely,

Karen Asp

Health/Fitness Writer

[my contact information here, including e-mail and phone]

COMMENTS BY KAREN:

I tailored this query specifically for this publication/publisher which manages a series of ten online magazines. After reading articles on the site, I knew that the tone of past articles was casual and conversational. Readers were often addressed as "you," and all of the articles contained service-oriented information with tips and advice.

So I put that information to work in my lead paragraph (which ended up being close to the actual lead). When I'm writing queries (and articles, too), I usually spend most of my time working on the lead. I want my lead to sizzle, if you will, maybe pop, or at the very least, catch the attention of the editor.

After the lead, I slipped in my credentials. I could have put them at the end of the query, which I used to do when I didn't have as much experience. But with such big credits behind my name and because this was the first time I'd queried this publication, I wanted the editor to know from the start that she was dealing with a professional writer, not a professional want-to-be writer. I also included a working title; this could always be changed later.

In the next two paragraphs, I discussed the information that I planned on including in the article. Of course, I had to research to find this information. Once I found what I needed, though, I simplified it and chose the main points about exercise-induced asthma (EIA) that my editor may or may not have known. Again, because I wanted to sell this article, I needed to give her enough information so that she could make a decision about this article. (Fortunately, she bought it!) Also, I wanted to point out that the information would include advice and suggestions for dealing with EIA. I even listed specific tips for preventing EIA.

Finally, I suggested the sources I'd contact. Again, I had to locate these sources, which I did through the Internet. Note, though, that I had not yet contacted these sources. Had these sources not been available, I figured I could locate other nationally known experts on the topic. But at the very least, I wanted my editor to see that I had direction and that I planned on interviewing top sources. I would suggest always including sources in queries, even if you have to change them once the article has been assigned to you. Of course, you may want to talk with your editor about the source changes.

There's one exception to this. If you're planning on interviewing a celebrity or high-profile professional, don't promise the interview unless you have it.

Finally, I closed the query and thanked the editor for her attention. I also included my contact information, which is important in an e-query. Unless you've designed electronic letterhead, include your phone number and e-mail address somewhere in the query.

Notice that this query didn't drag. Although you can write a novel on one electronic page, don't. I keep my electronic queries to one typewritten page, just as if I were submitting to a print publication. Yet I format electronic queries differently than printed queries. I line everything up on the left side of the screen, delete all tabs, and doublespace between paragraphs. Note, too, that even though I could have been more casual with the editor, I kept things professional and business-like. I included a date, the editor's name, and publication, and then addressed the editor as "Ms".

Query letters are the most important part of writing. I've spent anywhere from two hours to an entire day crafting a query. Some might call that wasted time, but if I don't write a good query, then I don't get the article.

There's another reason, though, why I spend so much time with queries: Editors often judge your writing by your query. If you don't deliver a high-quality query, then editors won't have confidence in your ability to deliver a high-quality article, and well, you can draw your own conclusion.

CINDY APPEL—Freelance writer

SAMPLE QUERY LETTER:

Dear [Editor name]:

Our family recently moved to the St. Louis area and discovered the joy of walking over the Mississippi along the Chain-of-Rocks Bridge. Formerly an important crossing along Route 66, the bridge is now open to pedestrian and bicycle traffic only. It's a wonderful spot to stroll on a warm afternoon, attracting locals and tourists alike.

I'm a freelance writer who has written on a variety of topics, married to a former photojournalist who adores the Chain-of-Rocks Bridge. Would you be interested in an article about the bridge? Thanks for your consideration of my query.

Cindy

COMMENTS BY CINDY:

My e-queries are usually this short—sort of a "one-two" punch, with my first paragraph giving the editor the reason why I'm contacting him or her and the second paragraph adding details as to why I feel I'm able to supply them with the article. I like to "hook" the editor quickly with a very brief summary of my proposed or written piece—not too much, but enough to give them an idea of the main thrust of the article. I used to list more of my "credits" or offer clips in the second paragraph, but have discovered that it doesn't seem to impress most editors one way or the other. Possibly this is due to the fact that my signature line "advertises" some of my work published online. If a particular writer's guidelines ask for more detailed info on my writing experience, I generally will send them my "writer's resume" along with my query. If I have published a similar piece to my proposed article or am offering an article as a reprint—or even if I have had a life experience that I feel makes me more than qualified to write the story—I generally give that info in the second paragraph, or possibly in a third, but no more than three short, to-the-point paragraphs. I've observed over the last couple of years that the shorter and less "cluttered" my query is, the more favorable the response from either print or online publications.

This query was a "first" for me—offering my hubby's experience as a photographer, but he adores the bridge and was very interested in capturing it on film, so I felt this couldn't hurt my chances of selling the piece—and it didn't. They've given us until the summer issue so we can have more favorable lighting conditions to shoot pictures and can actually get out and walk with the volunteers. It's too cold and cloudy in the winter around here—that's for sure!

SAL TOWSE—Freelance writer

SAMPLE QUERY LETTER:

More than 24 million people read, respond, ask questions, discuss, explain, complain and engage in "flame wars" in newsgroups on Usenet. Tens of thousands of Usenet newsgroups cover almost every topic imaginable.

Deja News, Inc., an Austin, Texas, company, has managed to harness all this knowledge. Since 1995 Deja News has been archiving Usenet newsgroup posts and offering free searching of their archives. At the end of last year Deja News' Usenet newsgroup feeds were receiving five gigabytes of posts daily, approximately 730,000 messages to over fifty thousand newsgroups.

How can Aunt Millie access this wealth of information (and smut and nonsense and flames)? How will she ever learn to tap into the Deja News archives when, according to the [Publication name] archives, you have not had a single article focusing on Deja News and you have a mere four articles which even mention its existence?

Let me know if you want me to write an article for [Publication name] with Deja News as its focus.

Qualifications to write the article for you? I'm the resident crank, evangelist, and Deja News wizard on misc.writing. Check Deja News <http://www.dejanews.com>. Pop in the search string: [e-mail address here] misc.writing deja*.

Hope to hear from you, Sal

COMMENTS BY SAL:

The start of my long relationship with this publication.

I knew the publisher, from a chance-met acquaintance on misc.writing, and checked out his print magazine online because I'm curious, insatiably curious. After reading the current and several back issues, I thought, "Hey. I could write articles their readers would like to see." I knew, however, that "knowing the publisher" might get me a look-see at the magazine, but I'd have to sell myself on my own merits.

The publication is a regional computer magazine with a popular bent. They have their guidelines online and encourage e-mail queries. Perfect! I decided I'd write something for their perhaps-not-so-very-techie readers, something about the Web. Deja News (now Deja) is a favorite resource, so I pitched an article on that. The editor replied that he'd be more interested in "a more general article about querying online databases, with reference to AltaVista- and InfoSeek-based engines as well as Deja News."

I took his thoughts and returned to him with a suggestion for "a *Zen and the Art of Surfing* sort of take aimed toward Aunt Millie." He bought the result. Another article followed and two years later, I'm starting my second year of writing a monthly "Surfing the Internet" column for the same publication. Guess you could say the query worked.

CHAPTER THREE

Types of Online Markets

THE INTERNET GROWS and evolves, and with it the number and diversity of paying markets for writers increases.

Print Publication Web Sites

Many print publications are establishing a presence on the Web as they realize the Web's tremendous marketing potential. The simplest of these Web sites are online brochures for the print publication, with basic information like how to subscribe and perhaps a table of contents from the current issue. Some magazine Web sites include sample articles from back issues. Still others will supplement these excerpts with online content unique to the Web site.

Web Guides and Portals

The amount of information on the Internet can be overwhelming. As a result, more and more "Web guides" or "portals" are being created both online and offline, designed to filter info and highlight the best resources for Internet users. These sites usually have in-house columns and sometimes pay writers to contribute additional articles and reviews.

Corporate Material

Businesses have recognized the Internet to be a valuable marketing tool. Many who have or want Web sites need to hire in-house staff or freelance writers to produce high-quality content.

E-zines

What exactly is an e-zine? As you might have already guessed, the term is an abbreviation of "electronic magazine." An e-zine could be considered an online equivalent of a print newsletter or magazine. E-zine publishing is a form of electronic publishing; you can find more information about e-zines and how to make money creating your own e-zine in chapter eight.

Some e-zines are published by a single individual; others by many. Some of the best-known e-zines include *Slate, Salon,* and *Suck.* Not all e-zines pay; check the submission guidelines carefully.

E-zines contain many types of writing:

1. Articles

Most e-zines use articles as the bulk of their content, just like regular print publications.

2. Reviews

Some online publications need reviews of all kinds—movies, restaurants, music, cities, stocks, comics, Web sites, software, books, and so on. This can be a good way of breaking into an online publication; several online writers have reported getting column assignments this way.

3. Columns

Columns range from straightforward opinion pieces, Q&A columns, and journalistic style to reviews. Of the writers I surveyed who were making a full-time living from their online work, most had at least one regular online column assignment. Writing a regular column helps establish you as an expert in a particular field, which could lead to other assignments and columns.

4. Fiction and poetry

"Online publications tend to be a better market for very short fiction or poetry," says writer Sabina Becker. "Haiku does very well (I got some of my first poetry acceptances from haiku sites), as does 'flash' fiction (anything under 1,000 words.) People's eyes tire easily from staring at a blazing screen, so bite-sized pieces of writing are just what the doctor ordered—they're literally a sight for sore eyes!"

Teaching Online Courses

Another way of earning online money is to teach an online writing course, either on your own or through a third party. "If you have knowledge in some other area, use those talents and combine them with your writing by developing a course," suggests freelance writer Bev Walton-Porter. For writers considering launching courses on their own, she emphasizes the importance of exposure and marketing; few people will find your course otherwise. "But more than the single issue of income, I think there's also an element of altruism involved—a 'giving back' to the writing community. It's a way to help new writers learn the tools and strategies they need to go out and get published, and paid, themselves."

More information about this topic in Paula Guran's article later in this chapter, "Earn Money Teaching Online Courses" (page 29).

WRITING FOR THE WEB
by John Hewitt

John Hewitt is an information developer at IBM and a successful freelance writer. He has also worked as a reporter, editor, and public relations writer. Hewitt runs the Writer's Resource Center, which may be accessed at www.poewar.com.

The Online Publishing Landscape

The Internet is a writer's revolution. It has reshaped industry, shopping, international relations, and just about every other aspect of life in the modern world. In no other area, however, is the Internet proving to be a greater revolution than in writing. To say that the Internet is the most significant development in the history of writing since the invention of the printing press is no exaggeration. Never before has anyone with something to say had the ability to put it in writing (or even in audio or video) and disseminate the information to a worldwide audience at such a nominal cost. Of course, there is more to e-publishing than just creating a Web page. Online publishing is an industry, just as magazine, newspaper, and book publishing are all industries. While most writers love the opportunity to see their names in print, there is nothing quite like having someone else publish your work. The knowledge that someone wants to publish what you have to say is one of the greatest thrills a writer can know, second only to getting paid. Web-based publishing doesn't have the cost and space limitations of print publishing. In addition, Web-based publishing can take advantage of its electronic medium to provide innovations ranging from hyperlinks to video and audio supplements. A profile of a politician, for example, may now contain video and audio files, transcripts, links to voting records and popularity polls, links to the candidate's white papers on key issues, and a discussion board where readers can comment on the candidate and the coverage. In addition, thanks to instantaneous statistical tracking, the publisher will know whether the readers are interested in any or all of this coverage. No other medium is this flexible and powerful. In the coming years, no other medium will provide as much work for writers.

The New Careers

Web-based publishing has created a variety of new job fields for writers. Most job titles focus on the word content: Web content writer, online content editor, content manager, and content developer to name a few. Most of these positions are with Web-based companies and companies with a strong Web presence. The majority of these positions fall into one of three categories: technical writing, copywriting/ public relations, or copyediting. Most technical writing employers now look for writers who can develop both online and hardcopy publications. These positions are similar to standard technical writing, but generally the writer is expected to have moderate to advanced Web skills. The writer should be able to competently use a Web-development package, and may be asked to have further knowledge of HTML, JavaScript, and other Web-based development skills. Writers are also expected to have some page design skills and to think in a customer-friendly way. Web copywriting and public relations positions focus more on promotion of the company. Writers often work on product descriptions, services descriptions, and press releases. Again, Web-development skills are valuable, and page design skills are important as well. Web copyediting is focused more on finding and developing content for a Web site. While these positions require traditional copyediting skills such as correcting spelling and grammar, there is an increased focus on customizing content for the company's needs. Frequently, the copyeditor is also a managing editor, determining which articles to place as well as writing articles for publication. By no means are online writing positions limited to writing for business, but, as with the writing industry as a whole, that is where most writers make their living, and it is the easiest area in which to get a paying job. There are, however, a growing number of more creative positions. Often, the key to finding these positions is to have a niche. If you like to write about childcare, for example, you should investigate the companies that sell childcare products. Companies are quickly finding that simply describing and selling their products isn't enough in today's online market. They need to give the customer value and a reason to return to their site. Content, in the form of articles and information, is a key to grabbing and keeping people at a Web site.

Freelancing Online

Freelance writing is thriving on the Internet. There are plenty of writing opportunities for freelancers. Traditional markets, such as newspapers and magazines, have expanded their content into the world of the Internet. No longer shackled by print costs, many weekly and monthly magazines are now publishing articles on the Web daily. This has increased the demand for articles and the opportunity for reprints. Magazines that would never publish reprints in their regular print runs are often less concerned with those issues online. In addition, traditional broadcast resources such as television and radio news networks are now publishing online editions of their news stories. The result is an increase in the number of stringer positions and other freelance opportunities. One of the benefits of dealing with online publishers is your increased ability to research their styles and content. No longer do you have to go to the library and wade through a dozen issues of a magazine to get an idea of its style and needs. Now you can read the magazine's online archives to find out what it runs, and topics it might have overlooked. Beyond traditional publishers, many Web-based publishers offer the opportunity to write to a specific topic. Sites such as About.com and Suite101 .com offer writers the opportunity to host subjects. These sites bring in people who will write an article or so a week and also look for links and other useful content. In some ways this is only a small step up from the personal home pages that were popular in the early days of the Internet, but the difference is that you have the promotional backing of a company that wants to direct traffic to your page. The pay for online freelancing often is below what you would expect from traditional publishers, but the opportunities to get published are far greater. For people who write short stories, poetry, and other more personal work, this rule is especially true. There are far more opportunities to get published than ever before. E-zines (small online magazines that are frequently run by individuals) often don't pay their authors, but with hundreds of e-zines on the Internet, it is much easier to find one interested in your work than it is with print magazines and journals that must battle space limitations. Another, more recent development has been the rise of the online book. Online books have been around since before the Web. Public domain works such as those of Milton, Shakespeare, and Mark Twain were available online when people still used gopher to surf text-only pages. These text-based books gave way to more creative HTML, which allowed illustrations and other innovations. Now, books are being published online in files such as PDF, which can be downloaded and viewed on a computer or printed on regular paper and read in the more traditional style. Even this innovation is quickly being superseded. Now, traditional booksellers such as Barnes & Noble are developing print-on-demand services that will print traditional books at the request of the customer. This innovation allows writers to publish their own books electronically, with low up-front costs. Writers will no longer be dependent on large publishing houses or have to pay the steep costs of vanity presses. Instead, booksellers will pay authors a royalty for each book that is printed.

Developing as an Online Writer

Building a career as a writer in the online marketplace is a challenge. The Web has made getting published easier than ever. If nothing else, you can put up your own page and publish your own work. With a few Web and marketing skills, you can easily bring some interested people to your site. To build a career, however, is more difficult. Not only do you need to develop your writing craft, but you also need to develop your technical skills. As a freelancer, your skills may not have to be as great. The ability to use some sort of Web-development program, such as Microsoft Front-Page, Adobe PageMill, or HomeSite, is sufficient for you to build stand-alone pages if your client wants more than a simple text article. You must, of course, be able to use an e-mail program to send files in text, HTML, PDF, or other formats. If you are seeking permanent employment, however, be aware that most employers value technical skills as much as writing skills. The most prized Web skills are the higher-end skills such as manual HTML and XML coding and knowledge of JavaScript, Java, VBscript, Perl/CGI, and Dynamic HTML. That's a long list of things to know, though, and too long a list for most people who consider themselves primarily writers. At the very least, employers want you skilled in the use of a Web-page development package such as the ones listed above. In this industry, however, you must always learn new skills and expand both your Web and writing abilities. Web technology moves fast, and if you want to be successful, you must keep up.

EARN MONEY TEACHING ONLINE COURSES
by Paula Guran

Paula Guran teaches, critiques, and edits a monthly e-mail newsletter for Writers on the Net (www.writers.com). She edits, writes about, and reviews horror for a number of venues online and off. Her weekly newsletter for horror writers, *DarkEcho*, was the first (and only) electronic publication to be awarded the Bram Stoker Award for Outstanding Nonfiction Horror and has also been nominated for the World Fantasy Award. Her own Web site is www.darkecho.com.

Good writers don't always make good writing instructors, but often the best writing instructors are writers themselves. Experienced writers can offer more than lessons in art and craft; they can also offer invaluable practical advice. Now, with the Internet, you can reach potential students literally all over the world right from your own home. You've heard the catchphrases—"e-commerce," "Web-based business," "dotcom economy" and more. Is online writing instruction your personal path to Internet riches and self-fulfillment?

Before you set up a Web page and settle back expecting eager students to flock to your virtual door, there's quite a bit to take into consideration.

1. Do You Have the "Write" Background to Be an Online Instructor?

Award-winning author Nancy Kilpatrick taught on the college level for a decade before starting to teach online for Writers on the Net (www.writers.com) four years ago. She's also taught and offered editorial services online directly herself. Kilpatrick feels that any instructor should know the subject. "Personally," she says, "I would not pay money to take a writing course from someone who does not have some years of both teaching and writing under his or her belt."

Stephen Morrill, the Dean of Writers University (www.iuniverse.com/marketpl ace/learn_online/wri_university.asp) feels that experience in the field is of prime importance for an online instructor. "I do not mean experience in teaching, or in knowing English, or in reading the great works of the masters," he explains. "I mean experience in *doing* the thing you propose to teach. Usually that means publication credits and the more the better."

"I look for teaching experience because it's the best indicator that the potential teacher will know what to do. And publishing credits are the best way to establish the credentials of the teacher," says Mark Dahlby, founder of Writers on the Net. He adds, "Identity is flexible on the Internet: anyone can claim to be a writing teacher. Since students don't have a chance to meet the teacher or tour the school, and because many people are still wary of sending their money to a digital, and therefore slightly abstract, company, I think it offers them some security when they can order the instructor's books from Amazon.com."

2. Are You Comfortable in the Online Environment, and Can You Readily Access the Net?

According to Amy Sterling Casil, a published writer with an MFA who teaches writing in the "real world" as well as online, "having experience in communicating online as opposed to in a real classroom is crucial to success. You may never see your online students, yet you are still obligated, as a teacher, to work as strongly with them as possible and to meet their educational needs." Morrill agrees saying that experience doesn't matter if "you can't communicate with the students because you are baffled by the technology. You need not be a programmer, but you do need to be able to get around online."

Instruction is handled in a variety of ways online. Some classes have specific times and "meet" for live interaction. Access to Web pages through a browser is needed for some classes. All have some dependence on e-mail. None of the technological knowledge required for any of this is particularly difficult, but both you and your equipment need to be able to handle it.

3. Do You Genuinely Care About the Students, and Are You Sincerely Concerned With Their Progress as Writers?

Blythe Camenson, director of Fiction Writer's Connection (www.fictionwriters.com), looks for instructors who can "be sensitive to the needs of individual students and be flexible in providing information and feedback. Enthusiasm for the subject matter and a supportive attitude are also important." Dahlby says, "I want people who enjoy teaching, are rewarded by it, and who feel that the growth of each student's skill is the point of the class."

4. Can You Handle Some Hard Knocks Yourself?

Kilpatrick advises that instructors develop a thick skin quickly. "You cannot please all of the students all of the time. Many people have great expectations of themselves (and others). They cannot take criticism at all. I agree with whoever it was who said that there is no bad fiction, just fiction that needs to be rewritten. The problem is, some people expect they will knock out a work of art in a first draft. And while that can happen occasionally, as Anton Chekov said, writing is rewriting. Someone, sometime won't believe that, so be prepared!"

5. Do You Have an Idea of How Teaching Online Is Done?

The path has already been beaten through the cyberjungle and is beginning to be paved. If you have never taken a course online, been involved in an online workshop, or have no one to mentor you in the field, it might be best to first investigate how it's already being done by others.

◆ ◆ ◆

Assuming you are undaunted by these first five criteria, the next choice you need to make is whether to try teaching/tutoring/editing on your own or whether you would prefer working with an established organization.

"When you offer courses on your own," says Camenson, "you can keep the entire registration fee. However, the advantages of working for an established organization can outweigh that. On your own, you have to do all your publicity yourself to find students, maintain a Web site, handle all the administrative details and have a merchant account. An established organization will do all of that for you."

"With an organization behind you," says Casil, "you have the benefit of a group and a number of writing classes. This helps to attract greater numbers of students and perhaps more dedicated students. However, on your own, you have a great deal more freedom and are not locked into a strict schedule."

If you opt for offering instruction privately, be prepared to spend considerable time (and perhaps some money) marketing your product. According to Dahlby, "On the Internet, the primary factor in the success of any business is getting people to visit your site. So people have to be prepared to do marketing, which is a lot harder than it seems it should be, at least for those of us who are not marketing types."

Lori Soard, who has taught through several online sites, through local businesses and clubs and now with her own Wordmuseum (www.wordmuseum.com), thinks "it would be a little more difficult to get the word out on your own, but if you already have a wide mailing list and a reputation for your writing, it's possible you could find students. It's a little like self-publishing: It takes more work and promotional time out of your schedule."

If you meet with success in promoting your services, then you must be willing to handle lots of e-mail and keep track of billing, students, potential students and much more. Obviously some degree of organization is needed.

You'll probably need to set up a system to handle credit cards and be ready to deal with the possibility of bounced checks and rejected card numbers. And you will have to handle accounting, tax, and other needs of what is, essentially, a small business.

Many freelancers are already used to dealing with pursuing payment and keeping track of things. Authors these days are quite aware of the necessity of self-promotion. Some folks enjoy responding to e-mail. But if you are daunted by any of it, or the time involved, you might think hard before trying it on your own.

And, of course, you will have to establish a workable, well-designed, informative Web site that will attract potential customers. Someone else can do this for you or you can do it yourself. Again, as a professional writer you may already have set up a Web site or have had one set up for you. But the time and cost of maintaining a site needs to be considered when contemplating the all-important topic of "money."

How much should you charge? How much will you make? It's hard to say because the courses and services offered online are difficult to compare. Plus, the number of writing courses being offered online is growing rapidly, so you can't price yourself out of what is a competitive market. Realize that only Web-based schools and individuals with established reputations seem to be able to charge a higher tuition.

Writers Club University's Morrill notes, "The majority of school efforts online consist of one enthusiast and a Web page. But this is a real business, no matter how virtual the presentation, and the usual business principles apply. It's very difficult to do this and make money at running any serious school. We can do it because the Writers Club University borrows programmers and administrative personnel from the 400-person iUniverse staff, and we have an AOL site to support us too. We can do it because we know how to run a business online. With about sixty courses we have the advantage of sheer size already. I do not envy the lot of anyone trying to enter the market all alone."

Further competition now comes from well-established, reputable writing schools like the Gotham Writers Workshop (www.writingclasses.com) and Writer's Digest (www.writersdigest.com) that are now on the Web. WritersOnlineWorkshops have been developed by Writer's Digest (the same company that publishes this book), an organization with a well-recognized "brand name" and plenty of associated marketing support through their print publications.

Other Factors Related to Compensation

- As an instructor for an online "school" you can expect to be paid per student. How much you make depends on how many classes you teach and how many students enroll in those classes. Classes need to remain relatively small to function well, and a maximum of twelve to fifteen is rarely exceeded. Usually you need a minimum of five or six students for the class to make it worthwhile to hold, but some special classes are limited to no more than that.
- The teacher's fee is usually a percentage of the tuition, and pay currently ranges from about $20 per student to about $200 per student. Some online formats require much more instructor input and time than others.
- Generally, the longer the class the higher the tuition. There are one-shot "seminars," and classes from two to fourteen weeks in length.
- Most individuals and schools offer one-to-one services as well as classes. If you are offering one-to-one services of any type—critique service, editing, individual tutorials—you'll need to set fees for this as well. Each new edition of the *Writer's Market* (Writer's Digest Books) lists pay rate information for a variety of writing, editing, and related work and can be used as a general guide for some services.

If you decide you'd prefer to work with an established organization, check for contact information on their Web sites. Many are looking for good instructors.

The Internet's opportunities are still uncharted. If you choose to teach online, you may not find immediate large financial rewards, but there is some income and the potential for more. For many writers the fact that you can do most of your work on your own schedule while wearing pajamas and bunny slippers is a form of compensation itself. By teaching online you will also gain from exposure to a wide variety of people with diverse ideas, backgrounds, talents, and experience. Teaching or working with others often hones your individual skills and offers new inspiration for your own writing. Finally, the true reward of online instruction is the same as any teaching role: the satisfaction you receive from helping others attain their goals.

Further Information About Sites Mentioned in This Article:

Fiction Writer's Companion

www.fictionwriters.com

Each e-mail course (most with ongoing registration) provides resource material, either in an online course library or sent via e-mail from your instructor. The instructor stays in "regular contact," sends lectures and assignments, and answers questions.

Costs:

Four-week courses: $48, $43.20 for members

Six-week courses: $55, $50 for members

(year's membership: $64)

Gotham Writers Workshop

www.writingclasses.com

Originally a bricks-and-mortar creative writing school in New York City providing classes for 4,000 students a year, GWW now offers online courses based on their real-time classes. During the ten-week courses, a lecture is posted to the site once a week. The student reads the lecture and makes comments or raises questions and the teacher responds. Other students can also respond, creating a "discussion" over the course of the week. Each student has an online "notebook" where writing exercises can be posted for the teacher only.

Costs:

Registration fee: $20 (waived for additional classes taken same term)

Ten-week online classes: $395; Returning students: $345 (some discounts available)

Wordmuseum

www.wordmuseum.com

Offers a limited number of classes via e-mail. Instructor critique included in some classes.

Costs:

Four-week courses: $25

Six-week courses: $35

Writer's Digest

www.writersonlineworkshops.com

WritersOnlineWorkshops are presented by the how-to-write giant, Writer's Digest. Courses offer peer review, instructor feedback, and writing practice. Their state-of-the-art technology is well-designed and user-friendly, but may frustrate some students who own less than state-of-the-art computers. Lectures are posted in a "Lecture Hall" that features a "discussion window" where questions or comments can be posted. A "Personal Notebook," a private space that only the individual student and the instructor can access, and a "Critics' Corner" for student-driven discussion are also provided.

Costs:

Eight-week courses: $199

Twelve-week courses: $299

Fourteen-week courses: $349

Writers on the Net

www.writers.com

Classes take place via a private e-mail list for each class. All members of the class receive the messages. (Private e-mail can also be exchanged.) Students responding to writing assignments post to the list so all students (as well as the instructor) can view and offer feedback on the assignment. Students are encouraged to offer feedback on one another's work and participate in additional discussions that take place on the list. A few classes use optional chats or material on the Web.

Costs:

Eight-week courses: $190

Ten-week courses: $240

Writers University (iUniverse)

www.iuniverse.com/marketplace/learn_online/wri_university.asp

The Writers Club started out on AOL, eventually expanded to the Web, and is now associated with iUniverse, which also has centralized publishing resources to offer writers a variety of publishing options. The many Writers University courses consist of e-mailed readings, homework, and special message boards. Some courses also have informal chats.

Costs:

Four-week courses: $60

Six-week courses: $80

Eight-week courses: $100

(They also have one-shot seminars and some special courses with different lengths/costs projected for the near future.)

CHAPTER FOUR

Where to Find Market Information

ONE OF THE BIGGEST advantages that the Internet offers writers is access to market information. Instead of investing time, money and postage for submission guidelines and sample copy of a particular publication, you can often find all the information you need by doing some online sleuthing.

Because content is updated more quickly online, the market information is more up-to-date, but how do you find it? "Take the truly good publications, both print and electronic," says Christopher Reynaga, creator of the Web zine *The Write Market* (www.writemarket.com). "Hide their Web sites in the random lists of a thousand poorly crafted e-zines that are born and folded every day. Bury that under a hundred thousand more electronic magazines that have nothing to do with writing or fiction. Scatter that into the Internet. You'll realize that finding the Web sites of publications that care to act professional, pay money, edit with heart, and stick around is like a mad crap-shoot."

Where Can I Find Online Markets?

One of the main benefits that the Internet holds for writers is its wealth of market research opportunities. Much of this online market information is free. The best market information sources are ones that contain an indication of when they were last updated and are also directly from the publications or publishers themselves.

Here are some ways you can find writing assignments online.

Guidelines databases

Several Web sites offer free guidelines databases for writers. Most are searchable, allowing you to browse listings by general category. Many have free e-mail newsletter subscriptions available, to keep users updated on recent additions.

Misc.writing Guide to Online Guidelines

www.snafu.de/~gadfly/

List of paying markets that accept electronic queries or submissions.

Writer's Digest

www.writersdigest.com

Web site of the popular writer's magazine. The database contains an abbreviated version of the annual print directory.

Writers' Guideline Database

mav.net/guidelines/

Browsable by topic category, or search for a particular term. Web site offers other resources for writers, such as a reminder service.

The Writer's Place

www.awoc.com/Guidelines.cfm

Flexible search capabilities (including pay category, last update, topic) and links include dated e-mails from market sources.

Writers Write

www.writerswrite.com/guidelines/

Includes links to the online submission guidelines of paying and nonpaying markets. Listings are not dated.

Web sites and electronic newsletters

As the number of writers and markets on the Internet increases, so does the number of Web sites devoted to providing market information and tips. Most are free resources, and some even offer the option of receiving new market information by e-mail.

Inkspot

www.inkspot.com

At the risk of tooting my own horn, I'd like to mention Inkspot here. Inkspot has several sections devoted to market information for writers, including a post-your-own markets listing classifieds section for publishers, a section devoted to paying online markets, and scrupulously researched market information in several of its newsletters.

Inscriptions

www.inscriptionsmagazine.com

This weekly e-zine, edited by Jade Walker, is one of my favorite online writing publications, extremely well researched and concise. You can find an interview with Jade Walker in the "Insider Views" chapter.

WritersWeekly.com

www.writersmarkets.com/index-twmr.htm

Weekly e-mail newsletter containing freelance jobs and new paying markets.

GENRE-SPECIFIC MARKET INFO WEB SITES

(Mainly speculative fiction, horror, fantasy)

The Market List

www.marketlist.com

Mary Soon Lee's List of Speculative Fiction Markets

www.cs.cmu.edu/~mslee/mag.html

Ralan.com

www.ralan.com

Spicy Green Iguana

members.aol.com/mhatv/

The Write Market Web-zine

www.writemarket.com

There are many more writer's Web sites and publications containing market information and market tips. I've posted a comprehensive list at www.inkspot.com/market for those interested.

The following are other tips on finding online markets.

Networks

According to my survey of online writers, many with regular assignments found them through contacts. See the chapter on networking for sales for tips, especially Dana Nourie's article on the topic.

Search engines

You'd be amazed at how much market information you can find by just using search engines. You can also get overwhelmed with useless information, which is why it's important to become familiar with efficient search techniques.

I strongly advise becoming intimately familiar with a few good search engines. Check out the "advanced help" section if available; learn all the extra commands that will enable you to fine-tune your searches. Most people know the basics of using a search engine, but very few realize how much time and effort they could save with advanced search features.

Just entering the term "submission guidelines" in a standard search engine, for example, turns up thousands of entries. Not all are writing related, however, and not all pay. Adding the term "writer" helps narrow the search, as well as the word "pay." Many search engines allow you to specify terms you *don't* want, which further narrows your search, such as specifying that you want to omit any entries containing the phrase "does not pay."

Electronic newsstands

Electronic newsstands are Web sites where users can browse descriptions of hundreds of publications. The main purpose of electronic newsstands is selling subscriptions, but they are also used as a valuable source of market information for writers.

Most are searched by publication title or category. If you've written an article about cats, for example, try entering "cats" in the search field, or look for publications that fit the general category of "pets" or "pet care."

Enews.com

www.enews.com

"The ultimate magazine site." Search by title or category, or browse alphabetically.

The Multimedia Newsstand

www.mmnews.com

Search by title or browse by category.

Newsdirectory.com

www.newsdirectory.com

Browse newspaper and magazine sites by subject or geographical region.

Publishers Web sites

According to a survey of 546 publishers by Book Zone (www.bookzone.com), nearly 80 percent of respondents have Web sites.

Many of these publishers have submission guidelines on their Web sites, saving you the cost of an SASE. Even if there are no guidelines available online, you can still learn a great deal by browsing through the publisher's Web site. Look for

- *A list of current titles.* Some Web sites will have searchable online catalogs. These can give you a better idea of what kind of topics the publishers are interested in as well as specific topics that have already been thoroughly covered.
- *Editorial contacts.* Find out the names (and correct spellings) of the editor who will be looking at your query or submission.
- *Newsletter.* Some publishers offer free updates or newsletters by electronic mail. This is another way of finding out about recent acquisitions, current needs, and industry news.

Other Resources:

BookWire Publisher Index

www.bookwire.com/index/publishers.html

Directory of publisher Web sites, categorized by topic.

Publishers' Catalogs Home Page

www.lights.com/publisher/

Searchable directory of publishers. You can also browse the listings by topic, type of material, city, state, country, or U.S. alphabetically.

Author associations

Many author association Web sites contain useful market industry news, tips, networking opportunities, job listings, and other resources. You can find a compilation of some of these at:

Author Association Directory

www.inkspot.com/tk/network/assoc.html

Job boards and job listing resources

Combing job boards is one of the best ways to find openings for regular online writing assignments. New Web sites often post job listings for columnists, editors, and freelance writers. Some offer other career resources.

Inkspot

www.inkspot.com/market/jobs.html

Inscriptions Job Opportunities

www.inscriptionsmagazine.com/Jobs.html

Telecommuting Jobs for Writers

www.tjobs.com/writers.htm

Newsgroups

Some newsgroups related to books, publishing, and writing occasionally contain news about new markets for writers. Be warned, however, that the noise-to-signal ratio in some newsgroups tends to be high.

Web site reviews and publishing news

Look for sites and newsletters that announce launchings of new Web sites. Often these sites are looking for new staff writers even if their submission guidelines aren't online.

Hardcopy sources

Regular market information publications are beginning to list online markets for writers. For example, the annual *Writer's Market* (Writer's Digest Books) now includes an "online market" symbol beside those publications that pay for online content. Anthony Tedesco's book *Online Markets for Writers: How to Make Money by Selling Your Writing on the Internet* is available from Owl Books/Henry Holt & Co.

Other Resources:

Gila Queen's Guide to Markets

www.gilaqueen.com

Mainly print markets.

Scavenger's Newsletter

www.cza.com/scav/index.html

Monthly small press market newsletter for writers and artists interested in science
fiction, fantasy, horror, and mystery.

Your favorite Web sites or online publications

What sites do you surf on a regular basis? What online publications do you read? As someone already familiar with the content and (presumably) interested in the topic, you have an advantage over writers who are approaching the publication for the first time.

"Just go to the sites you like and find the contact info for editorial, then pitch them," suggests Tracy Guth. "My experience working at a startup new media company is that it's crazy, and they are always looking for new ideas. Also they are not at all averse to e-mail, which some print editors still are!"

CAUTIONS FOR WRITERS

Before submitting material to an online publication, always verify the source of the market information. Some online market Web sites have not been updated in months or even years, and others may contain inaccuracies. I've seen several instances of market information newsletters or Web sites that cull their listings from other third-party resources without any indication that the information has been verified to ensure it is still up-to-date.

Also keep in mind that some online publications don't pay for submissions; be sure to confirm payment rates before submitting material. Read the submission guidelines carefully.

Author Michael Bracken says he is more cautious about submitting to an online publication than a print publication. "There appear to be a higher percentage of 'bad' markets online that offer poor presentation of material, little or no pay, and no knowledge of copyright law," says Bracken. "Because it is easier to start an online publication than a print publication, many more amateurs are starting publications." He strongly advises writers to research a market carefully before submitting.

How does one do this research?

Study the guidelines. Does the publication pay? What rights is it asking for?

Look at the site. How is material presented? Are there obvious typos? Is the layout clean and professional in appearance?

Ask around. Author Lori Enos advises writers to sign up for a writer's mailing list like WorkForWriters and ask if anyone has had problems with a particular publication.

Check Web resources. There are also several useful Web sites for this kind of research. "A few quick checks at places like Deja.com or agentresearch.com or Predators & Editors will turn up who's legitimate and who isn't, or even how well an agent performs," says Magee Gilks. "Writers now have the ability to band together and protect themselves and be, well, at risk of sounding maudlin, a brother/sisterhood."

Resources:

Writer Beware

    www.sfwa.org/beware

    Created and maintained by Victoria Strauss. Tips on how to recognize and avoid questionable agents, book doctors, and publishers.

CHAPTER FIVE

Contracts and Copyright

ALTHOUGH COMMUNICATION ON THE Internet tends to be more casual than in the "offline" world, it's still important to know what rights you are giving away. See Moira Anderson Allen's article below, "Electronic Rights: Your Hottest Commodity," for more information.

"Contracts are definitely less evolved," says Tracy Guth, freelance editor and writer. "Also, many online editors are not trained professionally as editors, which can be frustrating for someone used to working with journalists! It's getting better, I think, as more traditional media professionals start working online. I think the two will keep getting more and more similar."

E-publishing assignments are often made casually in e-mail. Whenever possible, however, try to get a formal contract. At the very least, save any e-mail correspondence in which you discuss the terms of your agreement.

ELECTRONIC RIGHTS: YOUR HOTTEST COMMODITY

by Moira Anderson Allen

Moira Allen has been writing professionally for twenty years, and is the author of *Writing.com: Creative Internet Strategies to Advance Your Writing Career* (Allworth Press). She is an Inkspot columnist and associate editor of *Inklings*, and contributes to a variety of electronic publications. The endnotes in this article are located on page 53.

If you thought "electronic rights" were important only if you sold your work online, think again. Today, there is almost no such thing as a purely "print" publication. Newspapers post their daily editions online, magazines offer archives of back issues, book publishers offer downloadable and CD-ROM editions, and major periodicals resell their content through fee-based databases. Even publications that don't yet offer a Web site or other electronic format may seek to claim a writer's rights not only for current media, but for all types of electronic media "yet to be developed." No matter where you sell your work today—to print periodicals, to book publishers, or online—your electronic rights will be in demand. This chapter will help you determine what rights to transfer and what rights you should seek to retain, and how to protect yourself against controversial "rights grabs."

Protecting Periodical Rights

Not so long ago, writers felt they could safely assume that when they sold an article to a newspaper or magazine, they were selling "First North American Serial Rights" (FNASR)—specifically, the right to publish that article "first" in a periodical. After the material was published, it was generally assumed that the publisher had no further rights to the material, and that the author was now free to sell it elsewhere. This was the assumption made by Jonathan Tasini and several other writers when they sold articles to *The New York Times* and other publications. When they discovered that their material had been resold to (or reused in) electronic databases, CD-ROM compilations, and similar format, without permission or compensation, they filed suit. In 1997, a judge ruled against Tasini et al., but in 1999, an appeals court overturned that decision. The 1999 ruling affirms that electronic rights are indeed separate from print rights, and that the right to reproduce material electronically (e.g., on a Web site or in a database) is not automatically included in a transfer of FNASR. In addition, the court ruled that "in the absence of a written contract, [the writer] transfers only FNASR and retains all other rights."[1] Though this decision has been widely hailed as a victory for writers, its ultimate impact is still unclear. While some publishers may make an effort to compensate writers fairly for electronic rights, others are already modifying their contracts to claim those rights without additional compensation, or worse, switching to "all-rights" or "work-for-hire" agreements. While some editors refuse to negotiate such contracts, others are more flexible. Here are some steps you can take to protect yourself (and your work) from excessive "rights grabs."

1. Read your contract carefully. Make sure a "rights grab" isn't hidden in legalese. If your contract's wording is difficult to understand (I received one that ran for four pages), talk to your editor and be sure you understand (and accept) the contract terms before signing. If necessary, ask the editor for written clarification.

2. Reject (or at least negotiate) unwanted clauses. Some publications insert "grabby" clauses knowing that many writers won't contest them, but will remove those clauses at a writer's insistence. If your editor refuses to remove a clause outright, suggest other options, such as a higher fee or the option to reclaim your rights later.

3. Know your rights under copyright law. A publisher can't legally claim freelance material as "work for hire" unless you specifically sign an agreement to that effect. This agreement must generally be signed before you've done the work. You also need to know that under the 1999 Tasini decision, a publisher cannot claim that "first use" means the right to be "first" to use your material in any medium. "First use" applies only to the primary medium of distribution (e.g., first print use); any other use is considered separate and must be negotiated separately.

4. Transfer nonexclusive rights whenever possible. Many publications seek exclusive rights only in their primary medium. Thus, print publications usually require exclusive "first" or "one-time" print rights, but are often willing to accept nonexclusive electronic rights. Similarly, electronic publications usually want exclusive electronic rights for a period of time, but are often willing to accept nonexclusive print rights (and some electronic publications don't ask for print rights at all). Nonexclusive rights allow you to sell the same material to more than one publication at the same time.

5. Ask for a time limit on the transfer of rights. When an article appears in print, it is considered "out of print" after the issue date has passed. When an article appears online, however, it may remain accessible to readers indefinitely. This can hinder your ability to resell that material; many editors won't want to buy a piece that can be accessed online for free. By specifying a limit on how long your material can be displayed online (e.g., "exclusive electronic rights for one year"), you improve your chances of reselling that material later.

6. Ask for a reversion of rights. Selling your rights doesn't always mean they're gone forever (though many publications would like you to think so). If an editor won't compromise on a contract, ask if you can add a "reversion" clause that will restore your rights after a period of time. Or, consider contacting an editor later to ask for some of your rights back. Print periodicals are most likely to reuse material within a year of its original publication—e.g., in an electronic database, on a Web site, or in an annual "best of" collection. If your material hasn't been reused within one to two years, an editor is likely to be much more willing to grant you the right to sell it somewhere else.

Nothing can protect you from a grabby contract that can't be negotiated. Vigilance, however, can protect you from publishers who attempt to claim more rights than you've authorized.

Protecting Book Rights

In recent years, book publishers have also become increasingly likely to demand electronic rights, not only for online or CD-ROM use, but in any future medium "yet to be developed." Here are some key issues to be aware of when negotiating a book contract:

1. Electronic editions and e-readers. In the past, electronic rights were usually lumped under "subsidiary rights" (e.g., translation rights, movie rights, etc.). Publishers rarely used those rights directly, but often sold them to third parties and authors usually received a 50 percent share of the proceeds of such sales. The development of electronic editions designed for use with handheld "e-readers" (such as NuvoMedia's Rocket eBook) has changed all that. Today, many publishers claim that electronic editions are simply another form of "distribution" of the print edition, and are offering authors nothing more than standard print royalties for electronic rights. Authors claim that this is unfair, given the lower costs of producing electronic editions; publishers respond that because of the heavy discounts demanded by e-reader companies, profits are too low to offer authors a higher share. For example, NuvoMedia (which distributes e-books through Barnes & Noble) demands a 60 percent "distribution fee" from publishers, and offers no advance for authors.[2] However, it is hard to believe that major publishers have been unable to negotiate better terms for themselves or their authors!

2. Reversion of rights. Traditionally, authors could reclaim their rights to a manuscript if the publisher allowed it to go out of print (i.e., did not make it available for sale for six months or longer). This, too, is changing. Publishers are exploring the option of printing "books on demand," a technology that enables publishers to print single copies of books rather than huge quantities. Authors' groups fear that when books can be printed "on demand," whenever a customer places an order, this will prevent books from officially going "out of print" and prevent authors from reclaiming their rights, even if a book is selling no more than a single copy a year. According to *Publishers Weekly*, at least one publisher claims that a book is "in print" as long as it is "displayed for sale" in any format, regardless of how many copies are actually being sold. Others are adopting clauses that specify the number of copies that must be sold per year (e.g., 300) to qualify as "in print." Still others leave contract language vague unless the author insists on a well-defined rights-reversion clause.[3] Authors who do regain their rights to out-of-print titles face another electronic dilemma: Whether to have their books reprinted by a "print-on-demand" firm. The Author's Guild has already partnered with one such firm, toExcel, to reprint its members' out-of-print titles. Other agencies offer similar services. Such reprinting, however, is usually handled on a "subsidy" basis, meaning that you pay a fee for publication and are primarily responsible for marketing your book. As with any subsidy arrangement, you should read the contract carefully before making a decision.

3. Electronic books. Many authors have turned to electronic publishing as an alternative to print publishing. While e-book sales are still lower than print sales, e-book contracts tend to be far more author-friendly than those of print publishers. Most e-publishers ask only for the rights they plan to use, and make no claims on print rights (unless offering a print-on-demand service) or subsidiary rights such as translation or movie rights. Royalties are higher (between 20 percent and 40 percent) and paid more often (usually quarterly). E-books are generally available in the major online bookstores (such as Amazon.com, Barnes & Noble, and Borders), but are rarely found in "real-world" bookstores (though they can be ordered at any bookstore). E-book publishers avoid the "out-of-print" dilemma by offering contracts that must be renewed every one to three years. This enables either the author or publisher to "opt out" at the end of the contract period, and also offers the author a chance to test a book's marketability in the electronic marketplace while still seeking print publication. Electronic subsidy publishing is also flourishing online, and costs an author far less than its print counterpart. While a print "vanity press" may charge $10,000 to $20,000 to publish your book, an electronic subsidy publisher will usually charge between $100 and $500. Reputable subsidy publishers usually offer the same royalties as commercial e-publishers (from 25 percent to 40 percent). Unfortunately, many electronic subsidy contracts are less author-friendly than those of commercial e-publishers. (One, for example, claims the right to reuse your material in its own publications—e.g., if you published a book of poetry, the publisher could "borrow" some of your poems for its own anthology, for which it would pay you a prorated share of royalties.)[4] Many offer minimal royalties (15 percent to 20 percent), despite the low costs of electronic publishing and the fact that you're paying a fee for publication to begin with, and many require longer time commitments than commercial e-publishers. Fortunately, nearly all e-publishers post their contracts online, which enables a writer to make an informed choice; be wary of any publisher who doesn't make this information available, or who leaves important clauses "to be negotiated."

Protecting Your Web Site

You'd think that material you write and "publish" yourself, on your own Web site, would be free from the contractual risks that plague commercial publishing contracts, right? Don't count on it! In 1999, Yahoo! triggered a wave of outrage when it acquired the sites hosted by GeoCities and developed a "Terms of Service" agreement that essentially amounted to a claim to all rights to all material posted on its customers' sites. Ultimately, Yahoo! was persuaded to change its contract language, but it is not alone.[5] According to Amy Gahran, editor of *Contentious*, free ISPs are more likely to incorporate such "grabby" language than fee-based ISPs, and their contracts should be reviewed with care. One ISP, for example, permits customers to use material found on the sites of other customers (though it acknowledges that in some cases, this could be a copyright violation).[6] You may also forfeit your rights to your work if you write for one of the various "Web guide" sites, such as About.com or Suite101. These two sites claim all rights to any material you produce for them, including your own columns and articles, and your lists of links and other resources. Your risk may not end there, however: Some guide sites also prohibit contributors from hosting a personal Web site on the same topic. Thus, if you wrote a "guide" column on horror novels, you could be prohibited from later offering a personal Web site on the same subject, even after you've terminated your contract with the guide site.[7] Another risk of posting material on your Web site is that if you later try to sell that same material, publications will regard it as "previously published" and treat it as a reprint (which usually means lower rates). Some publications won't accept previously posted material at all. Thus, it's usually far better to seek publication for your work first and post it online after it has been published (presuming you've been able to retain the rights to do so).

Writing for the Web can be highly rewarding, both financially and through the recognition you gain from appearing online. Electronic rights, however, are a tangled web all their own, and one that probably won't be disentangled for several years. For now, your only protection against "rights grabs" lies in knowing your rights, reading your contracts, and keeping abreast of the latest news and issues. In this way, you'll be better able to protect your property and reap its rewards in "all media now known or later developed through the universe." After all, who knows what those Klingon data crystal rights may be worth?

Other Resources:

American Society of Journalists and Authors (ASJA)

www.asja.org

Offers advice on contract issues involving electronic rights, including *Contract Watch*, a free newsletter alerting writers to publishers who offer "grabby" contracts.

The Authors Guild

www.authorsguild.org/welcome.html

Copyright Code

www.law.cornell.edu/uscode/17/

Copyright and Intellectual Property

www.arl.org/info/frn/copy/copytoc.html

Sponsored by the Association of Research Libraries, this site offers an extensive set of links to current legislation on copyright and related issues.

E-Publishing FAQ (by Moira Allen)

www.inkspot.com/epublish/articles/epublishfaq.html

National Writers Union

www.nwu.org

Check here for details of the Tasini decision, and other actions and controversies involving electronic rights.

SFWA Statement on Electronic Rights

www.sfwa.org/contracts/ELEC.htm

The Science Fiction Writers of America position on electronic rights, including an open letter from a lawyer on rights issues involved in handheld "e-readers."

Endnotes:

1. National Writers Union, "Tasini v New York Times Ruling: What Does It Mean for Writers?" (September 26, 1999): www.nwu.org/tvt/9909vic.htm.

2. The Authors Guild, "E-Book Agreements Are Bad Deals for Authors and Publishers," www.authorsguild.org/prebook.html.

3. Steven M. Zeitchik, "The Great Ether Grab," *Publishers Weekly Online*, (June 14, 1999): www.publishersweekly.com/articles/19990614_71279.asp.

4. Writers Club Press, "Publishing Agreement for New Manuscripts," (October 18, 1999): www.iuniverse.com/publish/wcpressagr.html.

5. Sandeep Junnarkar, "Yahoo Relents on GeoCities Terms," CNET News.com (June 30, 1999): news.cnet.com/news/0-1005-200-344341.html.

6. Amy Gahran, "Web Host Content Grabs," *Contentious* (August 9, 1999): www.contentious.com/articles/V2/2-4/editorial2-4.html.

7. Marla Milling, "Net Guides: Good for Your Career?" in Moira Allen's *Writing.com: Creative Internet Strategies to Advance Your Writing Career* (New York: Allworth Press, 1999).

CHAPTER SIX

Networking Online

The Online Grapevine

In some ways, networking online tends to be a more powerful tool than networking offline because information can be conveyed so much more quickly. This comes with its disadvantages; if you upset an editor or start a flame war, for example, chances are good that quite a few people will know about it before the day is over. My rule has always been: Never post a message in anger. Always let a few hours pass before you post anything, and then imagine how you'd feel if your posting was circulated to people outside of the particular conversation, likely out of context.

Always behave professionally, even in a casual environment like a chat room or friendly mailing list. You never know who might be lurking in the background, possibly misinterpreting your careless comments, such as editors or potential employers. "I get many writing solicitations through listserv groups I belong to," says Kim Swenson Gollnick. "As a result, I submitted to several projects, and got the good news that my essays were accepted and will appear in three different book projects this year."

Overcoming Isolation

In the response to my survey, many online writers said that online networking helped get their creative juices flowing again, inspiring them to be more productive. "Selling aside, the Internet has de-isolated writing," says writer Magee Gilks.

Children's book author Lee Wardlaw agrees: "Writing can be a lonely profession. It's just you and your pen. Or you and your word processor. But the Internet has changed that. I've made a number of writing friends through conversations and lectures in chat rooms. I've also made friends through an online writing club for professional children's authors. We cheer each others' sales, boo rejection letters, and send cyberhugs when books go out of print or contracts are cancelled. We often critique manuscripts, and have lively discussions about contracts, agents, editors, book signings, conferences, workshops, and school visits. With their wide range of knowledge, experiences, and personalities, these people are invaluable resources—as well as an important support system."

Networking for Sales

Don't underestimate the power of online networking to lead you to more sales. Of the online writers I surveyed, many said they got their assignments through contacts. Some contacts were made through regular print assignments, some through chat rooms, discussion forums, mailing lists, and still others by simple recommendations ("You need someone to review books? I know the perfect person!"). See Dana Nourie's article below, "Making Sales Through Online Networking," for more tips.

MAKING SALES THROUGH ONLINE NETWORKING
by Dana Nourie

Dana Nourie frequently writes for *Family Circle, Family Life, Walking*, and online markets such as KBkids.com, Inkspot, and Discovery Online. In addition, she maintains the Web pages of Writers' Guidelines Database (www.writersdatabase.com) and *Freelance Success* (www.freelancesuccess.com). You can network and trade publishing secrets with her on many online forums and lists.

In an online forum, I voiced a complaint, "I mailed my query five months ago and haven't heard back. This idea is perfect for *Fitness* magazine. Do the editors there usually take so long to respond?"

A woman who frequently writes for *Fitness* magazine responded to my frustration. After a bit of discussion about my idea, the writer sent me a private e-mail. "I called my editor at *Fitness*," she said. "I told her a bit about your idea and that I highly recommend that they use you." I was thrilled she had been so thoughtful and eager to help me get my foot in the door. She gave me her editor's e-mail address, and two hours after I e-mailed my query I heard back from the editor. Two days later, I had a firm assignment.

How often do writers meet such generous comrades? Frequently. Through online networking, writers share experiences, give advice, announce editorial changes, and divulge contact information. Most of this information isn't available in the paper world. What does appear in print is stale. By the time a job opening or an editor's e-mail address is published, the information is old if not changed or obsolete, and competition is fierce.

"The Internet is a powerful grapevine filled with all sorts of interesting news," says Janice Wells, a Californian who writes for numerous magazines including *Woman's Day, Parenting, Family Life*, and several newspapers. "Other professions hear about jobs, news and gossip by 'word on the street' but for writers like me who can't get away from their desk, it's now 'word on the Net.'"

Through job boards, forums, discussion lists, and e-mail, writers have discovered that online networking increases their sales. There is a lot of "I'll scratch your back, you scratch mine," going on online. But don't think it's just who you know. Ultimately your ideas have to be appropriate to your target market and your writing skills must be sound. Getting to know other writers well enough that they'll share an editor's name, recommend you to an editor, or let you know that a magazine has just folded takes a little time and lots of friendliness. Knowing where to go and how to or not to behave can mean success or failure in your online networking ventures.

Job Boards

You're likely familiar with the classifieds in the newspaper. Job boards on the Internet are similar. Like with the classifieds, you learn what kind of writing an editor wants, whom to contact, and sometimes how much the assignment or job pays. Listings for editorial positions, copyeditors, and copywriters fill these kinds of job boards. When you see one that suits the kind of writing you want to do, send your resume with a writing sample. Many writers have gotten writing work this way.

The problem with job boards is that many, many other writers are also reading these job ads, so the competition is fierce, and unfortunately some editors are reluctant to advertise on the boards for fear of being overly swamped with inappropriate material. And job boards are about as dry and dull as newspaper classifieds. Even so, peruse them regularly because the writing position you've been seeking may be posted and ready to be filled.

"I've had several writing jobs off of boards such as JAWS and *Inklings* Classifieds," says Terry Miller Shannon, health and parenting writer. "I'm now writing regularly for CBSHealthWatch.com and Planned Parenthood's teenwire.com due to ads on job boards."

Discussion Boards and Discussion Lists

Discussion boards and discussion lists have some advantages over job boards. Though they don't list the number of open writing positions that job boards do, they offer the inside scoop on many publications and Web sites. Depending on what list or board you participate on, you may get information about new contracts put out by a publisher, or you may learn that the editor you were going to send a query just left for a competing publication. You may discover the editor you're dealing with at *Family Circle* is open to negotiating terms, or that the magazine does indeed have a first rights contract. That information can yield you more income in the long run.

"What I learn from my writing buddies saves me lots of time and aggravation, too," adds Wells. "Often writers confirm my own suspicions, like a particular market may not be worth pursuing or is slow or low paying, or no longer accepting queries."

Besides learning about what editors don't want, or that they're not open to freelancers, writers often get wind of new magazines before the print world does.

Time is crucial, and when Rich Maffeo learned about a new women's Christian magazine, he fired off some of his articles and sold them as reprints.

Besides such helpful information about publications, job listings also get posted to lists and message boards. One such posting alerted me that KBkids.coms, formerly BrainPlay.com, needed writers. I responded immediately and have written for them frequently over the last year and a half. My experience is not unusual.

"I have a steady client I landed from a tip offered from an online buddy and another job that's in the works," says Wells. "I have to say that the only pitfall is spending too much time networking online. It's tempting to send a lot of messages and check out networking sites because feedback is instant. But, of course, the majority of a writer's time must be spent writing, working on paying assignments and jobs."

Public, Monitored, Private, or by Subscription?

"Writing is a solitary task," says Kathleen Purcell, member of several lists, public and private, and administrator of a private list that is part of the Internet Writing Workshop. "Prior to the Internet, my only opportunity to commune with other writers was at annual conferences. Everything I knew about the markets I discovered the hard way and through reading writers' magazines. Sharing marketing data, techniques, and contract expertise is a lot like meeting with a group of co-workers around the water cooler to compare working conditions and salaries."

Not all writers' message boards, forums, and lists are alike. While some have frequent helpful posts, job listings, advice from editors and writers, others suffer flame wars, off-topic discussions, and few messages of value. Others are aimed at beginners, filled with helpful how-to information and invaluable critiques. In addition, lists and boards have slightly different attitudes that work for some and not for others.

"If you're looking for a list to join," says Purcell, "you should know what you want from the list. Some lists may have requirements that you may find overwhelming, while lists without participation requirements may be monopolized by a handful of individuals, reducing everyone to lurker status."

Discussion types generally fall into public, private, and moderated. Public boards and lists are the most common, mostly because they're free and easily accessible. Just because they are public, though, does not mean people can say or do whatever they want on the list or board.

"Every list must be run by someone," adds Purcell. "Theoretically, they can remove problem individuals. Some lists are more open than others. E-mailed lists have more potential to be controlled, although some well-known e-mail lists are very open."

With the diversity of writers and variations on experience levels, opinions can be vastly different. Frequently flame wars break out on these lists. Be careful what you say online, as you never know what editor may be reading those posts or what writers you may offend. If a flame war ignites, ignore it. Bring up other topics of interest to you and wait out the arguments.

Private and subscriber-based lists and boards don't generally suffer the petty flame wars of the public lists. "These lists are under the control of individuals who can maintain order by removing problem members," says Purcell. "Private lists tend to be more focused, less argumentative, and reflect the personality of the list administrator. So it's important that you find a list that's comfortable for you."

Private and subscriber-based lists also tend to be more lucrative in terms of the information that is passed around, including editors' names, e-mail addresses, phone numbers, paragraphs from contracts, and recommendations. Besides writers sharing information, many of these lists also have a good number of working editors, some from big magazines such as *Family Circle* and *First for Women*. Experience levels are higher and attitudes more open. In addition, private and subscribers-only lists often have guest speakers visit, ready and willing to answer writers' questions.

"Because of a guest to a private list I belong to, I learned about the opportunity to apply for a vacant columnist position," says Jenny Rackley, health and parenting writer. "This guest got to know a bit about me and my writing, then I sent my proposal. It was accepted and I was a columnist for a year and a half. Had I not been a member of that discussion group, I never would have learned of the opportunity."

Private lists are not as easy to get into as public and subscriber-only lists. These are invitation-only lists, and once you join you are sworn to secrecy about its existence. So how can you get into one of these great discussion groups? By making your presence known on public and subscriber-only lists. Provide enough valuable input and information on these lists and soon you may receive an e-mail, inviting you to join a private list.

With public and private lists available, why join one that requires you to pay for a subscription? Subscription lists offer the same benefits that private ones do, but you can join any time you like. In addition to editorial contact info, market information, etc., these lists also invite guests to put on seminars on various topics such as taxes, contract negotiations, writing book proposals, etc. Guest speakers are experts in their fields, such as editors, authors of writing books, lawyers, publishers, and others. These seminars can last from a day to several weeks and allow interaction for writers to ask specific questions that are answered by the guest expert.

Subscription discussion lists also lack flame wars and pointless bickering. On the contrary, members are more likely to share inside information, knowing that it will go no farther than the list since everyone is paying a fee to be on board. In addition, most subscriber lists also include high-quality newsletters with invaluable market information.

"I had wanted to write for HealthGate.com," says Terry Miller Shannon, health, essay, and fiction writer. "Then it just so happened someone on the *Freelance Success* forum asked about this company. A writer responded that she had written for them regularly, that they were a tough market to crack but great to work for, and she provided the editor's e-mail address. I sent a query that day and got a 'We're interested, please call' e-mail within a week and got my first assignment with them."

Connecting With Writers and Other People

No matter what type of writing list or discussion board you join, connecting with other writers will prove invaluable to increasing your writing income. In addition to market information, writing instruction, and good advice, writers' experiences can help you earn more from the assignments you get.

Contracts lay out what a writer is paid and what rights are bought, but frequently contracts are not written with the writer's interest at heart. Mona Vanek, a Montana book and article writer, learned about negotiating better terms from lists and then through invaluable URLs she was given.

"I learned about the American Society of Journalists and Authors and the National Writers Union through networking. ASJA (www.asja.org) helped me with several contracts (free of charge)."

Mona has not only learned to negotiate better terms for her assignments, but she has turned her newfound knowledge into articles for *Writer's Digest, Freelance Success,* and *State of the Arts.* In addition, excerpts from her writer's conference notes, shared with many online writing groups, have been published in a Romance Writers of America newsletter in California.

As helpful to increasing your writing income as writing lists are, don't overlook discussion lists in other areas of interest. Joining lists that concentrate on your other interests and hobbies can yield information, contacts, and anecdotes for more writing assignments and sales.

"Probably my most lucrative liaison came from a message board for party planning," says Phyllis Cambria. "After writing numerous responses to questions on the board, a well-known party planning professional and author of eight party books, Patty Sachs, contacted me. She asked if I had considered writing a book about party planning. I sent her a book proposal I had written before (it had been rejected by numerous publishers). In response she asked me to co-author some articles with her, then when a major book publisher contacted Patty she asked them to consider me to write it with her. After viewing my resume and clips, they agreed. We've also been approached by several companies to write for their Web sites."

So be sure to keep your interests alive by joining a few lists in those areas, and don't hesitate to let folks know that you are a professional writer. You never know where your online networking may take you.

Online Discussion Boards:

Freelance Success

www.freelancesuccess.com

Subscription fee. Contains an excellent market newsletter.

Inkspot's Forums

www.inkspot.com/forums/topics.html

Free to the public.

The Literary Times Message Board

www.writerswrite.com/messages/

Free to the public.

Writers' Guidelines Database

www.writersdatabase.com

Free to the public.

E-Mail Discussion Lists:

Liszt

www.liszt.com/

Lists of Lists

catalog.com/vivian/interest-group-search.html

Tile Net

tile.net/

Private Lists and Boards:

Sorry but I've sworn secrecy on my decoder ring. Join lists and discussion boards and maybe you'll be noticed and receive an invitation.

E-Mailing Thereafter

Once you've established yourself on a few lists and boards and had some success in publishing, you'll find online networking increasing your sales as well as developing e-mail friendships with writers and editors that are invaluable.

"We trade industry information, critique each other's work and offer a shoulder when needed," says Carole Moore, humor writer in North Carolina. "I've made friends who don't think writing humor is an odd profession."

CHAPTER SEVEN

Online Promotion

THE INTERNET PROVIDES numerous promotional opportunities for writers, many for relatively low costs. "The Web is pretty much the cheapest form of self-promotion going," says Sabina Becker.

Before You Start Promoting . . .

Before launching into online promotion, take some time to familiarize yourself with the environment. Some people mistakenly believe that they can promote online the same way they do offline.

Let's make up an example to illustrate this point. Suppose we have an author, Gomer Glotz, who has just published a book about hedgehog care. He wants to promote it, and he has heard that the Internet is a cheap and easy way of doing it. Gomer is relatively new to the Internet. He knows how to use e-mail, does a little Web surfing, and has visited a chat room once. He does some research and finds a volunteer-run mailing list for pet owners.

The first thing Gomer does is to prepare an enthusiastic press release about his book and mails it to everyone in his electronic address book. Then he joins the pet owner mailing list and posts the message to the entire group. When he logs on the next day, he is shocked to find irritated e-mail messages from some of the people in his electronic address book, asking if he could remove their e-mail addresses from his list. He also finds several extremely angry messages from members of the pet owner list, and on the list itself, several others are publicly accusing Gomer of "spamming." Gomer is hurt and bewildered. What did he do wrong?

Don't spam

First, he e-mailed his press release to people who didn't ask for it. The term "spam" was originally created to refer to excessive posts and cross-posts in Usenet newsgroups but now is often used also to refer to off-topic posts in mailing lists, advertisements, and other unsolicited mail. People tend not to like spam, sometimes to the point of complaining to the ISP of the person who sent the spam (who may choose to terminate a spammer's online account as a result).

Avoid the "hard sell" approach

Secondly, he posted in the pet owner mailing list without lurking first. His message may not have been seen as spam if Gomer had taken the time to become an active member of the community, showing genuine interest in the list postings rather than viewing the list just as a promotional tool. And even then, online communities tend to react badly to the "hard sell" approach in a forum like the mailing list or chat room.

It would have been better to lurk first, then participate in the discussion without actively pushing the book. Instead Gomer could use a signature (text appended to every e-mail message he sends out) to mention the book.

You can find other promotion tips in Bev Walton-Porter's article on page 68, "How to Promote Your Work Online."

Making Your Own Web Site

Having your own Web site can be a valuable tool in promoting yourself and your writing. However, creating and maintaining one can be a time-consuming process. Whether you're considering making your own Web site or having someone do it for you, ask yourself the following questions to help you get started.

What do you want to accomplish?

Do you want to promote your newest novel with your Web site? Convince editors to give you assignments? Promote your editorial or writing services? Sell your books online?

Who is your target audience?

Is your Web site geared toward your already-existing fans or those who aren't familiar with your writing? Or both?

What type of Web site do you want?

Most author Web sites tend to be "brochureware." "Brochureware" is an informal term that refers to Web sites that contain the basic information about an author, but not much more. These sites are rarely updated, and are similar in function to business cards; they provide a simple source of reference information. There is nothing wrong with this type of Web site, but the content doesn't usually encourage repeat visits. You can enhance your Web site with other content and features, but this brings up the next question.

How much time are you willing to devote to creating and maintaining the site?

This question is important. Even if you decide to hire someone to create your Web site, you need to provide input to help guide the development and content.

Some writers expect that they can create a Web site and then just ignore it. At the very least, the Web site content would need to be updated on a regular basis to reflect new publications and other changing information. And if you plan to make your site more than a typical brochureware site, then you must commit time.

If you are an unpublished writer with few or no writing credits, ask yourself whether your time is better spent working on your own writing and building up credits first.

What kind of tone do you want?

Your site should be "professional," of course, in that content should be accurate and carefully checked for spelling and grammar errors. But do you also want to instill any kind of personality? Do you want your site to be merely a place where users can look up information, or an environment they would want to linger in and explore?

How Can I Enhance My Web Site?

There are many ways to encourage repeat visitors to your Web site and to help your site stand out from the rest. Here are just a few suggestions.

Update frequently

This is the most important factor in encouraging repeat visits. If your readers sense that you're actively involved in the Web site, they're more likely to come back more often to see what's been changed.

Inject personality

Even adding a scanned photo will make your Web site more personal.

Add graphics

A few well-chosen graphics will enhance any Web site. Be wary of size, however. If you include a 2MB graphic of your cat, for example, users will likely grow impatient waiting for the picture to download and will surf elsewhere, no matter how adorable your pet may be.

Include unique content

Consider adding an opinion piece or article that would be of interest to your readers, such as a description of your writing process or motivation for a particular story.

You might also include samples of your writing. You may feel that people should buy your books if they want to read your writing; this may be true, but posting choice excerpts free of charge could lure those who aren't familiar with your writing into wanting to read more. Before posting excerpts from already-published works, however, always check with your publisher to make sure you aren't breaking any copyright agreements. Always include full copyright information with each piece.

Make your Web site a resource

If you write nonfiction, you could include some useful resources centered on your topic of expertise. If you just wrote a Beethoven biography, for example, you could have a section of your Web site devoted to Beethoven content, such as links to good Beethoven Web sites and other online resources.

Encourage a sense of community

Posting reader comments and encouraging other user-contributed content makes your reader community feel more involved. You can do this by posting reader feedback (always get permission first), hosting chats, publishing an electronic news-letter, creating a message board, having giveaway promotions, and so on.

How Can I Sell My Books on My Web Site?

Basically, there are two ways of selling print books through your Web site: Sell them yourself, or sell them through an affiliate or associate program offered by an online bookseller.

Selling books yourself

If you choose to sell your books yourself, then you take orders, process payments, and mail the books directly to the purchasers.

The advantage of selling the books yourself is that you get to keep more of the profits. The main disadvantage is that you have to handle all the administration yourself, such as postage, calculating taxes, payment handling, and customs issues. You are also limited to certain types of payment options unless you are willing to invest some money to accept credit card transactions.

Selling books through an affiliate/associate program

Several online booksellers offer programs in which authors can get a percentage of any book sold by referral.

The main advantage of taking this route is that the company offering the pro-gram usually handles all of the customer service, fulfillment, shipping, and tracking of sales. Customers have the option of paying by credit card.

Another advantage is that people are more willing to give their money to an established company. "When I was selling my book myself, I tried to sell it from my site but found that people preferred to read about the book on my site and then order it through Amazon.com," says M.J. Rose, author of *Lip Service.* "I didn't expect that to be the case but now realize that people felt more comfortable ordering from a known entity."

The disadvantage, of course, is the author doesn't get as much profit. In the long run, however, many authors find it worth it not to worry about the administrative issues. All you have to do is provide an HTML link on your Web site.

Amazon.com offers other promotional services for authors as well. For more information, go to Amazon.com's Books section and click on the "Author's Guide" link near the bottom of the page. If authors have distribution rights, they may also want to check out Amazon's Advantage Program.

Other online booksellers offer similar programs. You can generally find more information by going to their main pages and looking for the words "affiliate" and "associate."

Selling electronic books

Some authors are also beginning to sell their electronic works via their Web sites. For more information, please read the chapter on e-publishing.

HOW TO PROMOTE YOUR WORK ONLINE
by Bev Walton-Porter

Bev Walton-Porter is a full-time freelance writer-editor with more than 150 published pieces to her credit. Her work has appeared in many well-known writer's publications, such as *Writer's Digest, ByLine Magazine, The Oklahoma Writers' Federation Report,* and *The Write Markets Report.*

Whether you're a seasoned professional or an absolute beginner, if you're writing for the Net, you must not only target your markets and define your audience, you also need to promote your product.

Sharp writing and research will highlight your word and reasoning skills, but if you don't put energy into promoting your writing skills, and yourself, online, you'll not only miss out on possible readers, you'll also miss out on potential writing projects!

Getting Your Name Out There

Word of mouth is all-powerful. That stands for sales and for you, as well. In fact, you *are* in the selling business, whether you want to admit it or not. When you write a piece and query an editor, you are, in essence, selling a piece of yourself—a product you birthed through the sweat of your brow, the virtue of your intelligence, and the fruits of your labor.

All too often, beginning writers prefer the isolation of the writing life and are shy about promoting themselves or their work. Why? Because when writers are in that "prepublication" mode, they are unsure of their talents and they need official affirmation (hence, publication) before they feel confident enough to step from the darkness of uncertainty into the light of assuredness.

Despite your record of publication, or lack thereof, your first step toward effective online promotion is to get your name and your work out in the open. A scary thought for beginners and even intermediate writers, but the benefits far outweigh the drawbacks.

Networking is akin to the pebble-in-a-pond analogy: Throw a pebble in a pond and ripples will form and move outward, expanding and growing with every movement of the water. Likewise, as writers interact with others in their field of interest, or similar fields, names become more familiar and the Web suddenly becomes a smaller place.

If you're a novice and aren't sure how to get your name out there and recognized in the online writing community, here are some ways to begin:

Use signature lines. Sig lines, or signature lines, are those lines of text at the bottom of a person's e-mail that include his name, e-mail address, occupation, Web site address, or anything else of importance. For writers, a sig line may include all of the above, plus a "teaser" about any upcoming article or book, such as: "Look for my new book, TREASURES OF LOVE (ISBN number can be included here), to be released by XYZ publishers in December 2000."

Each time you send an e-mail, include your sig line. It's an easy way to get your name and your recent work a second look!

Write a bio. Why write a bio, even if you're a new, unpublished writer? Because you never know when you'll need it. Put all pertinent information in your bio, such as any publication credits. If you're lacking those, insert how long you've been writing and the writing groups you belong to.

Keep your bio professional: No one needs to know you love needlepoint unless you're sending a copy to an editor who works for a needlepoint magazine. Keep it crisp, professional, and to the point. As your credits build, simply use your original "template" to add to your bio.

Build a Web site. Most writers have Web sites, so why shouldn't you? For professional writers, Web sites can serve as cornerstones of their online publicity and promotion efforts.

Before you build your site, determine if you'll be building your Web presence at a free hosting site, such as GeoCities, AngelFire, or FreeYellow, or if you're willing to purchase your own domain—a relatively inexpensive choice considering it will garner you a shorter address and higher rankings in the search engines once you're registered.

If you're unfamiliar with HTML or Java, use a page wizard at the host site or design your page using a simple HTML editor, many of which are available for downloading off the Net as trial versions, shareware, or freeware.

Keep graphics and music to a minimum (for quick download) and make it look professional and clean. Your site is a direct reflection of you, so be sure you're projecting the image you want others to see!

Join a mailing list. If you're interested in professional freelancing, join a list where such people reside. Always find people who are doing what *you* want to eventually do, and model their behavior. Once you join, don't lurk without posting. Familiarize yourself with the list, learn the etiquette, and then jump in. Don't be afraid to ask questions. Often, you'll find a mentor who will be happy to assist you with writing-related concerns.

Moderate a message board or chat room. Once you become comfortable interacting with other writers, you may want to start your own message board or chat room for writers.

Have a passion for haiku? Create your own haiku haven and schedule moderated chats or critiques. On your sig line, announce your new forum and invite visitors!

Start, or join, a Web ring. Web rings include a number of sites that cater to a specific topic. For instance, romance writers will find numerous rings devoted to romance writing or authors. Once you have your Web site up and operational, visit www.webring.com and scan the offerings of rings that may pertain to your site's topic. Once you become more familiar with the way these rings work, you can then build your own Web ring. Then, every time your ring is featured on another site, you'll earn instant promotion of your site!

Use an autoresponder. As visitors peruse your professional writing Web site, many of them may be eager to read articles or other samples of your work. If you're an author, they may also wish to receive the latest update on your soon-to-be-published book list. This, among many other offerings, can be provided twenty-four hours a day by an autoresponder.

Write an online press release. One item you may use in conjunction with your autoresponder is an online press release. Written in the same tone as a print release, online press releases are sent via e-mail or posted on the Web in an online "press room" where media and interested others may visit.

If you've been commissioned to write a monthly column for a prestigious online site, or if your first book has been released, write up an online press release and send it via e-mail (to your opt-in list) along with posting it in your Web site's "media room."

Become an expert. Write a column. Gain name recognition and an air of expertise about you by writing a column for guide sites such as Suite101 or About.com. By selecting a topic you're passionate about and churning out regular columns, you benefit twofold.

First, you're exercising your writing skills—and honing them—on a regular basis, as well as establishing yourself as an expert in a certain category of interest. And, although your topic may not be related to writing, your guide bio can make mention of your profession and provide a link to your writing Web site.

Publish an e-zine. There are a million e-zines in the online world, and perhaps you have the energy and gumption to edit and publish your own. Although an e-zine takes a lot of time and effort, smart promoters know they are effective in increasing product and name recognition. That goes for pencils, as well as for prose and poetry.

If you do take the step and publish an e-zine, always include this bit of information in your standard bio—it shows you have initiative and enthusiasm, not to mention creativity! Finally, use your autoresponder, mailing list, and message board to announce upcoming issues of your e-zine.

Conduct a workshop. If you have firm publication credits and experience, one way to promote your work is to facilitate an online writing workshop. By lending your experience and assistance to new writers, you do your part by giving back to the writing community, as well as raising the level of your professionalism.

If you're not ready to conduct a workshop, volunteer to lead a critique session or weekly writers' chat. Eventually, once you feel more confidence in your abilities, you can move up to workshop facilitation.

Final Words

Depending on your specific writing goals, you may choose to implement some, or all, of these promotion and marketing techniques. Consider what results you're looking for, then build your promotion strategy around them.

In the end, when it comes to writing, putting the words on the computer screen is only half of the equation. Online promotion is the perfect answer that will deliver the results you need to succeed!

ENCYCLOPEDIAS, DINOSAURS, AND THE INTERNET: TAKING A LESSON FROM ALL THREE AND MAKING THE MOST OF THE LATTER

by Brian A. Hopkins

Brian A. Hopkins is the author of more than sixty stories in a variety of professional and semiprofessional magazines and anthologies, including *Dragon Magazine*, *Aboriginal SF*, *Realms of Fantasy*, and the Stoker Award–winning anthology *Horrors! 365 Scary Stories*. Recently published is *Flesh Wounds* (Lone Wolf Publications), a CD-ROM story collection.

The metropolitan library system in Oklahoma City sells its older books every year. (The abundance of ex-library books for sale around the country tells me that other cities do the same.) This year, I was struck by the number of encyclopedias. For ten dollars you could own a complete set, *A* to *Z*, that must have sold originally for over a thousand dollars. What's worse is these encyclopedias *weren't* selling, not even at ten dollars a set. At the end of the sale, our library offers up everything that remains for a mind-boggling two dollars per grocery sack. An industrious individual could possibly load that complete set of encyclopedias into a single (admittedly heavy) grocery sack. You could literally take home an entire set of *Encyclopedia Britannica* for two dollars! Granted, these are older encyclopedias, perhaps ten years out of date, but it's still staggering to consider that not too long ago there were guys who made a living doing nothing but selling them. Where are these encyclopedia salesmen now? Gone, like the dinosaur. With a Grolier's or Microsoft Encarta CD-ROM included with most computer purchases, no one's buying bound encyclopedias anymore.

This is a serious indicator, not only of our times, but of things to come. The question is, will writers who don't grasp the significance suffer the same fate as encyclopedia salesmen and dinosaurs? And, more obviously, will books ultimately be replaced with more convenient electronic formats?

As one who loves the feel, the smell—indeed the whole *experience*—that can only be had with a *real* book, I'm happy to say that the Internet and electronic publishing are not, as of this writing, ready to put the traditional paper publishing industry out of business. However, they are making serious inroads, and authors asleep at the word processor are at serious risk of being left behind. Authors should be taking advantage of the current trends in electronic publishing. There are some very simple things that all writers should do.

The Internet is probably the best vehicle ever invented for advertising, and the real beauty is that much of its potential can be had for free. Every author should establish a Web presence by building a Web page. Hypertext Markup Language (HTML), the programming language used to code documents on the Internet, is simple to learn. If you haven't the time to figure it out, there are thousands of young Web programmers eager to help. Most Web programmers work at reasonable rates; however, most writers with an established fan base would have little trouble locating fans who'd gladly create and maintain an author's Web page for free. Make sure the location of your Web page is submitted to all the popular search engines—AltaVista (www.altavista.com), Yahoo! (www.yahoo.com), Lycos (www.lycos.com), etc. This is generally as simple as going to the search engine's Web site and submitting your Unique Resource Locator (URL), the Internet address by which your site may be found. Finding Internet space to host your site is relatively simple and generally free. Most Internet Service Providers (ISP) provide users with a certain amount of Web real estate. There are also providers oriented specifically to serving the writing community, most of which will provide free Web space and e-mail service to established writers. SFF Net (www.sff.net) and Dueling Modems (www.dm.net) are two that come to mind. In addition, there are dozens of providers such as Xoom (www.xoom.com) and Yahoo! willing to provide free Web space and e-mail service to all subscribers in exchange for the minor annoyance of being subjected to their advertising.

There are other Web-based vehicles for free advertising that authors should use to their advantage: guest spots in moderated chat rooms (unmoderated rooms are typically too chaotic for an author to use to advantage), newsgroups (again, offered free by providers such as SFF Net and Dueling Modems), e-mail newsletters (fan- or author-generated), and list-servers such as Onelist (www.onelist.com), to name a few. All of these vehicles provide an author with a forum for meeting with fans and discussing current and forthcoming work. No advertising works better than direct contact.

Internet e-mail gives fans a means of providing you with feedback and inquiring about other work you might have available. Your Web page should always include a means of sending e-mail to you. If you don't have time to answer the e-mail, have someone else do it for you, even if you have to pay him. Nothing keeps readers more interested in your work than being able to communicate with the author. Besides contact with fans, e-mail is the single greatest resource for networking with other authors, publishers, and agents. Cheaper than phone calls and nearly as fast, e-mail has become the communication tool of choice. In recent years, e-mail has even started replacing other types of communication. Need a fax machine to receive a proof of your latest short story? There are now free Web-based fax machines. Xoom offers one as part of its services. Faxes are received at a phone number specifically assigned to you, they're converted to a graphics format and e-mailed to you, where you can view them on the monitor or print them out. With a fax-modem card in your computer for sending faxes and a service like Xoom for receiving them, there's no need to spend hundreds of dollars on a machine that you probably don't have room on your desk for anyway.

Short story writers should offer reprint rights on the Internet every chance they get. Though most Web-based electronic magazines "e-zines" can't afford to pay, they're always eager to carry the work of established authors. The exposure will invariably lead Internet surfers to seek out the short story collections and novels you have in print. Reprints in e-zines are a good method of reintroducing stories that have long been out of print. There are only a few e-zines that offer payment approaching that of print publications, so marketing original fiction on the Web is a dicey prospect. Its only primary advantage is that nearly all Web-based publications accept submissions via e-mail, while print publishers seem to be lagging in the acceptance of this money-saving option. There are also a lot of unique formatting options involving color graphics and animation that are simply not available on the printed page. Otherwise, writing for the Internet is no different than writing for print publications. It's been my experience that the established e-zines are every bit as professional as their print brethren. Be sure the URL for your Web site and your e-mail address is prominently displayed with any of your work that appears on the Internet.

Novelists should consider making their out-of-print work available in electronic formats. Though none of the present electronic options are lucrative enough, in my opinion, to prove viable for original novels, this will likely change in the next ten years. Just remember the encyclopedias. E-mail has also been used by several authors now, myself included, to serialize novel-length work. In addition to the recent avalanche of downloadable e-novels, there's the compact disk option. With CD-ROM hardware and media prices becoming more and more reasonable, publishing on CD-ROM has never looked better. There are distinct advantages to publishing on CD-ROM when compared to print media. Like all electronic formats, the text of your work can include hyperlinks. These links might do nothing more than control the flow of the story, perhaps even making it interactive, or they might whisk the reader away to peripheral sites on the Internet or activate other programs stored on the CD. Compact disks allow for full color graphics and animation. Both audio and video tracks can be loaded on the CD and synchronized to the text. When was the last time you read a novel with a sound track? When was the last time you heard the author introduce his work or actually watched him give that introduction right there on the page?

Writers who don't embrace the electronic forum will be forced, eventually, to play catch-up, competing in a market where younger, more aggressive writers have already become well established. If not, these writers will be left behind. It's to their advantage to make the most of *both* electronic and print media for as long as both are with us.

CHAPTER EIGHT

E-publishing

What Is Electronic Publishing?

Electronic publishing (also known as "e-publishing") is a form of publishing where text is stored electronically. This text can be read on a computer screen or handheld reader, or printed for later reading. The term "e-book" is short for "electronic book," or a book with an electronic binding.

The advent of the Internet made it possible for anyone with access to the Net to become a publisher. This was both a good and bad thing. "The decentralizing of publishing is giving a voice to the voiceless; any individual, club, gang, or school can go online and start publishing," says Crawford Kilian, author of *Writing for the Web* (International Self-Counsel Press). "This is a welcome development. But the sheer volume of such publications is making them seem less important. A 'real' book still counts for more. This may change as Web documents acquire some of the beauty of books, but don't hold your breath. The Queen could ride in a Rolls to open Parliament, but she still takes a horse-drawn coach. The prestige of the book will be a long time dying."

E-books: Will They Ever Replace Paper Books?

There is much speculation about whether electronic books would ever replace paper books. I suspect traditionally bound books will be around for a long time;

it will be difficult to replace the distinctive experience of holding and reading a paper book. Handheld readers like the RocketBook and SoftBook have attracted much attention but are not selling very well, partly because of the hefty price tag and partly, say analysts, because consumers don't enjoy this new reading experience nearly as much as the old-fashioned way.

Technology will gradually improve this aspect, making it easier to read text on a screen. Researchers are also working on developing a kind of "electronic paper" that could help solve this problem. Anyone who has read Neal Stephenson's *The Diamond Age* (Spectra Books) will be familiar with this idea. Imagine reaching for the morning newspaper over breakfast and being able to program the "e-paper" to display the contents of your favorite newspaper. And having a different newspaper display when your spouse picks it up. The possibilities are endless.

Whether or not e-books eventually become more popular than regular printed books, many authors and publishers are beginning to investigate the possibilities of electronic books. Some authors choose this route because they have been unsuccessful in marketing to traditional publishing houses. Some want more direct control over the profits.

Still others opt for e-books because they are intrigued by the new technology and want to be a part of this new type of publishing. David Saperstein, author of the best-selling novel *Cocoon* (Jove), purposely decided to sidestep traditional publishing channels and publish a novel exclusively on the Internet (www.darkagain.com).

Just before this book went to press, Stephen King's book *Riding the Bullet* (Scribner), was released in electronic format, attracting a flurry of media and industry attention. Time-Warner also announced its new venture into electronic publishing, iPublish. The interest in electronic publishing is only beginning; it will be exciting to see what happens in the next five years.

What Is "Print on Demand," or "POD"?

Also known as "on-demand printing," POD is a new technology that makes short-run printing more affordable. POD publishers can convert an author's manuscript to electronic format, create a cover, and then list the book with online booksellers like Amazon.com and barnesandnoble.com. When readers order the title, the book can be printed and sent out within a matter of days.

Most publishers need to print at least several thousand copies of a book to make it economically feasible. POD makes it easier to revive books that are out of print as well as publish books with specialized topics that have a narrow audience. POD services seem to be a natural fit for the e-publishing industry. Since the text is already in electronic format, several e-publishers are offering the option of producing the book in bound hardcopy format as well as electronic.

Fees for POD services vary widely. Xlibris (now partnered with Random House and located at www.xlibris.com) recently made its core publishing service free. It will be interesting to see if other POD services follow suit. iUniverse (www.iuniverse.com) also offers publishing services for authors, charging $99 and higher for new manuscripts.

Policies regarding author rights also vary. Be sure to read the author contract carefully—what rights are you giving away? And for how long?

How Can I Turn My Book Into an E-book?

If your book is in hardcopy format only (i.e., paper sheets of typewritten text), then you will need to convert it to electronic format. You can do this yourself by typing the text into a computer, or by using a third party. Some authors are turning their out-of-print titles into e-books.

Companies are beginning to offer services to help authors determine whether their books are officially out of print and to help them digitize their books for use as e-books or as preparation for on-demand printing. E-Rights (www.e-rights.com) is one such service created by New York literary agent Richard Curtis.

Should I Sell My Writing Myself, or Through Someone Else?

The main advantage of selling directly, of course, is that you get to keep more of the profit. The main disadvantages are that you are likely limited in publication format (what if you want your writing in PDF format? Readable by Rocket eBooks?

Other formats?), and that you are completely responsible for your own marketing promotion as well as administration and transaction handling. If you want to accept online credit card payments, for example, you must research how to set this up, and pay the accompanying fees.

Commercial e-publishers. One solution is to be published by a commercial e-publisher. See "E-Book Basics" by Leta Nolan Childers for an overview of the e-book industry, and Jamie Engle's article "Tips for Selecting a Commercial E-publisher" on page 86.

Third-party services. These are varied in nature, from commercial e-publishers to pay-per-view to "display" services. Several of these are listed at the end of the markets listing section.

By the time this book is published, there will likely be many other models of online content publishing available to authors. Be wary of any that charge upfront fees—are they worth it? Does the site attract a lot of traffic? Ask for statistics. Read the contract carefully. What rights are you giving away? Can you sell your piece elsewhere? Can you remove it from the service anytime?

Also, be aware that some editors may consider your work already published if it's posted online (i.e., you may not be able to sell first-time rights to the piece).

Other Resources:

Electronic Publishing Resource

www.inkspot.com/epublish/

Includes an E-publishing FAQ and a Print-on-Demand FAQ by Moira Allen.

Electronic Publishing: The Definitive Guide

www.petalsoflife.com/karen.html

By Karen Wiesner.

E-BOOK BASICS
by Leta Nolan Childers

Leta Nolan Childers is the author of the number-one best-selling e-book of 1999, *The Best Laid Plans* (www.diskuspublishing.com), as well as twelve romantic comedies and five children's e-books. Childers also operates a business she co-owns that provides cover art, text conversions, and promotional materials to authors and publishers (www.pubpromos.com).

A new frontier beckons authors. Not since the invention of the printing press by Herr Gutenberg has there been such an explosion in the publishing business, an explosion that will reshape the world of publishing.

E-books are just like any other books except for one difference: Rather than being distributed in hardcover or paperback, e-books come in electronic bindings, in a variety of digital formats. Authors are finding new markets for their works because of this development.

Pioneers in this quickly growing market have a variety of methods from which they can choose to realize the publication of their books in digital format—almost a Chinese menu of options—from which authors can choose whichever methods best fit their needs.

Roughly, there are five types of publication available to authors: house, self, subsidy, cooperative, and broker. Though not publishers in the traditional sense of the word, brokers are included in this list so that authors can discern between the differences in services they offer and those of the more traditional publishers.

Types of E-publishing
1. House publisher

A house publisher is based most closely on the model of a traditional, royalty-paying publishing company. An author submits a query or a partial submission to the publisher. If the publisher is intrigued by the submission, a complete manuscript is requested. (Some electronic publishers in this category simply request that the full manuscript be sent, most often as a file attached to an e-mail, as the initial submission.)

If the publisher accepts the manuscript and the contract is successfully agreed upon, the house publisher provides most, if not all, of the services normally associated with a traditional, royalty-paying publisher. The manuscript is carefully edited; cover art and back cover information are collected; ARCs (advance review copies or advance reading copies) are sent to reviewers, and initial promotion and marketing is begun. Following publication, the author and the publisher work together to promote the book.

The benefit for the author using this form of publication is that there is little risk involved. The publisher pays for the costs of production and distribution, while the author receives (on average) between 25 percent and 50 percent royalties.

The disadvantage is that, as in the traditional world, final editing and creative control are left with the publisher rather than the author.

2. Self-publishing

Again, this type is based on the model of self-publishing in current publishing. The exception lies in the process in which the author prepares the book for publication. Rather than visiting a traditional printing press to arrange for print runs, the self-published author either prepares the book himself and converts it into digital format or arranges with an independent contractor to perform the conversions. The other facets of the publication—the cover art, editing, sending of ARCs, and promotion—are also left to the self-published author, as well as the creation of a Web site (usually with the added convenience of a credit card server) for sales.

The benefits of this form of publication are that the author has complete control of the final presentation of the book and that the author also receives all the proceeds from the sale. The disadvantage of this form of publishing is that the author must promote and market the book without the benefit of the awareness already afforded to established e-publishers. The author is also responsible for the cost of publication, which varies with the level of computer skills possessed by him.

3. Subsidy

Again, subsidy publishing is similar to the traditional model, but does not necessarily carry the associated negative implications. Authors who contract with a subsidy e-publisher choose from a menu of services, each with a separate fee or contained within a "package" deal. The subsidy e-publisher prepares and converts the book as well as provides exposure for it on the publisher's Web site.

The advantages of subsidy e-publishing are that the author who might not be computer savvy can obtain the services needed more easily and not have to worry about obtaining a credit card server or a Web site from which to sell his book. The disadvantage is that this form puts the author at financial risk if book is not successful in sales.

4. Cooperative publishing

Cooperative publishing is a hybrid form of publishing, rather unique to e-publishing. In this model, the publisher bases its operation on the traditional house model, with the associated book preparation and royalty payment. The cooperative publisher offers the basic editing, cover art, and Web site preparation, offers the book in its standard formats, and promotes and markets the book. However, if the author wishes to have the book presented in formats not normally offered by the publisher, the publisher will either convert the books, for a fee, or refer the author to a third-party contractor for the conversion. The publisher will then also offer that format for sale from its Web site. The same is true if the author desires to provide the cover art.

The advantage of cooperative publishing is much the same as for house publishing. However, the disadvantage is that the authors, if they choose, place some money at risk if they decide on obtaining conversions or original cover art.

5. Broker

A broker publisher simply offers the author the opportunity of displaying his book at the broker's Web site and takes care of the selling and distribution of the book.

The advantage of this sort of publishing lies in the fact that the author need not create a Web site from which to sell or worry about selling and distribution. The disadvantage is that the broker normally offers no services such as editing and cover art or promotion. If the broker does offer those types of services, it's usually at a cost in either a fee or in royalty points. Otherwise, this is left to the author, which again puts his capital at risk. This type of publisher normally charges between 25 percent and 75 percent for brokerage of an author's book.

As in any publishing endeavor, it's very important for an author to thoroughly research and investigate every aspect of a publisher before signing a contract.

Electronic Formats

There are a variety of electronic formats in which books are published, including HTML, PDF, PRC, RB, IMP, TXT, RTF, DOC, and WPD. More than just a collection of abbreviations, each of those is a format used in binding e-books. They are called file extensions, and determine the means by which someone reads an e-book.

HTML—hypertext markup language

HTML is the type of electronic file that is read by Internet browsers. There are variations of HTML, but basic HTML is most often used for e-books. The advantage of this type of format is that it allows readers to read the book either online or offline on their computers. Owners of some designated reading devices, such as the Rocket eBook, are also able to import HTML files to read on those devices. Multimedia effects, such as linking to Web sites, music and video files, and linking internally within a book, are also possible with the HTML format. HTML can also be read by those who have a handheld PDA (personal data assistant) that operates on the Windows CE platform. The disadvantage is that HTML is not usually encrypted and the files offer little security against recopying.

PDF—portable document format

PDF files are very popular in binding e-books. Essentially, when one creates a PDF file, using a special program from Adobe, it "prints" to a file an exact replica of the original document, but adds certain conveniences such as internal linking; linking to audio, video, and graphics files; and linking to external Web sites. Most information disseminated by the state and federal government agencies as well as manuals and schematics offered by manufacturing companies rely on the PDF format. The advantage is that it is an exact duplication with enhancements. The only disadvantage is that the files tend to be large and can only be viewed on a free reader, also available from Adobe.

PRC

PRC is the file format that can be imported to reading programs for personal, handheld devices operating the Palm Pilot platform.

RB and IMP

RB is the file type for Rocket eBook devices and IMP is the file type for SoftBook. Use of these types of files is limited to the devices and requires either a special program (Book Mill for the SoftBook) or specific coding (HTML or OEB, Open E-Book) for the Rocket eBook.)

TXT and RTF

TXT and RTF are basic word program file types. There is little formatting that can be accomplished with the basic files. TXT documents or books can also be uploaded to the Rocket eBook device. The advantages of these types of formats are that they are normally universal and can be read on most computers in any word program. Normally, these formats are not used for publishing e-books because there is little or no encryption for security.

DOC and WPD

DOC is the file extension for works created in the Microsoft Word program while WPD is the file extension for works created in the WordPerfect program. Normally, these formats are not used for publishing e-books because there is little or no encryption for security.

Normally, the publisher (or the distributor) delivers these files on diskette or CD or as a download over the Internet.

◆ ◆ ◆

Often, the question is asked about just how books in electronic bindings will be received in the future. E-books will probably never totally replace traditional bound books. However, writers will see a certain blurring in the distinction between traditional publishers and e-publishers. Inevitably, and it's already occurring with several, traditional publishers will begin to offer books in electronic formats. Likewise, many e-publishers are also beginning to offer books in traditional bindings—both paper and hardcover. Eventually, a publisher will simply be a publisher without any distinction as to the type of bindings in which it present its books. Of course, the ultimate winner in all of this is the reader, who will have choices in content and delivery as he has never before enjoyed.

TIPS FOR SELECTING A COMMERCIAL E-PUBLISHER
by Jamie Engle

Jamie Engle is a freelance writer and editor of the eBook Connections (http:// eBookConnections.com), the first Web site to review e-books exclusively.

You're exploring electronic publishing, but how do you recognize a reputable commercial e-publisher? Thoroughly evaluate and compare e-publishers' sites, guidelines, contracts, and sales before you submit your manuscript.

Web Site

Visit the e-publisher's Web site and look at it from a reader and writer's point of view.

First impressions
- The e-publisher Web site is a storefront. Is it easy to navigate and organized? Is it neat and professional looking? Does the publisher accept credit cards, and are the transactions secured?
- Look for an "About" page with information about the business itself and the people running it. A good company information page will tell you how old the company is, include real names of the people who work there and ways to contact them, and the business address and phone number. Also look for affiliations and memberships in trade groups such as the Association of Electronic Publishers (AEP) or other publishers' groups.

Authors published
Authors can reveal the size of the company and the caliber of writers who belong. Check that there are more than two authors, indicating the publisher is publishing work other than its own. If there are e-mail addresses for the authors, you could ask about their experiences with that publisher.

Books on the Web site

- Take a look at the titles offered. Neat Web page layout, eye-catching cover art, and reasonable prices are signs the Web site is designed with the customer in mind.
- Are ISBN numbers assigned to each book? "The acquisition of a publisher prefix (needed to receive ISBN numbers) shows the publisher is serious enough to put their money where their mouth is," says Bonnee Pierson, editor at Dreams Unlimited (www.dreams-unlimited.com). ISBNs also aid booksellers when ordering. Books are not required to have an ISBN, but it greatly increases the sales and marketing options for books.
- Check if the publisher offers out-of-print books. If the majority of books are out of print rather than original new releases, it could impact the level of editing per manuscript.

Final product

- Make sure the e-publisher delivers a professional-looking final product. Buy books and read them; it's the only way to verify the quality of the publisher's editing, book design, and layout. Try the free e-book download, if available, but also order a book or two to check the quality of new releases.
- If you have a mystery to submit, buy one or two. Are they similar to your book(s) in quality? Are they well edited? Is the book design easy to read, are page breaks and margins consistent?
- Look at the buying process as a consumer would—was it easy to find the genre, select books, and complete the transaction? How fast was delivery? Is there good customer service?

Does the Manuscript Fit?

Now it's time to determine if your manuscript fits the e-publisher's catalog. Notice the genre breakdowns on site. Does one fit your manuscript? If your book crosses genre lines, be sure to check for all possible genres. Remember that e-publishers favor nontraditional books, even though the genre listings might look traditional.

- Click to the Submission Guidelines. Here you should find more detailed information about the types of manuscripts that the e-publisher is interested in acquiring. If the guidelines are too general in nature, it could indicate the e-publisher has not defined a target reader market.

- Some guidelines mention "minimal editing." This could mean little more than a spelling and grammar check run on a word processor program. Good editing is essential, and it's important to have a clear understanding of how much editing the e-publisher does on a manuscript. If the guidelines are not specific, ask. Buying one or two of the books is the best way to evaluate the level of editing.
- Check to see if there's a Submission Tracking System available to authors. Many e-publishers have a system that can be accessed by the authors through the publisher's Web site, telling the manuscript's status.

Contracts and Sales

You've determined the e-publisher matches your manuscript. Look deeper, at the finer points of contracts and sales.

Contracts

A sample contract is usually on site. If not, ask for a copy. It could be the e-publisher doesn't use a contract, in which case think carefully before proceeding. E-mails are binding, but most advise using a contract; AEP requires its members use contracts. With or without a contract, keep a paper trail at all times.

ROYALTY RATES

- What is the royalty rate? Expect from 25 to 50 percent royalties.
- All royalty packages are not created equal. Because of the deep discounts required by some distributors or booksellers, royalties paid on books sold through them may be less than on books sold directly through the publisher. Is a percentage of royalties given up for using certain distributors or booksellers? For example, if e-books are offered through Amazon.com, do you get less royalty on sales through Amazon.com?

E-RIGHTS

E-publishers that publish only electronic editions ask for electronic rights, leaving you free to market the rest of the subsidiary rights such as print and audio.

- Does the e-publisher ask for electronic rights only, electronic and print rights, or all rights?
- If the publisher asks for print rights, is it going to produce print copies?

CONTRACT PERIOD

- Is a specific contract period stated? Are there start and end dates?
- Is there an "out" clause if either the author or publisher is not satisfied with the relationship?

OUT-OF-POCKET EXPENSES

The author should not be expected to pay for normal publishing expenses such as editing, cover art, or production expenses. Most e-publishers require the author to pay for registering the copyright. Other items to check include the following:

- If multiple file formats of the e-book are offered, who pays for the file formatting? The e-publisher will pay for the file formats it regularly publishes, but may offer to publish additional formats if the author pays the formatting cost. This is acceptable as long as the publisher pays for formats it regularly offers.
- How many author copies are provided? Are additional copies discounted?
- How many review copies are sent by the e-publisher, and in what format? Some e-publishers send print review copies, increasing the number of reviewers available to review their books.
- Are promotional copies discounted?
- Does the author pay for promotion? What e-publisher promotion is included in the contract? The author shouldn't pay for standard promotion, such as sending the book out for review.
- What advertising is included in the contract? Only advertising and promotion listed in the contract are guaranteed for your book.
- Are there additional costs?

Sales

- Besides your e-publisher's Web site, where can readers find your e-book? Will it be at barnesandnoble.com, Amazon.com, other online booksellers, or physical bookstores? Don't forget to check if your royalty rates are less on these sales.
- Good e-publishers actively promote their sites, titles, and authors with contests, newsletters, or other interaction to encourage repeat visitors. They also should keep their Web sites high on the search engines. Use a couple search engines and see where your e-publisher turns up on the list.
- Check whether the e-publisher offer formats compatible with handheld devices, such as the Palm Pilot, or formats compatible with dedicated handheld e-book reader devices, such as RocketBook or SoftBook. Dedicated handheld e-book reader devices are expected to make a huge impact on e-publishing when sales take off; however, sales have not taken off yet.

Networking

- Ask other writers if they've heard of the e-publisher or have had any experience with it. Ask the published authors about their experiences with promotion and sales support from the publisher. Listservs, either writers' or e-publishing, are good places to ask about e-publishers.
- The E-Pub list was formed November 1, 1998, and is an open forum for discussing the e-publishing industry and the business side of writing. Open to writers (published and unpublished), editors, publishers, and any industry professional interested in electronic publishing. To subscribe, go to www .onelist.com/subscribe/e-pub.
- Subscribe to eBookConnections.com's ePub Market Update for publisher tips and e-publishing industry news for writers (www.onelist.com/subscribe/ ebcmktupdate).
- The E-Authors list was formed in the fall of 1999, and is an information source for those interested in e-publishing, and a support group for e-published authors. To subscribe, go to www.onelist.com/subscribe/e-authors.

E-publishing is a new industry, but if you know what to look for, you can find the right e-publisher for you and your manuscript. Soon you will be celebrating the contract that makes you a published e-book author.

WHAT IS THE FUTURE OF ON-DEMAND PUBLISHING?
by John Feldcamp

John Feldcamp is the president of Xlibris Corporation (www.xlibris.com).

My, what an enormous question. And like all questions related to the future, there are some parts that are perfectly clear today, and some others that no one on Earth is yet sure of.

The first case I need to make is that publishing exists as we understand it today purely because of technology. Up until a few years ago, the current state of the art in publishing processes and technology had remained fundamentally unchanged for many, many decades. Offset printing technology dictated huge and unavoidable up-front manufacturing costs, and the craft processes of preparing a book for publication dictated another large up-front investment. Taken together, the technical state of the art of how publishing has worked up to now demanded that tens of thousands of dollars be invested, at minimum, to publish a book. Then of course there's warehousing, distribution, administration, and so forth.

So let's begin by understanding this simple thought: Publishing exists as it does today because the act of publishing a book costs so darn much. Almost nobody can afford to publish his own books; he needs the financial help of somebody else. Publishing doesn't exist in its current form because some power from on high dictated that it must be so—it has evolved that way because of the traditional technology and economics of publishing.

And the underlying technology and economics of publishing are what have now changed. It used to be that publishing was one big craft and industrial process. Typewritten text had to be keyed, and painstakingly laid out in metal type. Printing plates had to be made and checked and corrected. Huge presses had to be set up and run. And now that's all going away. Thanks to personal computers, books are now digital from the very moment of creation. The book design and production process is digital. The book distribution environment is digital. Digital printing systems now exist, which enable books to be printed in any quantity whatsoever, on demand, right down to single copies. And with the advent of companies like Amazon.com, even the retail environment is going digital.

Digital publishing technology is incredibly cheap and efficient, and the minimum cost to publish a book is currently falling like a stone. The costs of building these kinds of digital publishing systems are not trivial, but once they are built, the cost of publishing any single book using them is very, very small. So the technology and the economics that have defined how the publishing industry has worked since time out of mind are now suddenly and irrevocably changed.

Publishing is about to go through a series of extraordinary and inevitable changes starting from right now. It's inevitable that everybody is going to be able to afford to publish his own books. It's inevitable that companies like Xlibris, which live inside this new technology, are going to spring up to help authors publish on their own. And it's inevitable that the cost of publishing is going to be so cheap that all authors will ultimately publish their books. There simply won't be any barriers.

Let's be clear. Everybody who writes is going to publish what they write. This is not one of those things that is debatable anymore. It's perfectly clear to us at Xlibris that this is the case. It's clear to our competitors at iUniverse and elsewhere. It's clear to Barnes & Noble. It's clear to other major players in the industry that you'll know about by the time you read this. And, it really doesn't matter whether you think this is a good thing or a bad thing for the world of books and publishing—it is going to happen regardless of what any of us thinks.

So maybe the next question is, is this a good thing? My only answer is that, in the long run, I don't know. The world of publishing a decade from now will be radically different, in more ways than any of us can understand. All I know is that people will have exactly the same access to publication as they do to the Net, and in fact I think those two things will be very similar to one another. Every book written will be available from every bookstore (the stores will be able to make them on the spot), and every book written will stay in print forever.

A corollary to the question that started this paragraph is, won't a lot of bad books get published? And the answer to that question is, you bet. I would argue that there are already a lot of pretty bad books being published, and that there are a lot of great books that never see the light of day. The problem is, who gets to decide? Everybody has different interests and tastes, and a book that would have remarkable value to one thousand people has just as much of a right to reach those people as the next best-seller. There are no absolutely unbiased arbiters of what is good; everybody has to decide that on his own. And so while it's likely to be a very messy place, the future world of publishing that we see will be far less elitist and far more fair than today—which is inherently a good thing. Instead of living or dying in an inherently random and unfair way on the transoms of literary agents and publishers, every book will succeed or fail in the market itself. Nothing is going to change the fact that creating a best-seller is as hard and as rare as any other way to get rich, but everybody will have a decent shot at achieving his own goals and his own level of success in the market. That's what Xlibris and other companies like us are here to accomplish.

Will the traditional mass-market publishers, companies like Random House and HarperCollins, go away? We don't think so. Books will continue to break out and need far more attention and investment than companies like ourselves can provide. But instead of mass-market or nothing, there will be a lot more steps along the way in which publication is accessible and works well.

If you're an author, it's going to be an amazing, strange, exciting world, in which you have more power and more choices than ever before. Look forward to seeing you there.

MARILYN NESBITT, DiskUs Publishing
Marilyn Nesbitt is the CEO of DiskUs Publishing (www.diskuspublishing .com) and an active promoter of electronic books.

How was DiskUs Publishing created?
I loved the whole idea of electronic publishing right from the start. In early 1998 on the threshold of the new century, a century that will be a digital century, it just seemed the right time for this kind of venture. And having seen so many wonderful books turned down by New York publishers for various reasons, a friend and I decided to start up DiskUs Publishing to help some of these wonderful authors become published.

What type of promotion do you do for your authors?

We've done everything from joint ads in magazines, to interviews in papers, magazines, and online journals, as well as press releases. I also buy quite a few promo items like stickers, bookmarks, postcards, buttons, and send these to my authors as well as passing them out myself. I send my authors their books to use at book signings and conferences and help them with promo ideas, working with them as much as possible to get the word out there about their book.

E-book authors tend to receive less recognition than authors from traditional publishing houses. Any comments?

I think old habits die hard. People get set in their ways and don't like the idea of trying new things, so to them, e-published authors aren't really published. As we go into the new century, our young people of today will be the adults of tomorrow and they have been raised in the digital age and aren't intimidated by computers, e-readers, or e-books. Instead, they embrace the new technology with open arms. Children of today are the readers of tomorrow and they'll think of e-books as the norm and when this happens, there will be no difference between e-books or paper books.

E-book authors are starting to receive more recognition; I've had stories about my business and about my authors in various magazines and newspapers. Some of them are the *The Wall Street Journal, Salon, Wired, Writer's Digest*, as well as a forthcoming *Time* article.

What impact do you see electronic publishing having on the traditional publishing industry over the next five years?

Most if not all New York publishers will electronically publish their books in that time span. Some are already doing this and more will follow suit because more and more buyers like the idea of purchasing a book from the Internet and being able to start reading in a matter of minutes, all without leaving their home.

How do you think traditional publishers will respond?

I hope they'll lower the cost of their books to help further e-publishing. Some of the New York publishers who are electronic publishing their books right now have prices that are the same as their paper or worse their hardbound books and that just doesn't make a lot of sense.

CHAPTER NINE

Insider Views

JOSH DANIEL, online editor
Josh Daniel is the Managing Editor of *Slate* magazine (www.slate.com).

What tips do you have for those who want to write for **Slate***?*
Pitch stories that make an argument. Queries of the "I'd like to do a story about Bill Bradley" sort go nowhere. (It seems obvious, but you'd be surprised at how many pitches I see just like that.) Send original ideas that haven't been done elsewhere. It certainly helps to have a good writer's resume, but we do publish less-experienced writers when they can deliver the goods.

How does writing for an online publication differ from writing for print?
A couple of ways. One, thanks to hyperlinking, you have a bit more freedom to decide what must be included in your piece and what can be a link to another page. Writing on the Web can be more modular than writing for print; you don't always need to create the same sort of narrative. (Though often you still should do so.) Two, writing on the Web needs to be even more concise than writing for print. People simply don't want to read as much on their computer screens—yet. So you shape your ideas accordingly.

How does editing an online publication differ from editing a print publication?
Much the same way as writing: You must edit tightly, and make sure you're taking

advantage of the medium. Ask yourself, can I make this point even better with a sound file, or a video clip, or a hyperlink?

What is your opinion about the future of electronic publications?

I think electronic pubs have a great future—but then, I work at one. Right now print has one major advantage over digital forms: portability. But as the technology improves—as handhelds and other form factors become more prevalent, as screen fonts get easier to read, etc.—that gap will narrow. And then the advantages of publishing with bits instead of atoms will really show.

What advice do you have for someone considering starting up an online publication?

Online and print publications face many of the same sorts of problems. Distribution is always going to be a big one, but print pubs at least have the advantage of newsstands and subscription sales, which remind people that the magazines are there. You have to choose to visit a Web site. So if I were starting an online publication, I'd focus on figuring out ways to drive traffic back to my site. You can buy banner ads, but the clickthrough rates on those are still pretty low. Better to piggyback on established, popular sites: Find ones that might be interested in carrying your content, or links to it, and court them assiduously. Propose that you post some of your content on their site, with your branding and links back to your pub; or try simply to post headlines that send traffic to you. Keep in mind that they'll want something in return, and know what you have to offer. You'll also want to capture as much info as you can about your readers; one easy way is to offer a regular e-mail newsletter, which gives you a list of your readers' e-mail addresses and a way to remind them to come back to your site regularly.

JERRI LEDFORD, online writer

Jerri Ledford has sold about 150 articles to online markets. She writes online columns for several Web publications including Myria.com and MomsRefuge.com.

How do you find your online markets?

I use a variety of Web sites and newsletters. AJR Newslink, Craigslist, Writer's

Write, Writing for Dollars, Inkspot, and the Writers' Guidelines Database online. Also a ton of other places, like e-zine lists, Disney's Family site, and now that I am not sending out all of the posts, the Momwriter's Markets list.

How did you get your online column assignments?

I queried them. Nancy Price, the owner of the Myria, Interactive Parent, and ePregnancy sites, is also a Momwriter. And so I had a little "in" with her because we know each other from the list, but I still had to pitch the column, sell her on why it would work for her readers, and prove that I could actually write what I promised.

With MomsRefuge.com I answered a general call I found on a Web site. The call was for writers in general, but I took a chance and sent a column proposal. It took the editors a while to get back to me, but when they did they loved the idea. So, we're working out the details about slant and payment now.

I tend to take a lot of chances. What I mean is that like with a job posting for an in-house writer, I'll send my resume, bibliography, and a cover letter trying to persuade the editors to give me a shot as a freelancer. Many times it doesn't work, but I have had a number of editors come back to me with positive responses. Or, if a market is just a little bit outside my normal writing expertise, I'll query it anyway, and wing my way through getting the assignment. Then I spend a lot of time learning what I need to know to be knowledgeable on the subject.

What is ghostwriting, exactly?

For me, it means that I do all of the research, writing, and revision needed for an article, then the "author" pays me and puts his name on the work. The article has to be as accurate and well written as if it were carrying my name because often the writers I work for are well known in their field.

The pay for ghostwriting can be very good (my scale tops out at about $.50 per word, but I know ghostwriters who make $1 per word or more), but it does hinge on thorough, precise work that is often needed on a very quick turnaround.

How did you get your online ghostwriting assignments?

Those I get by responding to online postings with a resume and bibliography. The first one was through the Writer's Boards on AOL. Then that person referred me to someone else, and I found one on the job boards for what used to be Writersclub.com, and that lead to another referral, and so on.

Basically, I spend a lot of time selling myself. I teach classes over at the Writer's Village University, and in one of my classes I tell the students to be prepared to spend half of their time selling themselves and the other half selling their work. The writing part is easy. It's the selling that's tough. I have developed a resume that I use for everything. It's short on actual jobs but long on the bibliography part, which I think is what is important.

How do you organize/keep track of your online submissions/queries, etc.?

I have built a tracking system into my Day Planner. It's a foldout page that lists the month and then has columns for where a submission was sent to, who the contact is, what exactly was sent, what the reply was, what specific comments were made, and a follow-up column. Everything I do goes into that whether it's a query, resume, completed article, or something else.

Then I follow that with a letter-sized legal pad where I cross-reference all of the queries I have out by subject because I do a lot of simultaneous queries. For that, I list the topic of the query at the top of the page, then list the market on the lines, with the pay scale down one column on the left and the response down another. I send all of my queries out in the three-tier format (highest paying, mid-paying, and low-paying), so this helps me to keep up with who has what and what kind of income I am generating.

Finally, I track all of my income in a separate folder. As I complete an invoice for an article, I write down how much the finished assignment was and when it was invoiced. Then as the payment comes in, I check it off the list.

I guess I am a little compulsive about tracking. I've tried electronic programs but this system works better for me.

AMY GAHRAN, online editor

Content consultant Amy Gahran (gahran.com) is the editor of *Contentious* (contentious.com), a Webzine for people who create content for online media. She also co-edits the online newsletter *Content Spotlight,* and is VP of Content Exchange (htpp://content-exchange.com), a new service for content professionals and online publishers.

Why did you create Contentious?

I was just starting out as a freelancer at the time, after several years in print publishing (including Managing Editor stints at a monthly magazine and niche publishing company). I was very interested in doing more work for online media and also wanted to explore content issues specific to online media.

At that time, however, few people seemed to be interested in content issues— or at least, not many people were talking about it. I could find lots of resources for writers and editors who were doing work for print media, but there was very little focused on content specifically for online media.

That frustrated me. Since I couldn't find a resource that met my needs, and since I'd amassed some knowledge and experience about content for online media, I thought I'd stick my neck out and start a resource on the topic. I figured it would be fun, useful for myself and others, and good marketing for my own work as a freelancer/consultant. It's exceeded my expectations in all regards.

In fact, I was completely floored by the initial strong and positive response to *Contentious*. On the day I published the first issue, I just sent out a few announcements to discussion groups for writers, editors, Web developers, etc. I went out for lunch, and returned an hour and a half later to about four hundred e-mail messages, most of which were from people asking to receive announcements of future issues. There I was, worried that no one would care that I put together this publication (or worse, that my colleagues would think I was stupid or crazy for focusing on this topic, since no one else seemed to be doing so) and it turned out that I put out a resource just as everybody was ripe to discuss the topic.

The guy I had lunch with that day happened to be Steve Outing, whom I was meeting for the first time. Steve is now my partner in Content Exchange. I called Steve (after I scraped my jaw off the floor from seeing the response from my readers) and told him about the strong response to *Contentious*. We decided to catch the wave by founding a discussion group about the practice and business of creating and managing content for online media—the Online Writing list (OWL). That list just exploded when we started it in late April 1998, and now averages about eighteen hundred subscribers. We've since made OWL a free service of Content Exchange.

Who is your target audience?

As the tagline for *Contentious* indicates, I target that publication toward writers, editors, and others who create content for online media. That's all kinds of content, for all kinds of audiences, and for all kinds of online venues—not just Web sites, but also e-mail publications, intranets, discussion groups, etc.

Based on a survey of *Contentious* readers that I did early in 1999 (with more than four hundred respondents), just over half of my audience (53 percent) classifies themselves as writers or editors. An additional 15 percent are Web designers or programmers, and 11 percent are online publishers. (See www.contentious.com/articles/1-11/results1.html)

What is Content Exchange?

Content Exchange is a marketplace that brings together all kinds of content professionals ("talent") with all kinds of online publishers ("venues"). In other words, it's a nexus for the online content industry.

We offer several services for online content talent and venues. The ones that currently are of greatest interest to writers are our talent database, our newsletter *Content Spotlight*, and the Online-Writing list. All of these services are currently free.

Any writer or other content creator who wishes to do work for online media can create a free detailed profile for himself in our talent database. There, you can specify your areas of expertise, offer information about your background and prior experience, discuss what you require in terms of rates or rights, etc. While it's possible to create a profile containing only minimal information, we recommend that content professionals provide as much information as possible. The more information you include, the more likely it is that your profile will turn up in a targeted search.

Online venues can search the talent database for free, and contact talent via their database profile. Several writers have already been contacted for work this way.

Content Spotlight (www.content-exchange.com/cx/html/newsletter/index.htm) is a weekly newsletter covering the online content business: practical advice for online content professionals and publishers, profiles of interesting talent or venues, etc. This is an especially useful resource for writers who are just getting started in online media.

The Online-Writing list is an open discussion forum covering the practice and business of creating, managing, and publishing content in online media. This is a great place to ask questions about the online content business and benefit from the experience and perspectives of others in the field.

In the near future we will be introducing other services, such as classified ads, a venue database, a content brokerage, and more.

How do you feel about the claim that the caliber of online writing isn't nearly as high as in print publications?

OK, you hit my hot-button here.

Personally, I think that's crap. It's true that there's a lot of amateurish, awkward, inconsistent, or even misleading content available on the Internet, but the same is also very true of print and broadcast media—if you look at all of those media in their entirety. I've found that a lot of people who make that claim consider major daily newspapers or network TV to be representative of print and broadcast media, respectively. That's not a fair comparison. Print media also includes marketing brochures, technical manuals, supermarket tabloids, local weekly papers, tax instructions from the IRS, photocopied newsletters with a circulation of four, and even handwritten flyers posted on coffee shop bulletin boards. Meanwhile, audio/video media includes not just ABC News, NPR, or CNN, but also public-access cable shows, commercials, televangelists, VH1, the Pacifica Network, pirate radio, training videos for convenience store employees, etc.

The difference is this: The Internet immeasurably increases the availability of niche publications/programming, and also makes it easy to hear about (or track down) print or broadcast publications that aren't directly available online. Since people now can access a conspiracy theorist's personal Web site as easily as a feature story on ABCNews.com, people get exposed to a lot of information on the Net that they couldn't easily access before. It's not that this information didn't exist before, it's just that it was difficult or expensive to learn about and access. Therefore, online media does not represent lower quality or credibility than print or broadcast media—I think for the most part it equals what you find throughout the "spectrum" of traditional media.

This includes production/editorial quality. Yes, many personal Web sites look terrible and are fraught with errors, but there are plenty of professionally produced online venues that are very slick, coherent, and reliable. Just like a home video will look terrible compared to a feature film from Miramax—but there are innumerably more home videos in the world than feature films; we just don't have easy access to the universe of home videos.

There's another aspect to this issue. I've been in journalism for a while and know many journalists from all kinds of news outlets. Based on what I know, I contend that a lot of the print and broadcast news venues that are held up to be paragons of journalism are not all they're cracked up to be. Look at newspapers—the quality of newspaper reporting has been steadily deteriorating, at least since I got out of journalism school in 1990. Most newspapers, even major ones, pay their writers very little and thus can't attract or keep good journalists. They often skirt stories or issues that would alienate major advertisers. They focus on providing news that will attract wealthy eyeballs, rather than on information that's truly useful to people in all parts of the economic or social spectrum. In local TV newsrooms, news budgets have been slashed drastically—leading to a proliferation of stories about fires and the weather, topics that generally require scant expertise or resources to cover. TV newsrooms also often run "B-roll" provided for free by PR firms, add a few pre-scripted voice-overs, and run it as news with no additional reporting. Sure, all of that may all end up looking slick and superficially professional, but it doesn't take much digging to realize that many popular news sources have serious credibility and quality problems. On the Internet, if you're confronted with shoddy journalism at least it's easy to dig further on your own. You can't do that easily with TV or newspapers. Also, on the Internet it's easier to find out about stuff that the major media aren't covering, or angles that aren't being explored. On the Internet, you can even directly consult original sources if you want to.

What tips do you have for traditional print writers who wish to make the shift to writing for online media?

I've written a lot about that in *Contentious*, Content Exchange, and in an article for *Writer's Digest* magazine. If I had to hone it down to a few key pieces of advice:

1. Spend a lot of time checking out various kinds of online venues. Get a feel for what works and doesn't work in the online world.

2. Remember that there's a lot more to online media than writing articles for online magazines. There are plenty of opportunities writing for corporate sites, e-mail publications, intranets, etc. Also, there are probably more jobs and projects that require people with editorial skills than writing alone.

3. Be willing to learn and use at least basic HTML. It's not hard, and it's definitely not programming. You don't have to design Web pages, but you should be familiar with how to create links, etc.

4. Consider narrowing your focus. The Internet is not really a broadcast me-

dium as it is a various collection of niches. There are a lot of paying opportunities for people who can write about specific topics (like utility deregulation, or dog grooming), or for very specific audiences (new parents, or tax accountants).

5. There is a *lot* of paying work in online media. There also are a lot of underfunded or just plain unscrupulous publishers who will ask you to write for little or no pay. You don't have to do that if you don't want to. Only accept such offers if there is demonstrably something for you to gain. Be skeptical about claims of "exposure"—often the content you are providing is much more valuable than the exposure you'd receive from a rinky-dink site.

6. Pay close attention to copyright issues, and pursue infringements of your copyright for work that you have published in online media. As with print work, avoid selling (or giving away) all rights. Here's a good reference on this point: www.content-exchange.com/cx/html/newsletter/1-7/tt1-7.htm.

DAVID SAPERSTEIN, author

David Saperstein is the author of seven novels and twenty-seven screenplays, and has directed two films. One of Saperstein's best-selling novels, *Cocoon* (Jove), which was turned into a movie by director Ron Howard, ended up winning two Academy Awards. In November 1999, Saperstein decided to sidestep traditional publishing channels and publish a novel exclusively on the Internet. For more information, see www.darkagain.com.

Why did you opt to release* Dark Again *exclusively on the Internet?

I am a novelist, screenwriter, and director. So I write visually, but more to the point, I see the Internet as a way to tell a far richer story using the multimedia promise of the Web. I am also a student of the new technologies as they apply to entertainment and communication. Someone had to be first, so why not me? In one stunning moment I have bypassed agent, reader, editor, publisher, marketing committee, administrators, bean counters, rack jobbers, store managers, and critics. I am directly in touch with my readers/audience. Just like a painter or musician, the Internet removes all those people that I did not create my work for, and instead lets it be judged by those I wish to reach.

How did you decide on Cybergold as your payment mechanism?

I talked with Nat Goldhaber about the future of publishing and found that we were on the same page with the same vision. He treated the book as it developed into an Inter-novel with professional enthusiasm. All the Cybergold people, management, legal, creative, and technical, have been excellent to work with, and fun. It is a pleasure to be with people who want to find ways to *do* things rather than finding reasons *not to.*

Do you think e-books will ever replace regular print books?

No. This is a new form of publishing. But I do think we will see the Inter-novel develop into a major interactive, multimedia storytelling medium. We have plans to eventually release the book in a bound version.

Do you plan on continuing to release novels exclusively on the Internet, or also through traditional publishing channels?

Both. It will depend on the story. Does it lend itself to becoming an Inter-novel? I do think, from what I have learned with *Dark Again,* that I know how to write an Inter-novel and utilize the medium. Being first, we literally wrote the Inter-novel manual and continue to add to it every day.

What advice do you have for writers thinking about publishing their novels online?

"Normal" publishing, text alone, is fine on the Internet. The problem is getting your readers to find your work. With Cybergold I have 3.5 million people on notice. And Cybergold is backing me with publicity and PR—something very difficult to get from a "normal" publisher if your name isn't Clancy or King.

But the real challenge is in writing and designing a true Inter-novel with all the adjunct and collateral material that is possible to present on the Web. You can have pictures, sound, music, art, articles, information to enrich the story. Eventually (within months) we can add video! Not all stories lend themselves to this. I think being a screenwriter and director certainly helped me in this process and will on my future Inter-novels.

M.J. ROSE, author

M.J. Rose (http://mjrose.com) made literary history when her self-published novel, *Lip Service,* was discovered online and chosen as a featured alternate selection for both the Doubleday Book Club and The Literary Guild (September 1999). It was the first time the clubs had bought an independently published novel. In September 2000 *Lip Service* was re-released by Pocket Books as a hardcover. Rose is the coauthor of *The Secrets of Our Success* (Deep South Publishing), an e-book about how to self-publish and self-promote on the web.

To what extent was the Internet responsible for* Lip Service *'s wild success?
Completely responsible. First, because I was able to test-market the book on the Net and find out if it had an audience.

When I found out I did have an audience, I had the book printed. Then I got in my car and started going to independent bookstores, asking them to stock it. I thought they would (especially the ones in my area), but I was wrong.

The bookstore owners said that with all the competition from the giant chains, they couldn't afford to give up shelf space to a book that had no promotional and marketing dollars behind it.

So I took to the virtual highway and got the book stocked on the virtual shelves of the online bookstores. Not only did it sell, but that's where it was discovered by the New York publishing giants.

What self-promotion techniques did you use online?
I got my site linked to many sites that my target audience visited. Most of those sites also reviewed my book. In addition, I wrote articles in exchange for live links on other sites. I spent about six hours a day, six days a week for four months working the Web and it paid off. I've been told by my editor and publisher that if *Lip Service* weren't a great read it would not have taken off the way it did and no amount of promotion would have made any difference. Using reviews as a promotional device was the most important factor in my success. Getting a word-of-mouth campaign going on the Net is what has motivated readers to buy my book.

My Web site has been invaluable. It gives me a place to post news, reviews, events, links, and articles I've written. I offer the prologue to my book on my site and also give readers a way to contact me.

What is your opinion about print-on-demand?

I think that POD and e-books are part of the future for big publishers, the first real way for the giants to test books they aren't sure of (which will, by the way, give new authors new hope). The midlist author will have a rebirth because a publisher who likes a book but isn't sure of it can do it POD and as an e-book and test it. If it sells well, the publisher can do a big print run. If it doesn't, the publisher hasn't lost much.

Returns are the bane of every publisher's business; POD can solve that. In addition, books that might otherwise go out of print can have a much longer life and will be available to readers forever.

For the small press or independent author, POD is part of the present. In addition to an e-book—which is still hard to get reviewed—a self-published author can do a POD run of just a few dozen books for review purposes.

What is your opinion about electronic books?

I think in the next few years we will see e-books for every print title that is published.

Nonfiction e-books, which contain live links, and cross-genre fiction books are already doing incredibly well. And the more "comfy" e-readers get, the faster the transition from print to "e" will be.

What impact do you see the Internet having on traditional print publishers?

I think the Internet will prove as important to the publishing industry as Gutenberg's press. It will take some time for the traditional publishers to figure out the best ways to use the Internet, but the marketing techniques being developed now are more sophisticated than anyone ever thought possible. In just the past two years we've moved at warp speed. The first e-book publishing company is only two years old! Who knows what the future will hold?

PAMELA WILFINGER (pen name Jade Walker),
editor of *Inscriptions*

Pamela Wilfinger began *Inscriptions* (www.inscriptionsmagazine.com) in August 1998 after she lost her editing job for another magazine. The three hundred freelance writers working for her at the time lost their jobs as well, inspiring her to start *Inscriptions* to share the job opportunities and paying markets she found on the Internet.

Is there a difference between writing for an online market and a regular print publication?

Absolutely! Writing for the online market is more immediate. Work can easily be edited and posted on the Web without having to travel through a printing press and distributor's hands. Your readers aren't limited to subscribers or local folks—you can publish to a global audience. The actual style of writing is different, as well. Writing for the Web requires adopting a hip, compelling voice that can present information in a concise and scannable fashion.

Some writers claim that online writing isn't nearly as high caliber as writing in print publications, and also doesn't pay as well. Any comments?

High caliber? Oh, please! Writing for online markets takes vision, talent, and hard work. Five years ago, the thought of publishing online was just starting to take seed. Today, a writer isn't worth a dime if he doesn't have a computer, Internet access, an e-mail address and competent Web skills. As each of the major publishing houses and magazines turn to the Web to provide online content, the need for content providers will increase. With that need will come the necessity of providing decent wages.

Strictly online markets have difficulty paying decent wages to writers because they haven't generated enough profit to do so. Publishing online only brings in a profit through advertising or investors. In the past five years, few investors were willing to make the leap into the electronic world. That's changing every day. So is online advertising. If a magazine can prove the existence of a sizable audience, it can now get advertising.

These two trends will continue in the future. Investors are flocking to the Web, seeking profit and a global marketplace. Advertisers are doing the same thing. Both groups will turn to the best-looking sites providing interesting, up-to-date, and compelling content. That content doesn't come cheap. Thus the pay rates for writers will increase. It simply takes time. Until then, it's wise to get in on the ground floor of lesser paying markets. That way you'll be remembered once the money starts coming in.

***Inscriptions** has a reputation of providing quality market and industry news. How do you do your research?*

I have a huge amount of bookmarks! I've been on the Net since 1989, and I occasionally teach a class called Writing Resources on the Net, for Computer Coach (www.computercoach.com). Each week, I visit about one hundred writing- and publishing-related Web sites. I subscribe to more than eighty mailing lists and e-zines, and I make dozens of requests for submission guidelines. Yes, any writer can do the same thing I do. But most just don't have the time or energy. So I do it for them, and condense the information for quick reading.

What advice do you have for writers doing online market research?

Inscriptions publishes the most recent submission guidelines from various magazines and publishers. However, it's always wise to request these guidelines again for any new changes. Follow these guidelines to the letter. Address the editor by name in your query. Target your query to fit the publication. Finally, sign up for various writing-related e-zines and mailing lists to keep up-to-date on the latest needs of online publications.

What advice do you have for writers wishing to break into the online market?

Obviously, the first thing to do is get online. Obtain a decent computer, a second phone line, fast Internet access, and a reliable e-mail host. Start reading online magazines and books. Notice the difference in writing style between print and the Web. Create a Web site of your own, or an ASCII resume and clips. Then, simply start requesting guidelines and sending out queries.

What impact has the Internet had on the craft and business of writing?

There was a recent article in *The Online Journalism Review* about working as an online freelancer. The editors of various online magazines were complaining about the quality of submissions they received in e-mail. They felt putting a stamp on a query made a writer more serious about his craft. Let me tell you. If a magazine *doesn't* have a Web site or e-mail address, I don't even bother with it.

Print is dying. The world of publishing needs to address this death and focus on the new beginning—publishing on the Internet. It no longer costs a writer to live in the boonies. Writers can live on a boat, in a log cabin, or on a deserted island. As long as you can access the Internet, you can research, write, and publish your writing.

Editors no longer have to trudge through rush hour to get to work. Using my fully loaded iMac, I do all of my work from the comfort of my home. I can work naked. In the middle of the night. By candlelight. And someday, I can stay home with my kids and still make enough money to support us.

You don't even have to waste gas to visit a bookstore anymore. With the electronic publishing industry growing, and the popularity of online booksellers, everything can be produced and distributed with the click of a mouse. You don't even have to leave your house to get great discounts on the best-sellers; you can order books and have them sent by mail.

The Internet offers people in the publishing business a great deal of flexibility. Communication is immediate. Response occurs almost instantaneously. And fame no longer exists on a local scale—if you write a good book or article, people around the globe can now enjoy it.

KAREN ASP, health and fitness writer

Karen Asp is a freelance writer who specializes in health and fitness issues. For the past four years, she has worked as a freelancer full-time and now contributes regularly to print magazines such as *Shape, Fitness, Walking, Fit Pregnancy,* and *Oxygen.* She also contributes frequently to online magazines. She is a regular contributor to HealthGate's series of online magazines (www.be well.com) and a contributing editor for *FitnessLink* (www.fitnesslink.com).

How do you find information about online markets?

I search everything and anything I can find about markets. I subscribe to print trade journals and e-newsletters for writers. I visit various writing Web sites to look at market listings. When I have time, I'll even do searches on the Internet for health and fitness publications. I subscribe to dozens of health and fitness magazines for fitness professionals (I happen to be one as well) and consumers. Those magazines often list new Web sites. I also receive press releases and various industry reports about health and fitness through several Web sites. Through those reports and press releases, I often hear about new online sites that might need writers.

Then I log any market information into a database on my computer. When I'm looking for a place to send a query, I open the database to find a market.

Ironically, though, having a presence on the Internet has brought clients and markets to me. For example, after learning about *FitnessLink* (www.fitnesslink .com) through *Writer's Digest*, I queried the site. One assignment led to another and now three years later, I'm the Fitness Professional Contributing Editor for *FitnessLink*. As such, I handle a monthly department that profiles professional and Olympic athletes and celebrity fitness professionals. At the end of each profile is my bio, which includes my e-mail address. Thanks to that, I've earned dozens of assignments from other online publications as well as health and fitness sites.

I'm also listed as a contributing writer for HealthGate at www.bewell.com. Over a year ago, I learned through *Writer's Digest* that HealthGate was looking for experienced health and fitness writers. I threw a query together to see what would happen. That one query has now turned into dozens of assignments.

Have you found writing for online publications different from print publications? If so, how?

Yes, I have. Online writing has to be different from print writing because online readers differ from print readers. Readers who are browsing online scan material quickly, and their attention spans are short. If something doesn't interest them, they're not going to stick around. So when you write for an online audience, you have to keep that in mind. Your leads, for example, have to be that much more appealing and catchy to hook the readers. Your sentences have to be shorter and crisper. And your text has to be easier to read. That's why online writing usually involves more bullet points and subheads.

You also have the option of using links in online writing, which affords you greater opportunities. By clicking on a highlighted word, readers can learn more in-depth information about a topic. For example, for an article that I wrote about exercise-induced asthma, I learned that many people who have asthma don't know how to use inhalers properly. That didn't necessarily pertain to the point of my article, but it did make a good sidebar. So I wrote it up, let the editor know what I was doing, and then when the piece was published, the word "inhaler" was underlined in the text. When readers clicked on it, my sidebar about using an inhaler popped up on the screen. The publication might also link a word in your text to an article that's already been written for that Web site.

The way that you address the audience is also different. Online publications tend to be more casual than print publications. So your tone when you're writing for online publications might be a little more casual than if you were writing for print publications. This will, of course, depend on each publication, but generally, most online sites prefer a casual, conversational tone, as if you're sitting next to the reader and having a friendly chat. Many writers use slang and clichés to make them seem more hip or friendly to their readers. I tend to stay away from slang and clichés for the same reason that I don't use them in print writing: I think you can always find better ways to say things.

Because online publications are accessible to anybody around the world, it's sometimes tougher to write to the specific audience. It's easy, for example, to write for a print publication whose audience is, let's say, females ages thirty-five to fifty. But the audience for an online publication might be much broader. Readers might include both genders, all ages, maybe even people from around the world. Of course, good online sites will have a target audience in mind. If you do start working with an online publication, always ask for its reader demographics and find out what kind of audience it's looking to attract.

Along with the physical act of writing, there are other differences between writing for online publications versus print publications. Although some print publications do take e-queries (electronic queries), especially once you've worked your way into the publication, every online publication that I've worked with has accepted e-queries, saving me postage and time.

Online publications also pay differently. Many online publications can barely afford to pay writers, which is why many look for inexperienced writers, making the online arena a wonderful place for beginning writers. Others, though, offer competitive pay. Yet if you're used to writing for top magazines at one dollar or more per word and you want to match that pay through online publications, you'll be hard pressed to find many markets.

Of course, there's also the issue of rights. Just as I try to avoid selling all rights to print articles, I don't like to sell full electronic rights to online publications. If a publication wants to buy exclusive electronic rights, I'll often renegotiate a deal where, after the first few months, the rights revert to me. But what rights you sell to online publications tends to be trickier and less loosely defined than rights purchased by print publications.

This brings up another point. Protecting your work on the Internet is much harder than in print publications. I've had dozens of situations where people have stolen my work from an online publication and then posted it on their own Web sites without having obtained my permission or having paid for electronic reprint rights. Unfortunately, these people think that because something is on the Internet, it's in public domain and, therefore, able to be used at will. That's not the case. Monitoring this can be tough, though. I'm sure there are dozens of other times my articles have been stolen that I don't even know about.

Finally, if you're sending e-queries (obviously for online publications but this may also apply to print publications that accept e-queries), you'll have to find a user-friendly way to include your clips. I usually paste clips and a brief bio into the e-mail. Some writers, though, attach their clips in a separate text attachment. Check the writer's guidelines to find out how the publication prefers to receive this material. Sometimes, editors don't accept unknown attachments so keep that in mind.

How has the Internet helped you in your writing career?

Without the Internet, I wouldn't be where I am today. In fact, I've often wondered how writers twenty years ago used to do things without the Internet. Frankly, I couldn't live without it. Or at the very least, my job would be much harder.

First, the Internet has made it possible to work from anyplace. Thanks to e-mail, I can communicate with editors in California just as easily as I can with those in New York. (I live in Indiana.) I should mention, too, that the Internet has eliminated lots of paperwork and postage. I send a majority of my queries and finished articles via e-mail. Plus, the Internet has made communication easier. If editors have questions, they can simply zap me an e-mail. Or if I have questions or need to send information to one of my clients, I can do so easier in an e-mail than through a phone call, which takes time and may interrupt an editor at work. E-mail just provides a more timely, less intrusive way of communicating.

Second, the Internet has provided a wealth of resources for doing research. Whereas I might have spent hours in a library perusing for information, I can now easily access information on the Internet. Not just information, though. I also find many sources for articles on the Internet. Maybe I need to locate an exercise physiologist or a physical therapist or a university professor. Or maybe I just need to find ordinary people to talk about their experiences. It's all on the

Internet. For example, I posted a note on a fitness forum for an article I was writing about women's addiction to exercise. I received dozens of e-mails from women who abused exercise, all of whom willingly filled out a questionnaire about their struggles. I would never have found them had it not been for the Internet. Interestingly enough, one woman wrote to tell me not only about her addiction to exercise but also her struggle with a rare eating disorder. That led me to write an article about that eating disorder, my first for *Shape* magazine.

Also, the Internet has provided additional markets to sell my writing.

Most importantly, though, as much as I hate to coin a cliché, the Internet has opened doors. I've received several freelance jobs because people have seen my work on the Internet. A surgical center in Iowa, for example, has assigned me several articles for its publications; without the Internet, there's no way I would be working with that center. Likewise, an online syndication company in San Francisco also saw my work and contacted me about syndicating my health and fitness columns online. Again, without the Internet, chances are, I would never have had this opportunity or the ability to search Web sites for job listings about freelance projects and assignments.

I could probably write tons more about the Internet, but I wouldn't want to write without it.

ANGELA ADAIR-HOY, author, editor, publisher
Angela Adair-Hoy is the editor and publisher of *WritersWeekly* (http://writersweekly.com) and *The Write Markets Report*. She has authored a variety of how-to books for writers and also owns the e-book publisher Booklocker.

How does the pay rate online compare to that of print publications? Do you see this changing, and why?
Freelance pay, on a whole, is lower for online publications. However, this is not always the case and is changing quickly. I've been offered $500 from a Web site and then offered $150 from a print magazine for the same article. As with traditional publishing, the circulation and advertising income of a publication plays a major role in determining how much it pays freelancers. As the Internet explodes, online publications can afford to share their increasing profits with freelance writers.

The quality of market info online varies widely. What advice do you have for writers who aren't sure what info is reliable?

The quality of paying markets information was what spurred me to launch *The Write Markets Report*. I was frustrated with out-of-date information that hurt my chances of succeeding as a new freelance writer. The Internet helped me offer new paying markets to the freelance community, often within two weeks of my interview with each editor.

The primary problem with most online markets coming over the e-transom is that the publishers of these e-zines and Web sites aren't willing to go the extra mile to deliver quality content to their readers. Most market publications simply rewrite old market listings they find or cut and paste writer's guidelines (often outdated) into their publications. Since this information is often old and also widely available, it is not beneficial and merely acts as a filler in these publications.

My advice is to find publications that speak directly with the magazine editors and book publishers; publications that investigate markets, obtain each editor's current needs, and deliver them in a timely manner to their readers. There are only four publications on the market right now that do this in generous quantity and high quality: *Writer's Digest* magazine, *Inklings*, *The Write Markets Report*, and WritersWeekly.com, our free weekly e-mag of freelance jobs and paying markets.

PAULA GURAN, online horror author/editor

Paula Guran teaches, critiques, and edits a monthly e-mail newsletter for Writers on the Net (www.writers.com.) She edits, writes about, and reviews horror for a number of venues online and off. Her weekly newsletter for horror writers, *DarkEcho*, was the first (and only) electronic publication to be awarded the Bram Stoker Award for Outstanding Nonfiction Horror. Her own Web site is www.darkecho.com.

How has the Internet helped you in your writing career?

It *is* my writing career for the most part. Although I write for print media, too, the Net has been my bread-and-butter and established me as a professional.

How did **DarkEcho** *start?*

It began in 1994 as a weekly newsletter via e-mail for members of a horror writing workshop on AOL. I was encouraged, by professional writers in the horror community, to keep expanding it and to make it available to anyone with e-mail. It just grew.

How did you hook up with **Omni Online?**

Ellen Datlow had been the fiction editor for *Omni* magazine for about fifteen years by the time it went completely online. She continued in that role (along with other duties) and Pam Weintraub (who had also been with *Omni* as long as Ellen) was the overall editor. Ellen had been reading the newsletter, knew my Web site and we had met at a couple of conventions. At that point (1996) just the fact that I had a decent Web site and was learning how to interview and write specifically for e-media made me pretty experienced. I was working with a local real-world company then, too, that was trying to develop commercial Web sites so I was learning more daily. *Omni* hired me to produce and write the horror section of *Omni Online.*

The job for Universal's New Media Department for *HorrorOnline* was similar. Joe Sena was a long time *DarkEcho* reader and he eventually started a Web site, The Dungeon of Darkness, concentrating on his love of horror films. He eventually convinced Universal to give the *HorrorOnline* concept a shot and contracted with me to do the "book" section.

What is the online horror market like?

Good and bad. The fiction in *Omni* and then *Event Horizon: Science Fiction, Fantasy and Horror* (with fiction edited for both by Ellen Datlow) was of the highest quality. *Omni*, of course, is no more and *EH* is on "hiatus." But both established that professional genre fiction could be published and read on the Web and won literary awards to prove it. Unlike some genres, horror and fantasy people accepted electronic publication as legitimate early on.

And now we've already gone through a "first generation" of people trying to convert printzines to Webzines and others launching Webzines with much enthusiasm and then eventually finding out (1) how much time it takes to do and (2) there's, as yet, no feasible way to make enough money to cover costs.

There are tons of no-pay Webzines out there that specialize in dark stuff, but setting up a Webzine and saying you are an editor doesn't make you one. Most are extremely amateurish operations. If you are dying to get published, these sites will "publish" you, but don't expect such publication to be accepted as valid. At best the quality is tremendously uneven. Some compare it to an earlier era when fanzines and (then new) desktop publishing combined for a surge to printzines. The best survived; the worst quickly died. The analogy isn't quite accurate however. Being on the Web makes the playing field equal for a professional publication like *Event Horizon* and for anyone with a computer and time on his hands. A printzine might never be seen by more than a few hundred people due to a lack of distribution. A Webzine? Well, the *potential* is there for it to be seen by millions. Most are still not seen by many—and that's good because they aren't usually worth reading.

As far as fiction, *Gothic.Net* (www.gothic.net) was the first to pay minimal pro rates for dark fiction and modern horror—three cents a word. It is now up to four cents. Seth Lindberg is the fiction editor there now. He was my assistant when I became the first fiction editor. *Deep Outside* (www.clocktowerfiction.com/ Outside), another monthly Webzine pays three cents a word for "dark imaginative" fiction. *Pulp Eternity Online* (www.pulpeternity.com) is supposed to start paying five cents a word for SF/F/H. There are also sites that sometimes use "dark erotica" that pay well.

Below that there are several that pay one cent per word, notably *Chiaroscuro* (www .gothic.net/chiaroscuro) and Jackhammer (SF/F/H/humor/personal essays—www .eggplant-productions.com). There are even a couple of "no-pays" that are at least interesting Webzines that may have a future, like *Errata* (www.sfgoth.com/errata)."

What advice do you have for writers wishing to break into the online market?
In general:

1. Writing for the Web requires a new approach. Don't expect all hard copy to translate well.
2. Read your contracts. Know exactly what rights you are selling and for how long.
3. Have enough technical knowledge of how to send readable text and files to do so; a basic knowledge of HTML helps.
4. Be able to handle deadlines and offer up-to-the-minute information for the Web.

NANCY PRICE, online editor

Nancy Price is the editor and co-owner of *Myria* (myria.com), *Interactive Parent* (interactiveparent.com), *SheKnows.com* (sheknows.com), and *ePregnancy* (epregnancy.com). She and Managing Editor Betsy Gartrell-Judd use freelancers for all but *SheKnows.com*. Price has been a freelance writer since her teens.

How were each of your publications created?

Myria was our first site, and we created it to fill a gap we saw in the marketplace for a publication that addressed women but realized we are mothers, too. There is parenting information on the site, but in equal amounts to other sections, such as time for you, money/home/work, leisure, health and fitness, and others.

ePregnancy began because I was pregnant and Betsy was planning a pregnancy, and we found we just had so much content on this topic, and so much we wanted to say! Very much the same story with *Interactive Parent*—it was really a natural extension of our interests. We feel that each of our sites has several elements that make them unique, while, of course, also providing the sorts of information people would expect from a pregnancy or parenting site.

In your opinion, is writing for the online market different from a print publication?

One great thing about the Web is that we don't need to keep within very specific formatting guidelines, such as you would when dealing with a printed page in a magazine. Also, the time between when a story is written to when it is published can be a matter of days, instead of months. I always like how fast we can move.

Do you see e-publications ever becoming more popular than regular print publications?

I can see them becoming an equal force in the marketplace, simply because distribution is so simple—information about almost any topic is only a few clicks away. But I can't imagine a day when people won't want something the Web can't currently offer—something they can read at the table or in the bathtub, something they can cut out and save in a scrapbook. In that way, the Internet must become more like print publications—that flexibility of use is vital.

What mistake do writers tend to make when submitting to your publication(s)?

It's what a thousand editors have said before—they don't study the publication before approaching. A lot of people come to us with ideas that clearly fall outside our topic area, or with article ideas about issues we have already covered recently. Also, sometimes their ideas are too plain. We love a new creative twist—but something that really makes sense! We're also open to articles with an interactive component: a poll, a checklist, something to download, where to get more information. This was the concept upon which we based our *Interactive Parent* site.

What advice do you have for writers hoping to break into your market(s)?
Visit our sites and see what we're about. We want people writing for us who aren't just looking for another gig, but who really like what we're doing. Each one of our sites has a very distinctive feel.

We have had tremendous success with new writers, and feel very fortunate. They have been very dependable and turn out great work (proofread, spell-checked), which is fantastic because we're overwhelmingly busy most of the time. It's also great for us to be able to support new writers, and to sort of give them a first toehold in the marketplace.

THE FUTURE OF ONLINE JOURNALISM
by Steve Outing

Steve Outing is a journalist and Internet entrepreneur. He is CEO and founder of Content Exchange (www.content-exchange.com), a digital marketplace for online content creators and publishers. He also writes a column, "Stop the Presses!," about interactive media for *Editor & Publisher Interactive*, and is recognized internationally as an expert on online journalism.

Thanks largely to the meteoric growth of the Internet, the future for practitioners and students of journalism looks bright. As online has grown into the newest mass medium, jobs and opportunities have expanded and will continue to grow even more quickly. More people will have the opportunity to make their careers in journalism, because of a wider array of media job openings.

There are several key trends that should hearten established journalists looking for a better lot and those looking to break into the journalism field:

- "Old media" have established new-media operations, creating new journalism jobs.

- Purely online news ventures with no old-media affiliation represent a significant and fast-growing employment source.
- The Internet has opened up options for expression by journalists. Odd or unique journalism that couldn't find a home in the world of old media can succeed online.
- Journalists who cover narrow niche topics can leverage the Internet's ability to find audiences that are thinly sliced.

Old Media Tries Something New

The world of journalism in recent years has been split into "new" and "old." New typically means the Internet and other forms of interactive media, CD-ROMs, etc. Old means every media that came before online: newspapers, magazines, newsletters, radio, TV, film, wire services, etc.

When old-media companies realized just how fast the interactive media industry was growing, most of them focused some of their attention and resources on new media—both to protect themselves against possible competition from new-media companies, and to take advantage of new business opportunities.

Today, just about every significant newspaper, magazine, wire service, TV station, TV network, and radio station operates a Web site. Some of these operations are quite large. WashingtonPost/Newsweek Interactive, for instance, employs well over two hundred people. Others, such as the Web site of a small newspaper, operate with a staff of one. Some operate independently of their old-media parent. Others are part of the traditional newsroom.

Opportunities abound for journalists to work in these environments. They get to practice online journalism with the backing of established news media companies, trying out new things while having a parent organization that can absorb losses if the new-media business plan doesn't profit right away.

Increasingly, old-media companies will earn a significant portion of their revenues from their new-media operations. A newspaper company of ten years from now, for instance, might publish to print and online, earning an equal share of its income from each.

The Pure New-Media Crowd

Journalists working at pure new-media news organizations live closer to the edge. They are trying to build businesses with no blueprints to follow, crafting business models that may or may not work. While that may sound risky, it's more likely that a pure new-media company will do better on the Internet than an old-media company trying to understand new-media models. It gets to devote 100 percent of its intelligence and resources to figuring out how to make an online news business work. For old-media companies, new media is just a sideline, a single component of the entire operation.

For this reason, pure new-media news companies likely will be among the most profitable news publishers of the future. And thus, they will represent some of the biggest opportunities for journalists of the future.

Consider CNET, one of the largest and most-trafficked news Web sites at this writing. Specializing in technology news and consumer advice on technology, CNET's Web sites operate with more than one hundred editorial employees—the staff size equivalent of a decent-sized metro daily newspaper. Many of tomorrow's journalists will work for media companies that don't print on paper, or broadcast over the airwaves, but employ as many journalists as companies that do.

Digital Home for the Unique and Quirky

What online journalism does and will do is widen the type of journalism that can find an audience. The traditional journalistic marketplace has a limited number of outlets—a finite number of newspapers, magazines, TV, and radio stations. But on the Web, publishers count their competitors (other Web sites) in the hundreds of thousands. Every Web site out there, from the multi-million-dollar news site with hundreds of employees to the Webzine with a staff of one, is competing for Internet users' attention. And hundreds of new Web sites continue to launch every day.

What the Web will do is increasingly bring unusual, unique, and quirky journalistic content before a willing audience. Content that "wouldn't fly" in print can work using the Web as the medium. For example, a successful Webzine called *Nerve* (www. nerve.com) publishes what it calls "literate smut"—thoughtful, nonprofane essays and journalism about human sexuality that fit somewhere between pornography and erotica. The Webzine *Blue Ear* (www.blueear.com) features high-minded essays and journalism on international issues from a smattering of writers around the world. Both of those ventures probably wouldn't have succeeded as print publications, for the traditional publishing world would have found the content unsuitable *(Nerve)* or the business model lacking *(Blue Ear)*. Yet they work on the Web.

The future will see more quirky journalistic content find a willing audience. Journalists with a dream of producing content that traditional markets shun will find that they can make a living by publishing online, and consumers will have a more diverse content plate from which to dine. And, as some of these online publications attract large audiences, they will spin off into traditional media as well. It used to be that print publications created Web sites. In the future, some successful Web sites will subsequently create print editions or TV shows.

Slicing It Thinner

Perhaps the most significant journalistic future trend to be brought on by the growth of the Internet is the primacy of niche content. What the Internet is much better at than any other communications medium is assembling audiences with very narrow, specific interests. And that will mean huge opportunity for the journalists of tomorrow to serve niche audiences.

Future journalistic entities might serve such narrow audiences as women snowboarders; families of cancer patients; recreational vehicle enthusiasts over fifty; fans of science-fiction writer Orson Scott Card; etc. Those are examples of topics too narrow to support even a specialty print magazine, but they're not too narrow to support a Web or e-mail publication.

Yesterday's business journalist might have covered technology stocks for a traditional media outlet. Tomorrow's online journalist might make a living by being an expert commentator on something as specific as online jewelry retailing. And because of the high value of the content this expert journalist produces, there's the potential for high earnings. In online journalism, the "stars" of the future will be the experts in narrow fields who gain the respect and adoration of an audience seeking very specific information and news, and there will be many such online journalism stars.

If you're old enough, you may remember a line from the 1960s movie *The Graduate*, where a well-meaning party guest succinctly tells college graduate Dustin Hoffman where the future lies: "Plastics!" Were I at a modern-day party for a new journalism graduate, I'd whisper: "Niche content."

BITS AND BYTES: FOUND IN THE WEB
by Sal Towse

Sal Towse's waking hours once were spent writing, surfing the Net (research!), and loitering in Usenet newsgroups. Now she squeezes time for her freelance writing from what's left after her multitasking job as employee number six at a hot Silicon Valley dot-com startup. A source for article topics? Of course!

"We are starting a new free computer and internet magazine in Texas. I have seen your work and was wondering if you would like to contribute articles for our paper. Please let me know and we can discuss this in further detail."

People ask why I'm online. Do I find the Internet useful for my writing? My answer usually mentions the above e-mail I received last fall from a publisher/ editor I'd never heard of, asking me to write for his new startup magazine. The editor found my monthly Net-surfing column (for the regional print magazine *Computer Bits*) as he surfed the Web, liked it, and asked if I'd write for him, too.

Gainful recognition is great, but I'm also online because the Internet is a powerful resource for writers.

I'd used Usenet since the 1980s, but in 1992 I quit my day job and lost my connection. In 1994 I got a modem and an ISP and connected to the Internet again. Things had changed! Usenet newsgroups had proliferated and, thanks to Tim Berners-Lee, the World Wide Web was a reality and expanding at a rapid pace. With NCSA's Mosaic, and, later, Netscape, I surfed, watched the Web-cam pointed at the coffeepot in Cambridge, and became infatuated with the Web.

In 1994, interesting URLs were passed back and forth between fellow Web enthusiasts. Links within sites and "favorite link" pages provided other surfing opportunities, but there was no good way to research, for example, Bingo enthusiasts or Web sites about Bingo for an article. All that changed when Jerry Yang and David Filo, two graduate students at Stanford, turned their huge collection of favorite links into Yahoo!.

Search engines and Web portals made finding information much easier. By the late 1990s, the Internet was not just a substitute but, sometimes, a much better resource than the library. My favorite search engines are FAST (www.alltheweb.com), Northern Light (www.northernlight.com) and AltaVista (www.altavista.com). I also use Web Ferret, which searches many different search engines simultaneously, available free from FerretSoft (www.ferretsoft.com/netferret/download.htm).

The Web's usefulness for a writer isn't just as a reference tool, though. Writerly advice available on the Web and on Usenet in 1994 was invaluable. Today, it's even more so.

In 1994, I chanced upon fellow writers in the Usenet newsgroup misc.writing. I was a naïf who'd known few writers in real life; what I knew of the business I'd picked up from books and workshops. On Usenet I found a helpful bunch of folks who wrote, some of them full-time. Jack Mingo was exceedingly generous with help and advice when I was first starting out. Bill Quick nagged me to write. Patricia Cronin Marcello inspired me when she wrote about how she made the switch from a "regular" job to that of a full-time writer. I discovered writers weren't charmed Algonquin Table people. The ordinariness of the writers I met in misc.writing, their foibles and flaws, their tempers and insecurities, helped me realize that if they could do it, I could, too.

These days, other favorite writing newsgroups include rec.arts.sf.composition, misc.writing.screenplays, and alt.journalism.freelance. I also subscribe to writing mailing lists, including MAGWRITE and WorkForWriters.

Valuable writing-related Web sites include Stephanie Kwok's "official misc.writing Web site" (www.scalar.com/mw). The site has all sorts of useful information and links, including Writers' Marketplace ("packed with information covering the business aspects of writing, from manuscript format to rejection letters, plus an inside look at the publishing industry"), Starting Point ("a collection of recommended WWW Sites for information on writing"), and Writing Basics ("a collection of articles whose topics range from 'writer's block' to world-building").

Lars Eighner's Web site (www.io.com/~eighner) includes his online writing course (www.io.com/~eighner/qamain.html). Crawford Kilian's "Advice on Novel Writing" (www.steampunk.com/sfch/writing/ckilian) is another excellent resource.

Over the years Terry L. Jeffress compiled the misc.writing Recommended Reading List (www.xmission.com/~jeffress/mw/rrl_toc.html) and Charlie Harris wrote "Using the Internet for Research FAQ" (www.purefiction.com/pages/res1.htm). Andrew Burt's "Critters Workshop" (www.critters.org), a free critiquing workshop for writers of horror, fantasy, and science fiction, also has links, useful information, and market leads.

Jon Bard's Children's Writing Resource Center (www.write4kids.com) is another free resource. Jon also publishes the *Children's Book Insider* newsletter. The Science Fiction Writers of America (SFWA) site (www.sfwa.org) is chockablock full of useful information, discussion groups and other information, not specifically targeted toward SF/F writers.

Inklings (www.inkspot.com/inklings), the biweekly writers' e-newsletter from Inkspot (chosen one of *Writer's Digest*'s "101 Best Web Sites for Writers") has articles and markets information. One of my regular writing jobs is as markets editor for *Inklings*, and that job is an excellent example of the serendipity the Net offers for writers. I was researching paying markets for a misc.writing-related volunteer project and offered to swap markets information with Inkspot. Debbie Ridpath Ohi needed a markets editor and offered me the job. Serendipity.

That sort of serendipity happens on the Net more often than people realize. I've sold articles to editors I met while I had my markets-editor hat on. I've sold articles to people who knew me from my Usenet posts. People I know from the Net have offered introductions, advice, and more.

Which brings me to another benefit for the writer on the Net—immediacy. I was asked to write an article about Tim Berners-Lee, the "father" of the World Wide Web. I dropped Berners-Lee a note asking, among other things, "Are you available at all for short-brief-quick questions in e-mail?" Thirteen minutes later, I received an e-mail back, answering the questions I'd asked and telling me he'd be willing to answer others "If they are short!"

That's what I love about the Internet: There is a wealth of information about almost anything you want to research, a community of supportive writers, and "the father of the World Wide Web" answers e-mail from some writer he's never met thirteen minutes after I send it.

CHAPTER TEN

Market Listings

THE FOLLOWING ARE paying online markets. Please note that Web sites move and submissions guidelines change; be sure to verify information through the site information before submitting material. Also see the "Cautions for Writers" sidebar on page 45. If you discover a site has moved with no forwarding link, use a search engine to look for the publication name. If you still can't find it, then it's possible that the publication has folded or changed its name.

The basic rules of submission apply here as much as for print publications. Before submitting, be sure to (1) read back issues of the publication, (2) read the guidelines, (3) include a self-addressed, stamped envelope if you are making a submission by surface mail.

Online Publications

About.com Mysteries—mysterybooks.about.com/library/flash/blfl_menu.htm
Mysteries in a Flash. Cathy Gallagher, as an independent contractor for About.com, P.O. Box 669, Snoqualmie, WA 98065. Fax: (847)574-1311. Cathy Gallagher, Guide (mysterybooks.guide@about.com). "*Mysteries in a Flash* is a special section of About.com Mysteries in which we feature quick-solve, flash, and short story mysteries written by freelance mystery writers." Subject: Mysteries. Frequency:

Weekly. Format: Web magazine. Est. November 1999. Circ. 32,000. 100% free-lance written. Pays on publication. Kill fee: 25%. Rights: All rights. Byline given. Submit seasonal material 2 months in advance. Queries: Post, e-mail, fax. Reports in 1 week on queries. Reports in 2 weeks on mss. Lead time: 1-2 months. Mss published average of 1 month after acceptance. Sample: Free on Web site. Guidelines: mysterybooks.about.com/library/flash/blfl_submit.htm. FICTION: Mystery. Pays: $15-50. Mss bought/yr: 75-100. Length: 250-2,500 wds. How to submit: Send complete ms. Does NOT want: "Hard-core violence or sex (PG-13 at most), over 2,500 words, degrading."

accenthealth.com—www.accenthealth.com

Information for Healthy Living. AccentHealth, Inc., 1901 Research Blvd., Suite 350, Rockville, MD 20850. Tel: (301)545-0710. Fax: (301)545-0720. Karen-Lee Ryan, Managing Editor; Chris Lindsley, Senior Producer (clindsley@accenthealth.com); Tammy White, Producer (twhite@accenthealth.com). "Authoritative, practical information designed to help people live healthier, happier lives. Extensive database, plus regularly updated features, news stories, and interactive tools on topics ranging from medical conditions to nutrition to mind-body wellness. Writers should know that we focus on how to stay well and help people live healthier lives. As a Web-based publication, articles are on the short side (400-600 wds). The writing style is consumer-friendly and crisp—every word counts." Subject: Consumer health information targeted at women aged 25-54. Frequency: Daily. Format: Consumer Health Web site. Est. April 1999. Circ. Anticipate 400,000 unique visitors/month by January 2000. 85% freelance written. Pays on acceptance. Kill fee: 25%. Rights: All rights. Byline given. Accepts simultaneous submissions. Submit seasonal material 3 months in advance. Queries: Post, e-mail. Reports in 2-3 weeks on queries. Lead time: 2-4 months. Mss published average of 1 month after acceptance. Sample: Free on Web site. Guidelines: E-mail clindsley@accenthealth.com or rsanchez@accenthealth.com. COLUMNS: My Experience With . . . , 400-500 wds; Food for Thought, 400-500 wds; Healthy Traveler, 400-500 wds; The Fitness Link, 400 wds; Men's Health in the Know, 500 wds; Women's Health in the Know, 500 wds. Contact: Chris Lindsley. Pays: 75¢-$1 wd. Mss bought/yr: 100. How to submit: Send published clips. NONFICTION: General interest, humor, inspirational, interview/profile, personal experience, travel. Contact: Chris Lindsley. Pays:

75¢-$1/wd for assigned articles. Mss bought/yr: 120. Length: 400-600 wds. How to submit: Send published clips. Does NOT want: "Opinion pieces, technical copy written more for a medical expert than for a consumer." TIPS: "Get familiar with the specific columns we regularly run on the site and target queries to specific columns."

Active Trader—www.activetradermag.com

555 W. Madison St., Suite 1210, Chicago, IL 60661. Fax: (312)775-5423. Mark Etzkorn, Editor-in-Chief (metzkorn@activetradermag.com); Amy Brader, Managing Editor (abrader@activetradermag.com). "The goal of *Active Trader* is simple: to be the reader's personal trading support department. Every month we will produce a 100-plus page magazine explaining all the strategies, issues, products, and news you wish you had the time to investigate yourself." Subject: Trading strategy. Format: Web magazine. Est. April 2000. Rights: *Active Trader* retains copyright on all material published in its issues, and reserves the right to produce and distribute reprints of articles, as well as use them in special publications or promotions, or in any other way it deems fit. Authors may not reproduce or reprint articles in any format, print or electronic (including the Web), without express written permission of *Active Trader* magazine. Byline given. Sample: Free on Web site after April 2000. NONFICTION: How-to. Pays: Varies. Length: 1,350-3,000 wds. How to submit: Query, send published clips. Does NOT want: "We have no interest in articles like 'Top Trader Mistakes,' 'Traits of Successful Traders,' 'The New Trading Technology,' or other general articles." Other: Specific trading strategy articles from professional traders—the how, why, and when of buying and selling stocks, options, and futures on a (mostly) short-term basis. TIPS: "Authors should be able to confirm trading ideas and performance claims through brokerage statements, third-party trade auditing, responsible historical testing, or some other reliable source. We reserve the right to judge the validity and veracity of an article, and accept or reject it based upon our conclusions."

Adventureseek—www.adventureseek.com

569 Mission St., San Francisco, CA 94105. Diana Grossman, Associate Editor (dgrossman@adventureseek.com). Subject: Active vacations. Format: Web magazine. Rights: Nonexclusive first-time or secondary electronic rights for a period of 1 year, with an option for renewal. Byline given. Accepts previously published material.

Submit seasonal material 6 weeks in advance. Lead time: 6 weeks. COLUMNS: Destinations: Destination pieces that will inspire and inform our members with a unique look at a region's cultural and geographic essence; examples: Hawaii's Best Trails (Regional round-up), Festivals of New Zealand (Cultural), and The Heart of Nepal (Destination-specific); 500-1,000 wds. Activities: Should focus primarily on the activities we currently cover, although articles on other activities may also be of interest; how-to articles, skill-related articles and activity round-ups can also be submitted; examples: Trekking in the Andes (Destination-specific activity), The Top 5 Day Hikes in California (Activity round-up), and How to Pack your Backpack (How-to); 500-1,000 wds. How to submit: Send complete ms. TIPS: "As a comprehensive yet evaluative active travel site, Adventureseek.com demands accurate and reliable information for our members. We may spot-check facts before acceptance and will reject any article that is not factually correct and up-to-date. We welcome the submission of photographs along with completed articles. Electronic submissions of photographs are strongly encouraged, although mailed versions are acceptable. U.S.$75-200 per article, depending on the article's length and complexity, as well as the experience of the author. Rights to associated photos will earn an additional U.S.$25-50, under the same terms."

AlienQ—www.alienq.com

Science Cyber Fiction and Fact E-zine. 11231 San Fernando Rd., San Fernando, CA 91340. Fax: (818)890-7834. A.W. Bacon, Managing Editor (editor@alienq.com). "*AlienQ* is centered around an alien living on Earth. The premise is all beings are immortal but the residents of Earth have total amnesia. Stories should slant towards past life experiences, future conditions of existence created by the waking residents of Earth, out of body activities, telepathy, psychic powers, and the extraordinary abilities sometimes displayed by individuals." Subject: Science fiction. Frequency: Monthly. Format: Web magazine. Est. May 1996. Circ. 10,000. 50% freelance written. Pays on publication. Rights: First-time electronic rights. Byline given. Accepts simultaneous submissions. Submit seasonal material 2 months in advance. Queries: E-mail. Reports in 2 weeks on queries. Reports in 8 weeks on mss. Lead time: 2 months. Mss published average of 3-4 months after acceptance. Sample: Free on Web site. Guidelines: On Web site. FICTION: Science fiction. Pays: $50-100. Mss bought/yr: 35. Length: 2,000-7,500 wds. How to submit: Send complete ms.

All-Story Extra—www.zoetrope-stories.com/extra

Stories From the On-Line Workshop. *Zoetrope: All-Story*/AZX Publications, 1350 Avenue of the Americas, 24th Floor, New York, NY 10019. Barbara Garret, All-Extra Coordinator (ragbag@isoc.net); Hilary Bachelder, All-Extra Coordinator; Adrienne Brodeur, Editor (print publication only). "*All-Story Extra* was founded by two members of the on-line workshop to showcase the talent of our workshop members. Stories posted by workshop members are automatically considered by both *All-Story Extra* and *Zoetrope: All-Story.*" Subject: Literary fiction. Frequency: Monthly. Format: Web magazine. 100% freelance written. Pays on acceptance. "Join the writers' workshop to be considered for *ASE.*" Rights: First-time electronic rights and first look and last refusal for film/TV options. Byline given. Accepts simultaneous submissions. Reports in 6 weeks on mss. Lead time: 1 month. Mss published average of 1 month after acceptance. Sample: Free on Web site. Guide-lines: On Web site. FICTION: Contact: Barbara Garrett and Hilary Bachelder. Pays: $100. Mss bought/yr: 24. Does NOT want: "Genre fiction." TIPS: "The online submission process enables writers to simultaneously workshop their stories and submit them for publication. Most writers develop helpful friendships with other site members."

allpets.com—www.allpets.com

888 W. Sixth St., Suite 1500, Los Angeles, CA 90017. Marva Marrow, Editor-in-Chief (marva@allpets.com). "Focus: Pets/animals. We strongly stress responsible pet care. Our philosophy is pro-animal WELFARE but NOT pro-animal RIGHTS—although of course the two groups share interest in many issues. We accept only very qualified writers (experts, people with lots of hands-on experience with the animals they write about), or human interest subjects regarding pets/society/culture/news." Frequency: Other. Format: Web magazine/zine. Est. May 1, 1996. Circ. 50,000 visitors/week (3,500,000 hits). 60% freelance written. Pays on acceptance. Frequency: Triweekly. Rights: First-time electronic rights; second serial (reprint) electronic rights. Other: May not be published in other competing commercial PET Web sites (or . . . depends if material is already published or is written for us. Material remains available for reference to readers in our Article Archive). Byline given. Accepts simultaneous sub-missions and previously published material. Submit seasonal material 3 months in advance. Queries: E-mail. Reports in 2 weeks on queries. Mss published varied number

of months after acceptance. Sample: Free on Web site. Guidelines: E-mail marva@allp ets.com. COLUMNS: Pets N' People: Interviews/profiles: 700-2,000 wds; Features: Varies/How-To's, Problem Solving, Human Interest; NewsBreak: Current events/ controversial topics. Pays: $50-100. Mss bought/yr: Varies. How to submit: Query. NONFICTION: Book excerpts, essays, general interest, how-to, humor, interview/ profile, opinion, personal experience, technical, travel. Pays: $50-100 assigned or unsolicited (this will change later this year or early next year). Mss bought/yr: Varies. Length: Minimum 800 wds. How to submit: Query. Does NOT want: "Technical articles or how-to's from unqualified individuals." Other: How-to: Technical, behavior, training, veterinary. Interview/profile: Only people dealing with these pets. Strong personalities who deal with pets, work against the odds, or have unusual occupations, or organizations dealing with pets and/or other animals, celebrities profiled about their pets.

American Woman Road & Travel Magazine—www.americanwomanmag.com

Caldwell Communications, Inc., 2424 Coolidge Rd., Suite 203, Troy, MI 48084. Fax: (248)614-8929. Courtney Caldwell, Publisher/Editor-in-Chief (courtney@am ericanwomanmag.com). *AWRT* provides content on auto, travel, and safety-related issues from which working and professional women can make informed decisions. 29-60 yrs. Frequency: Bimonthly. Format: Print and Web magazine. Est. 1988. Circ. 500,000. 75% freelance written. Pays on publication. Rights: Makes work-for-hire assignments. Byline given. Submit seasonal material 6 months in advance. Queries: Post, e-mail, fax. Lead time: 3 months. Mss published average of 3-6 months after acceptance. Guidelines: americanwomanmag.com/writerguide.html. COLUMNS: Automotive, travel, and safety-related topics. Profiles on women of accomplishment. How to submit: Send complete ms. NONFICTION: How-to, humor, inspirational, interview/profile, travel. Pays: Varies. Mss bought/yr: Varies. Length: 500-1,500 wds. How to submit: Send complete ms. Does NOT want: "bimbo stories." Other: Auto tips, safety on the road, world travel; land or air. FILLERS: Anecdotes, facts, gags to be illustrated by cartoonist, newsbreaks, short humor. Pays: Byline. Mss bought/yr: Varies. Length: 25-50 wds. TIPS: "Send full manuscript of work covering our topics of interest. Include photos when possible. Submit disk or e-mail. Accept bylines for starters. Pay fluctuates from $0-250, depending on quality."

Anotherealm—www.anotherealm.com

287 Gano Ave., Orange Park, Fl 32073. Jean Goldstrom, Editor (goldstrm@tu.infi.net). "We seek quality science fiction, fantasy, and horror stories. 5,000 word limit to stories." Subject: Science fiction, fantasy, horror. Frequency: Weekly. Format: Web magazine/zine and e-mail newsletter. Est. September 1998. Circ. 5,000/week. 100% freelance written. Pays on acceptance. Rights: First-time electronic rights. Byline given. Open to submissions for 2001 from Jan. 1 to March 31. Queries: E-mail. Reports in 8-12 weeks on mss. Sample: Free on Web site. Guidelines: On Web site. FICTION: Fantasy, horror, science fiction. Pays: $10. Mss bought/yr: 104. Length: Maximum 5,000 wds. How to submit: Send complete ms.

Apogee Photo—www.apogeephoto.com

Apogee Photo, Inc., P.O. Box 730, Conifer, CO 80433-0730. Fax: (303)825-0430. Michael Fulks, Editor (mfulks@apogeephoto.com); Susan Harris, Managing Editor, Submissions (submissions@apogeephoto.com). "The readership tends to be mostly beginning to intermediate in skill range who are looking for how-to's and inspiration. We try to provide content that will interest an international readership (rather than just U.S.)." Subject: Photography for beginners to advanced photographers. Special sections for young people. Frequency: Weekly. Format: Web magazine/zine. Est. 1994. Circ. 90,000 readers monthly. 80% freelance written. Pays on publication. "E-mail submissions preferred; query first, then send actual mss if requested (a request for a ms does not mean we have agreed to publish it)." Rights: First-time electronic rights or second serial (reprint) electronic rights or makes work-for-hire assignments, and contract includes rights to have work included in CD edition. Byline given. Accepts simultaneous submissions and previously published material. Submit seasonal material 3 months in advance. Queries: Post, e-mail. Reports in 1 month on queries. Reports in 1 month on mss. Lead time: 1-3 months. Mss published average of 6 months after acceptance. Sample: Free on Web site. Guidelines: On Web site. NONFICTION: How-to, interview/profile, photo feature, technical, travel. Contact: Susan Harris, Managing Editor (submissions@apogeephoto.com). Pays: 10¢/wd minimum, $150 maximum for assigned articles. 3¢-$150 for reprinted articles. Mss bought/yr: 36. Length: 1,000-2,000 wds. How to submit: Query. Does NOT want: "Self-promotion." TIPS: "When writing your piece, please keep in mind that 30% of our readers speak English as a second language, that our readership is international, and that we also target young people and beginners who appreciate a simple writing style. When in doubt feel free to e-mail us with a question. We are easy to work with and gladly will help you with your submissions."

The Art Bin—www.art-bin.com

Nisus Publishing, P.O. Box 55518, Stockholm, Sweden 10204. Fax: (786)513-2450. Karl-Erik Tallmo, Editor (tallmo@nisus.se). "A Swedish/international forum for art, literature, music, cultural politics, etc. Here you will find articles, essays, poetry, fiction, paintings, and music, as well as some rare classical or other source texts. Much of this material could be useful for educational purposes. No special requirements, other than well-written interesting texts." Subject: Art, literature, other cultural subjects. Frequency: Quarterly. Format: Web magazine/zine. Est. April 1995. Circ. 9,000-15,000 visitors/issue. 50% freelance written. Pays on acceptance. Kill fee: 100%. Rights: First-time electronic rights. Byline given. Queries: E-mail. Lead time: 3-4 months. Mss published average of 3 months after acceptance. Sample: Free on Web site. FICTION: Experimental, historical, humorous, novel excerpts, science fiction. Pays: Varies, approximately the same as nonfiction. Mss bought/yr: 0-3. How to submit: Query. Does NOT want: "Fantasy, New Age stuff." NONFICTION: Essays, interview/profile. Contact: Karl-Erik Tallmo, editor (tallmo@nisus.se). Pays: $100-650. Mss bought/yr: 4. Length: 800-7,000 wds. How to submit: Query. Does NOT want: "Short reviews." POETRY: Avant-garde, free verse, haiku, light verse, traditional. Pays: Varies. Mss bought/yr: 4. Other tips: All poetry types accepted. TIPS: "If writers have a good idea for an essay or article, they may query the editor first."

At the Fence—www.atthefence.com

Relationships and Parenting. 6002 Whippoorwill Rd., Tampa, FL 33625. Nora Penia, Editor/Managing Editor (editor@atthefence.com). "Articles should explore relationship problems and offer solutions. Although articles do not have to relate directly to religious or Christian issues, articles should fit in with Christian principles as far as basic moral issues." Subject: Relationship issues including couples, marriage, divorce, singles, dating, parenting, work, neighborhood, and spiritual. Frequency: Monthly. Format: Web magazine/zine. Est. Site December 1996; magazine format April 1999. Circ. 9,700 visitors/month, approximately. Page views: 84,000/month.

20% freelance written. Pays on publication. Rights: One-time electronic rights and one-time excerpt for newsletter. Byline given. Accepts simultaneous submissions and previously published material. Submit seasonal material 3 months in advance. Queries: Post, e-mail. Reports in 3 weeks on queries. Reports in 3 weeks on mss. Lead time: 1-3 months. Mss published average of 3 months after acceptance. Sample: Free on Web site. Guidelines: www.atthefence.com/guidelines.htm. NONFIC-TION: Book excerpts, essays, general interest, humor, inspirational, opinion, personal experience, religious. Pays: $10. Mss bought/yr: 48. Length: 900-2,000 wds. How to submit: Query, send complete ms. Does NOT want: "Poetry, travel accounts, gay subjects, or erotica." TIPS: "Articles should be well written and focused, as close to ready-to-publish as possible. If sent without a query, be sure to introduce yourself, tell me a little about your background and why you are interested in my magazine. Don't be afraid to run an idea by me as I am interested in new topics and approaches. Please, do not send attachments unless given an OK by me."

Atevo Travel—www.atevo.com

1633 Bayshore Hwy., Suite 225, Burlingame, CA 94010. Editor (tom@atevo.com). "Atevo Travel is a full-service travel Web site providing editorial coverage, reservations services, and interactive community forums. Our only out-of-house writing assignments go to published destination specialists (guidebook writers, local writers, etc.), who can help us to expand and maintain our database of guides." Subject: Travel. Pays 30 days after final acceptance. Rights: All rights. Queries: Post, e-mail. Guidelines: www.atevo.com/contact/submit_guidelines/0,3890,0,00.html. NON-FICTION: Travel. Pays: Varies. Pays for guidebook-type files, and updated files (not actual articles). The pay scale on this varies widely, based on the assignments. How to submit: Query, send published clips.

Back2College.com—www.back2college.com

"*Back to College* is a news/information e-zine for adult re-entry students who are pursuing professional development or an advanced degree. Most readers are motivated by the desire to excel in their studies and accelerate their degree plans as much as possible." Frequency: Weekly. Format: Web magazine/e-zine. Pays 60 days from publication. Rights: Exclusive, first-use, one-time electronic rights only. Byline given. Queries: E-mail. Lead time: Wednesday afternoon before 5 p.m. PST for the upcoming week. Guidelines: www.back2college.com/guide.htm. NONFICTION:

Pays: $45. Length: 1,000-1,500 wds. How to submit: Send complete ms, query. TIPS: "Articles must address issues that are of importance to the older student: obtaining financial aid, distance education, finding the right program (comparing costs and quality of curriculum), graduate school, or attaining academic excellence. Career management and articles on successful transition are appreciated. Articles of preference may be anecdotal, or include examples, illustrations, direct quotes, and resources where readers can obtain more information. Web resources cited are desirable for an online publication. We are an electronic publication. Articles must be submitted via e-mail, as a (Microsoft Word or WordPerfect) attachment, or on a floppy disk. Use online submission form (www.back2college.com/submit.htm) to submit articles. Queries must include full details on the article idea, biographical information, prior articles or references, estimated length of article, and a writing sample. Articles should be concise, tight, and professional. If accepted, you will be notified within 30 days. No phone queries, please."

Backpacker—www.backpacker.com

The Website of Wilderness Travel. Rodale, Inc., 33 E. Minor St., Emmaus, PA 18098. Tel: (610)967-8296. Fax: (610)967-8181. Tom Shealey, Editor. E-mail: tshealey@backpacker.com. "We are far more literary in nature than most people suspect. Journal entry and pedantic, linear style articles ('me and Joe went hiking') need not apply. We have high standards for writing, both in quality and the take-away information value. Upon finishing an article, the reader should not only want to go to that place, but know why and how. On the Web, high information content to words ratio is expected." Subject: Self-propelled, overnight, low impact wilderness travel primarily in North America. Frequency: Daily. Format: Web magazine/zine and online directory. Est. 1995. Circ. Several hundred thousand visitors/month. 10-20% freelance written. Pays on acceptance. Kill fee: Varies, stated in contract. Rights: Typically offers all-rights contracts that include both print and electronic publications. Will offer first-time rights to some authors. Byline given. Queries: Post, e-mail, fax. Reports in 4-6 weeks on queries. Reports in 6-8 weeks on mss. Lead time: 1 month. Mss published average of 1-6 months after acceptance. Sample: Free on Web site. Guidelines: On Web site. COLUMNS: Most of the online-only columns are set by sponsor demand. Contact: Varies, see Web site. Pays: 50¢-$1/wd typical. Mss bought/yr: 10. How to submit: Query, send published clips. FICTION: Adventure, confession, experimental, fantasy, historical, humorous, mainstream. Pays: 50¢-$1/wd. Mss bought/yr: Maybe 1. How to submit: Query, send published clips. NONFICTION: Book excerpts, essays, exposé, interview/profile, inspirational, how-to, historical/nostalgic, general interest, personal experience, photo feature, opinion, technical, travel. Contact: Tom Shealey, Editor (tshealey@backpacker.com). Pays: 50¢-$1/wd. Mss bought/yr: Hundreds. Length: 100-3,000 wds. How to submit: Send published clips, query. Other: Interview of a national figure.

Balloon Life—www.balloonlife.com

The Magazine for Hot Air Ballooning. Balloon Life Magazine, Inc., 2336 47th Ave. SW, Seattle, WA 98116-2331. Tel: (206)935-3649. Fax: (206)935-3326. Tom Hamilton, Editor (tom@balloonlife.com). "*Balloon Life* covers the sport of hot air ballooning with educational and safety articles, current events, and personalities of the sport. Each issue has a special report that looks at one subject in-depth." Frequency: Monthly. Format: Other. Est. February 1986. Circ. 3,500. 80% freelance written. Pays on publication. "Reporting time depends on work load/traveling. Can be same day or several months." Rights: Nonexclusive one-time rights for all media and reserves the right to reprint, paying another fee if used again in a different context. Byline given. Accepts simultaneous submissions and previously published material. Queries: Post, e-mail, fax, phone. Mss published average of 1-6 months after acceptance. Sample: Free on Web site or $2 SASE for hard copy. Guidelines: On Web site or $2 SASE for hard copy. COLUMNS: Hangar Flying: Interesting balloon flying stories that have experiences others pilots can learn from, 800-1,600 wds; Balloonmeister: Profiles an interesting personality in ballooning 800-900 wds; Logbook: Short pieces about recent balloon events, 400-800 wds. Pays: $35 for Hangar Flying, $20 for Logbook, $50 for other stories. Mss bought/yr: 40-60. How to submit: Query, send complete ms. FICTION: How to submit: Query, send complete ms. Other tips: "Rarely use fiction but worth a shot." NONFICTION: How-to, interview/profile, new product, opinion, personal experience, technical. Pays: $50/article. Mss bought/yr: 30. Length: 800-3,000 wds. How to submit: Query, send complete ms. Does NOT want: "First-time balloon rides." FILLERS: Facts, gags to be illustrated by cartoonist. Pays: $20. Mss bought/yr: 5-10. Length: 100-300 wds. TIPS: "Material needs to be specific to ballooning. The magazine is written for the individual who is actively involved in the sport and is generally familar with it."

Bible Advocate Online—www.cog7.org/BA

General Conference of the Church of God (Seventh Day), P.O. Box 33677, Denver, CO 80233. Fax: (303)452-0657. Calvin Burrell, Editor; Sherri Langton, Associate Editor. E-mail: bibleadvocate@cog7.org. "We address the 'felt needs' of readers (grief, depression, sickness, etc.). We also use articles on current social and religious issues, Bible topics and personal experience. Material in our magazine is seeker-sensitive." Subject: Looking at life and life issues through a Christian worldview. Frequency: Monthly. Format: Web magazine/zine. Est. October 1996. 50-100% freelance written. Pays on publication. Rights: First-time electronic rights and second serial (reprint) electronic rights. Byline given. Accepts simultaneous submissions and previously published material. Submit seasonal material 6 months in advance. Queries: E-mail, post. Reports in 4-6 weeks on queries. Reports in 4-8 weeks on mss. Lead time: 3-6 months. Mss published average of 3-6 months after acceptance. Sample: Free on Web site. Guidelines: On Web site. NONFICTION: Inspirational, personal experience, religious. Pays: $25-55 honorarium. Mss bought/yr: 20-25. Length: 750-1,500 wds. How to submit: Send complete ms. Does NOT want: "Christmas or Easter pieces." FILLERS: Facts. Pays: $20-25 honorarium. Mss bought/yr: 5-10. Length: 50-250 wds. TIPS: "Stay away from religious jargon. Think broadly about who could be reading your piece. How would you say things differently if a non-Christian read your work? Be fresh and real in personal experiences."

Big World Magazine—www.bigworld.com

Big World Publishing, P.O. Box 7656, Lancaster, PA 17604. Jim Fortney, Editor (jim@bigworld.com); Karen Stone, Managing Editor. "Highly targeted toward on-the-cheap, down-to-earth world travellers." Subject: World travel. Frequency: Quarterly. Format: Web magazine/zine and print publication. Est. February 1995. Circ. 10,000. 75% freelance written. Pays on publication. Kill fee: 50%. Rights: One-time electronic rights. Byline given. Accepts simultaneous submissions and previously published material. Submit seasonal material 4 months in advance. Queries: Post, e-mail. Reports in 7 weeks on queries. Reports in 7 weeks on mss. Lead time: 4 months. Mss published average of 4 months after acceptance. Sample:

Online edition free on site; print version available for $3.50. Guidelines: www.bigwo rld.com/iwrite.html and by e-mail from botguides@bigworld.com. COLUMNS: Dispatches: Slice-of-life travel tales, 250-500 wds; Music reviews: World music, 100-200 wds; Film reviews: Current foreign films, 100-250 wds; Cybertravel: Internet site rundowns or software reviews, 500-1,000 wds. Contact: Jim Fortney. Pays: $10-25. Mss bought/yr: 6. How to submit: Send complete ms. NONFIC-TION: Book excerpts, essays, exposé, general interest, how-to, humor, opinion, photo feature, travel. Contact: Karen Stone. Pays: $25-50 for assigned articles. Pays $25-50 for unsolicited articles. Mss bought/yr: 25. Length: 250-3,100 wds. How to submit: Query, send complete ms. TIPS: "*Big World* is a friendly, laid-back magazine reflecting the travel philosophy of its readers. We also encourage writers to explore the non-touristy side of travel . . . politics, culture, language, all are fair game in *Big World.* We encourage and often prefer first-time writers to submit their stories."

Blue Murder Magazine—www.bluemurder.com

Fresh Pulp on the Web. Blue Murder, Inc., 2340 NW Thurman St., Suite 202, Portland, OR 97210-2579. David Firks, Editor (info@bluemurder.com). "Crime fiction publication." Frequency: Bimonthly. Format: Web magazine/zine. Est. March 1998. Circ. Tracking 500 copies of *BMM* are downloaded each day, world-wide. 75% freelance written. Pays on publication. Rights: First-time electronic rights. Byline given. Accepts simultaneous submissions. Queries: Post, e-mail. Mss published average of 4 months after acceptance. Sample: Free on Web site or by e-mail. Guidelines: E-mail info@bluemurder.com. COLUMNS: Pays: $20-100. Mss bought/yr: 30. How to submit: Refer to guidelines. FICTION: Mystery, suspense. Pays: $20-100. Mss bought/yr: 60-70. Length: 250-3,000 wds. How to submit: Send complete ms. Does NOT want: "No cozy/cat mysteries, please." NONFICTION: Interview/profile. Pays: $20-100. Mss bought/yr: 20. Length: 500-2,000 wds. How to submit: Query. TIPS: "Know our magazine. Our audience enjoys hard-hitting crime noir fiction. Study any of our issues to understand what we're looking for. *BMM* is always in search of unique approaches to this genre and enjoys when writers break the rules."

Bovine Free Wyoming—www.xpi.net/users/pome12/bovine

Dan Knestaut, Editor (pome12@xpi.net); Katie Kusmaul, Co-Editor. Subject: E-zine dedicated to literature and arts. Frequency: Quarterly. Est. February 1, 2000. Pays on acceptance. Rights: FNASR—one-time electronic rights. All rights revert back to author/artist once accepted piece has been posted. In the event of future print version or anthologized version, *Bovine Free Wyoming* will seek permission from author/artist for use of work again. Byline given. Sample: Free on Web Site. Guidelines: www.xpi.net/users/pome12/bovine/submit.htm. FICTION: Novel excerpts. Pays: $5/piece. Length: "Open to any length, but the lengthier the submission, the more critical we become." Other tips: "Literature—poetry, short stories, novel excerpts, music reviews, essays will be considered. Preference is toward post-modern and free verse." POETRY: Pays: $5/piece. Maximum line length: "Open to any length, but the lengthier the submission, the more critical we become. TIPS: "Our guidelines are vague, so the best way to determine what we're looking for is to read an issue."

The Breathless Moment—www.breathlessmoment.com

Romantic Fiction and Features of Interest to Women. Perrine Publishing, Inc., PBM #236, 12329 Fondren, Houston, TX 77035. Tel: (713)728-1678. Fax: (713)729-4843. George Perrine, Editor (submissions@breathlessmoment.com). "Our fiction is in the romantic genre and requires feel-good endings. We do not publish pornography, although sensuality as written within the genre is acceptable. Our articles furnish information about subjects of interest to women, such as family life, pets, make-up, relationships, crafts, etc. We focus on a specific city in each issue and provide articles about that city." Subject: Romance fiction and features of interest to women. Frequency: Bimonthly. Format: Web magazine/zine. Est. November 1999. Circ. 2,500 hits/month. 90% freelance written. Pays on publication. Rights: 2 years e-rights and first rights for hardcopy publication. Byline given. Accepts simultaneous submissions and previously published material. Submit seasonal material 4 months in advance. Queries: E-mail. Reports in 1 week on queries. Reports in 4 weeks on mss. Lead time: 4 months. Mss published average of 4 months after acceptance. Sample: Free on Web site. Guidelines: On Web site. COLUMNS: Family Living: Tips from a family therapist, 500 wds; Hints From Hellacious: Humor, 250 wds; Tourist Ideas: Fits the focus city, 1,000 wds; Your Pet: Veterinarian's advice, 500 wds. Pays: 7¢/wd. Mss bought/yr: 30. How to submit: Query. FICTION: Romance. Pays: 7¢/wd. Mss bought/yr: 48. Length: 1,000-5,000 wds.

How to submit: Query. Does NOT want: "Porn." NONFICTION: General interest, historical/nostalgic, how-to, humor, inspirational, personal experience, photo feature, travel. Pays: 7¢/wd. Mss bought/yr: 36. Length: 250-2,500 wds. How to submit: Query.

Business Life Magazine—www.bizlife.com

4101-A Piedmont Pkwy., Greensboro, NC 27410. Tel: (336)812-8801. Fax: (336)812-8832. Kay Meekins, Editor (kmeekins@bizlife.com). "As long as the 'slant' includes the topic's relevance to the general business community, we accept most any piece for consideration." Subject: Business. Frequency: Monthly. Format: Company Web site. Est. April 1989. Circ. 13,000. 15% freelance written. Pays on publication. "Sample not available." Rights: First-time electronic rights. Byline given. Submit seasonal material 4 months in advance. Queries: Post, e-mail, fax. Lead time: 4 months. Mss published average of 3 months after acceptance. Guidelines: E-mail editor. NONFICTION: How-to, interview/profile, opinion. Pays: $250-350 maximum for assigned articles. Mss bought/yr: 24-40. Length: 1,000-2,000 wds. How to submit: Query. Other: Any topic with broad business-based appeal, especially local business. TIPS: "Call to discuss particular writing style and interests."

The Cafe Irreal—home.sprynet.com/~awhit

International Imagination. G.S. Evans, Editor; Alice Whittenburg, Editor. E-mail: cafeirreal@iname.com. "*The Cafe Irreal* presents a kind of fantastic fiction infrequently published in English. This fiction, which we would describe as 'irreal,' resembles the work of writers such as Franz Kafka, Kobo Abe, Luisa Valenzuela, and Jorge Luis Borges. As a style of fiction it rejects the tendency to portray people and places realistically and the need for a full resolution to the story; instead, it shows us a reality constantly being undermined." Subject: Irreal fiction. Frequency: Semiannual. Format: Web magazine/zine. Est. June 1998. 100% freelance written. Pays on acceptance. "Submissions accepted by e-mail only." Rights: First-time rights. Byline given. Queries: E-mail. Reports in 2 months on queries. Mss published average of 6 months after acceptance. Sample: Free on Web site. Guidelines: On Web site or e-mail cafeirreal@iname.com. FICTION: Experimental, fantasy, science fiction. Pays: 1¢/wd for unsolicited fiction. Mss bought/yr: 18. Length: 2,000 wds maximum. How to submit: Send complete ms. Does NOT want: "Slice-of-life vignettes, horror." Other tips: "Fantastic, absurdist, surrealist." TIPS: "We're interested in stories by writers who write about what they don't know, take us places we couldn't possibly go, and don't try to make us care about the characters. We would also suggest you take a look at the current issue, archives, and theory pages on the Web site."

Career Magazine—www.careermag.com

4775 Walnut St., Suite 2A, Boulder, CO 80301. Nicolle Fogleson, Content Editor (nicolle@careermag.com). "Online magazine serving as a comprehensive resource for job hunters and networking-oriented readers." Circ. 400,000 unique user log-ins per month. Rights: One-time electronic rights for the period of 1 month, after which the rights revert back to the author. Article is then maintained in an archive (sort of like back issues of a magazine); author can ask *Career* to remove the article from the archives whenever he wishes. Byline given. NONFICTION: Pays: $50-100 per article, depending on relevancy, timeliness of topic, and placement. TIPS: "Practical and useful articles dealing with the topic of careers (human resources, labor relations, job seeking, interviewing, resume writing, diversity in the workplace, college student career issues, employment law, etc). Guidelines: Keep articles 1,750 wds and under, adhere to AP style guidelines, and include short author biography and contact info. Postal: submit manuscript on computer disk, preferably in an IBM-compatible format. E-mail: submit as an attachment or as text in the body of the e-mail."

CaregiverZone.com—www.caregiverzone.com

CaregiverZone.com, Inc., 2855 Telegraph Ave., Suite 601, Berkeley, CA 94705. Tel: (510)981-5000. Fax: (510)981-5099. Ms. Mignon Fogarty, Managing Editor, Director of Content (mignon@caregiverzone.com). "We strive to enable seniors to live in the community as long as possible, and to maximize their independence. Our content is directed to the caregivers and attempts to meet all of their caregiving needs (coping, caregiving in the home, insitutional care, financial, legal, medical, etc.)." Subject: Caregiving for the elderly. Frequency: Daily. Format: Web magazine/zine. Est. November 1999. 80% freelance written. Pays on acceptance. "Experts in their field (e.g., elder law attorneys or geriatricians) do get a byline. We sometimes use ghostwriters." Kill fee: $30. Rights: All rights. Byline given. Accepts simultaneous submissions and previously published material. Submit seasonal material 1 month in advance. Queries:

Post, e-mail, fax. Reports in 2-3 weeks on queries. Lead time: 1 month. Mss published average of 2-4 weeks after acceptance. Sample: Free on Web site. Guidelines: Sent after query. NONFICTION: How-to. Pays: 30-60¢/wd. Mss bought/yr: 200. Length: 300-1,500 wds. How to submit: Query, send published clips. Does NOT want: "Caregiving articles that are too general in nature. Pieces need to be focused and in-depth." Other: Caregiving topics.

CBA Frontline—www.cbaonline.org

The Premier Training Resource for Christian Retail Sales Staff. CBA/CBA Service Corp., P.O. Box 62000, Colorado Springs, CO 80962. Tel: (719)265-9895. Fax: (719)272-3510. Steve Parolini, Editor; Debby Weaver, Managing Editor and Editorial Contact (submissions) (publications@cbaonline.org). "Writers must be knowledgeable of retail and able to specifically address sales clerks in Christian retail stores." Subject: Christian retail/Christian products industry. Frequency: 11 times/yr. Format: Traditional magazine publication with portions published also on the Web. Est. January 1997. Circ. 6,500. 100% freelance written. Pays on acceptance. "All articles are by assignment only." Rights: All rights. Byline given. Submit seasonal material 7 months in advance. Queries: Post, e-mail. Reports in 4 months on queries. Lead time: 4-5 months. Mss published average of 3 months after acceptance. Sample: Free on Web site or $5 from above address. NONFICTION: Pays: 20-30¢/wd for assigned articles. No payment for unsolicited articles. Mss bought/yr: 24. Length: 750-1,250 wds. How to submit: Send published clips. Other: Subjects applicable to Christian retail sales staff, by assignment only. FILLERS: Pays: $25. Length: 20-300 wds. TIPS: "We look for writers with a thorough knowledge of retail business operations, excellent reporting and writing skills, knowledge of the Christian industry, and related previous experience."

CBA Marketplace—www.cbaonline.org

The No. 1 Resource for Christian Retailers and Suppliers. CBA/CBA Service Corp., P.O. Box 62000, Colorado Springs, CO 80962. Tel: (719)265-9895. Fax: (719)272-3510. Sue Grise, Editor; Debby Weaver, Managing Editor and Editorial Contact (publications@cbaonline.org). "Writers must be knowledgeable of retail and able to specifically address the retail audience." Subject: Christian retail/Christian products industry. Frequency: Monthly. Format: Traditional magazine publication with portions published also on the Web. Est. June 1969. Circ. 8,500. 25%

freelance written. Pays on acceptance. Rights: All rights. Byline given. Submit seasonal material 9 months in advance. Queries: Post, e-mail. Lead time: 4-5 months. Mss published average of 3 months after acceptance. Sample: Free on Web site or $7.50 from above address. COLUMNS: Book News: Book product and supplier news, 150-600 wds; Music News: Music product and supplier news, 150-600 wds; Kids News: Kid's product and supplier news, 150-600 wds; Apparel News: Apparel product and supplier news, 150-600 wds; Gift News: Gift product and supplier news, 150-600 wds; Video News: Video product and supplier news, 150-600 wds. Mss bought/yr: 12. How to submit: Send published clips. NONFICTION: Essays. Pays: 16-25¢/wd for assigned articles. Does not pay maximum for unsolicited articles. Mss bought/yr: 36. Length: 150-3,000 wds. How to submit: Send published clips. Other: Subject applicable to Christian retail, by assignment only.

Centura Pro—www.propublishing.com

2056 Rancho Canada Rd., La Canada, CA 91011. Mark Hunter, Editor (CenturaPro@ visto.com). "*Centura Pro* is a newsletter for the intermediate to advanced, professional Centura programmer. Write with this person in mind. Don't talk down to them, but at the same time don't be afraid to explain obscure concepts that they may be unfamiliar with." Subject: Centura development. Pays on publication. Byline given. Guidelines: www.propublishing.com/WriterGuidelines.htm. NONFICTION: Pays: Tips receive $20; articles receive $60/newsletter page. How to submit: Query. TIPS: "*Centura Pro* publishes articles and tips for experienced users of SQLWindows, Centura, and SQLBase. We're interested in all topics in these subject areas. See Web site guidelines for current topic needs. Read back issues before submitting. We're looking for tips, technical articles, technical case studies, and utilities. All material, prose, and source code must be original and must be owned by you. We generally don't print articles that have already been printed elsewhere (talk to the editor if you think you have an exception). Please inform us if other publications are considering your article. Pro Publishing reserves the rights to all articles published in *Centura Pro*. Be aware that your articles, and particularly your code, may be used by readers in the development and implementation of applications. All material submitted for publication will receive fair and judicious treatment; however, we can't guarantee publication. For full submission details, please see guidelines on Web site."

Chiaroscuro—gothic.net/chiaroscuro/chizine

Treatments of Light and Shade in Words. The Chiaroscuro. Brett A. Savory, Managing Editor, Editor-in-Chief (brett.savory@home.com); Patricia Lee Macomber, Associate Editor; Steve Eller, Associate Editor; Sandra Kasturi, Poetry Editor (kasturi@globalserve.net). Subject: Dark fiction. Frequency: Quarterly. Format: Web magazine/zine. Est. July 1999. Circ. 8,000 hits/issue. 100% freelance written. Pays on acceptance. Rights: Exclusive electronic rights for 3 months, then the right to archive it for another 9 months, equaling 1 yr total, and the right to include it in a "Best of *Chiaroscuro*" anthology. Byline given. No previously published material. Queries: E-mail. Reports in 1 week on queries. Reports in 1-10 weeks on mss. Mss published average of 1-2 months after acceptance. Sample: Free on Web site. Guidelines: On Web site. FICTION: Experimental, fantasy, horror, mainstream, mystery, slice-of-life vignettes. Pays: 1¢/wd (USD). Mss bought/yr: 12. Length: 5,000 wds maximum. How to submit: Send complete ms. Does NOT want: "Cliché, tired vampire, werewolf, mummy stuff." Other tips: "Almost any type of fiction, as long as it's dark." POETRY: Traditional, haiku, free verse, avant-garde. Contact: Sandra Kasturi. Pays: $2/poem. Mss bought/yr: 36. Maximum poems/submission: 10. Maximum length: 3 pages (not a hard-and-fast rule). Accepts work previously published in print magazines (applies for poetry only). Does NOT want: "Rehashing of J.R.R. Tolkien material. Clichéd love poetry. Nothing racist." Other tips: Genre poetry (horror, dark fantasy, dark science fiction), disturbing stuff, erotica, black humor. TIPS: "We're looking for material that is dark and well written."

CityTripping.com—www.citytripping.com

Your Urban Style Source. CityTripping Productions, Inc., 151 W. 25th St., 4th floor, New York, NY 10011. Tel: (212)924-5683. Fax: (212)924-5845. Tom Dolby, Editor (editorial@citytripping.com). "We specialize in covering the hip, edgy, and trendy in New York and Los Angeles. We are not interested in coverage of mainstream happenings, unless the writer has an unusual slant." Subject: "CityTripping.com is your urban style source for nightlife, restaurants, shopping, and culture from New York, Los Angeles, and beyond." Frequency: Weekly. Format: Web magazine/zine. Est. August 1998. Circ. 100,000 hits/month. 80% freelance written. Pays on publication. "We do not currently have the staff to respond to all queries, though we reply to as many as we can. If you don't hear back, please assume that your work is not right for us at this time, though we will certainly keep it on file for the future." Kill fee: 50%. Rights: All rights. Byline given. Accepts simultaneous submissions. Submit seasonal material 2 months in advance. Lead time: 1 month. Mss published average of 1 month after acceptance. Sample: Free on Web site. Guidelines: E-mail editorial@citytripping.com. COLUMNS: What's Hot Now: Current trends in restaurants, nightlife, fashion, media, pop culture, etc. Please see Web site for examples. 200-400 wds. Pays: 10-25¢/wd. Mss bought/yr: 40. How to submit: Query. NONFICTION: Book excerpts, essays, exposé, general interest, interview/profile, new product, opinion, personal experience, photo feature, travel. Pays: 10-25¢/wd. Mss bought/yr: 75. Length: 200-1,200 wds. How to submit: Query. TIPS: "Please always query with specific ideas. Do not just send clips or a resume. Please, no phone calls. Request writer's guidelines and check out the site before querying."

CNSNews.com—www.cnsnews.com

Media Research Center, 325 S. Patrick St., Alexandria, VA 22314. Tel: (703)683-9733. Fax: (703)683-7045. Scott Hogenson, Executive Editor (shogenson@cnsnews.com); Dorothea Cooke, Managing Editor. Subject: Focus on political and cultural news. Frequency: Other. Format: Company Web site. Est. June 1998. 15% freelance written. Pays on publication. "General news publication. Publishes hourly." Kill fee: 0%. Rights: All rights. Byline given. Submit seasonal material 3 months in advance. Queries: E-mail. Mss published average of 2 days after acceptance. Sample: Free on Web site. Guidelines: On Web site. COLUMNS: Commentary on politics, environment, culture, defense. 600-1,000 wds. Contact: Scott Hogenson, Executive Editor (shogenson@cnsnews.com). Pays: $30 minimum. How to submit: Send published clips, query. FICTION: Humorous. Contact: Scott Hogenson, Executive Editor (shogenson@cnsnews.com). Pays: $30 minimum. Mss bought/yr: 50. Length: 600-2,000 wds. How to submit: Query, send published clips. Other tips: "Satire." NONFICTION: Exposé, general interest, humor, inspirational, interview/profile, opinion, religious. Contact: D. Cooke (dcooke@cnsnews.com). Pays: $30 minimum for assigned articles. Mss bought/yr: 150-400. Length: 250-1,200 wds. How to submit: Send published clips, query. Other: Religious issues germane to the Constitution. TIPS: "Best approach is to contact via e-mail with interest, bona fides, and a few clips. Next step is to pitch a specific story idea; include sources, approach, and length."

The CollegeBound Network—www.collegebound.net

Ramholtz Publishing, Inc., 2071 Clove Rd., Suite 206, Staten Island, NY 10304. Tel: (718)273-5700. Fax: (718)273-2539. Gina LaGuardia, Editor (editorial@collegebound.net); Dawn Kessler, Assistant Editor (dawn@collegebound.net). "Writing for a teen audience (lighthearted tone)." Subject: College/educational. Frequency: Monthly. Format: Web magazine. Est. 1996 (Net version). 60% freelance written. Pays on publication. "Reprints OK if material hasn't appeared in a national publication or Web site specifically geared toward college-bound teens." Rights: First-time electronic rights or one-time electronic rights or exclusive electronic rights or second serial (reprint) electronic rights or all rights. Byline given. Submit seasonal material 5 months in advance. Reports in 4 weeks on queries. Reports in 5 weeks on mss. Lead time: 4 months. Mss published average of 4 months after acceptance. Guidelines: E-mail editorial@collegebound.net. NONFICTION: Essays, how-to, interview/profile, personal experience, travel. Pays: $25-100. Length: 400-800 wds. How to submit: Query, send published clips. Does NOT want: "General 'How to get into college' pieces. We like very specific, well-thought-out articles." Other: First-person college success/struggle stories; big scholarship winners, scholar athletes; study abroad in college. FILLERS: Anecdotes, newsbreaks, short humor. Pays: $15-75. Mss bought/yr: 15. Length: 50-200 wds. TIPS: "We're looking for well-researched articles packed with real-life student experiences and expert voices."

ComputerCurrents—www.currents.net

Doug Dineley, Managing Editor (ddineley@computercurrents.com); Robert Luhn, Editor-in-Chief (rluhn@computercurrents.com); Stephen Lee, Associate Editor (slee@computercurrents.com). "Our readers run small businesses, manage midsized firms, and serve as department heads in large corporations. Although our style is informal and lively, every story has to deliver assistance, opinion, and resource information to the reader. 80% of our readers use PCs and Windows 95/98, while the rest use the Mac." Circ. 612,000 readers. Byline given. Guidelines: www.currents.net/magazine/writeguide.html. TIPS: "*Computer Currents* editorial needs fall into 3 categories: Product news ("Currents"), cover stories and features, and various review/how-to/opinion columns. Columns created in-house. Freelance opportunities are available in 3 areas: Short reviews for our Previews & Reviews section, buyers' guides, and feature-length cover stories. Previews & Reviews runs short pieces (300-600 wds) on shipping and prerelease (beta) software and hardware. Previews and reviews are lively, critical, and to the point. Payment: $50-100. Buys all rights. Contact: Doug Dineley. Cover Stories range from 2,500 to 3,500 wds and fall into one of several categories: How-to, consumer investigation, reviews. See guidelines for full details. Payment: $1,500-2,000. Contact: Robert Luhn. Buys FNASR, right to post piece on Web site, and nonexclusive reprint rights. Reassigns rights to author on request. Buyers' guides: These 2-page pieces show readers how to buy products or services. Payment: $500-800. Contact: Stephen Lee. Rights we buy: All rights, but will reassign rights to author on request. Note: All software and hardware obtained for a review must be returned immediately to the manufacturer upon request by *Computer Currents*. How to submit: Query before submitting any feature or review. Query with photocopied clips of your work that has appeared in other publications. All queries/submissions should be accompanied by a self-addressed, stamped envelope with sufficient postage. Otherwise you will not receive a reply. Queries and clips can be sent to: Computer Currents, 1250 Ninth St., Berkeley, CA 94710. No phone calls please. E-mail queries are acceptable."

ComputorEdge—www.computoredge.com

The Byte Buyer, Inc., 3655 Ruffin Rd., Suite 100, San Diego, CA 92123. Tel: (858)573-0315. John San Filippo, Editor (editor@computoredge.com). "*ComputorEdge* provides nontechnical, entertaining articles on all aspects of computer hardware and software, including productivity, advice, personal experience, and an occasional piece of computer-related fiction." *ComputorEdge* is published in print version in San Diego and Denver. Another print counterpart, *ComputerScene*, is published in Albuquerque. All buy online material. Other surface mail addresses: 10200 E. Girard Ave., Bldg. B, Suite 222, Denver, CO 80231; 2400 Louisiana NE, Suite 255, Bldg. 3, Albuquerque, NM 87110 (the New Mexico version is called *ComputerScene Online*). Denver Tel: (303)671-6675. Subject: Computers/technology. Frequency: Weekly. Format: Web magazine/zine. Est. 1997. Pays 30 days after publication. Rights: First-time electronic rights. Byline given. Queries: E-mail. Guidelines: On Web site. COLUMNS: Mac Madness: 750-900 wds; I Don't Do Windows: 750-900 wds. Pays: $75-100. How to submit: Query. FICTION: Pays: $50-150. Other tips: "Buys the occasional piece of computer-related fiction." NONFICTION: How-to, personal experience, technical. Pays: $50-150. Length: 500-1,000 wds.

How to submit: Query. Does NOT want: "Forced humor, flowery wordiness, and 10-year-old concepts. Don't send single-product reviews." TIPS: "Editorial schedule is available online with deadlines for articles."

ConsumerSearch.com—www.consumersearch.com

ConsumerSearch, Inc., 487 Columbus Ave. #3R, New York, NY 10024. Derek Drew, Editor (derekdrew@consumersearch.com); Damon Mcclure, Managing Editor and Editorial Contact (damonmcclure@consumersearch.com). "See the editor's and writer's page off the home page of www.consumersearch.com. *ConsumerSearch* editors write about the results of competitive product analysis across all consumer product areas." Subject: Consumer interests. Frequency: Weekly. Format: Web magazine/zine. Est. February 2000. 50% freelance written. Pays on acceptance. Kill fee: Varies. Rights: Makes work-for-hire assignments. Queries: Post, e-mail. Sample: Free on Web site. NONFICTION: New product, how-to, personal experience, opinion, technical. Pays: Ability level and experience determine payment. Correspondents: $125-150/day; Outside Writers: $200-250/day; Sr. Outside Writers: $300 minimum/day. Mss bought/yr: 100 minimum. How to submit: Query, send published clips, send complete ms. Other: See Web site for further information. TIPS: "The easiest way to break into our market is to examine what we are doing, and then take a crack at doing it better. We will publish and pay for any unsolicited material that is superior to material that we are already publishing on a product area. Alternatively, submit coverage of new product areas that we have not yet covered. If your work is good, this will pretty much guarantee that you will be drawn into our stable of freelancers."

Conversely—www.conversely.com

Premiere Online Magazine About Relationships. Editors (writers@conversely.com). "Our goal is a publication for men and women dedicated to exploring relationships—every aspect, every stage—through different forms of writing: essays, memoirs, fiction, etc." Format: Web-zine. Pays on publication (within 15 days). Rights: Exclusive rights for 60 days, nonexclusive thereafter. Byline given. Accepts simultaneous submissions and previously published material. Reports in 4 weeks on mss. Guidelines: www.conversely.com/write.htm. COLUMNS: Antidote—Essays: Opinion, observation, satire. 750-1,500 wds; Personals—Memoirs: Up close, from inside the head. 750-2,500 wds; Stories—Stories that deal with romantic relationships: At any stage, any age, from any angle. Not to be confused with "romance genre" writing, which is not for us. Maximum 3,000 wds; Say What?—Reviews of cinema, theater, books—with a twist. Perhaps between 500 and 1,000 wds; Unhinged—Quirky, amorphous nonfiction that fits nowhere else. Maximum 3,000 wds. At this time, we do not need writers for our advice column. Pays: Minimum $50. Pay tends to be higher for pieces that were assigned, requires little or no "editorial" effort prior to posting, comes from writers who have published with us before, and have a higher word count. *Conversely* also provides a "home page" on the site where writers can present a short bio and list other publications. TIPS: "Seeking material that is well written, intelligent, witty, engaging, and fun. Writers should have a lively interest in, and strong opinions about, relationships, as well as a passion for writing about them. No attachments; please paste text into the body of the e-mail message. E-mail submissions only. Indicate which section you are submitting to, and include a brief bio (optional)."

Crescent Blues—www.crescentblues.com

Crescent Blues, Inc., P.O. Box 3121, Arlington, VA 22203. Jean Marie Ward, Editor/ Managing Editor (crescentblues@hotmail.com). "Reviewers should judge books, movies, CDs, etc., on their individual merits, not as stalking horses for their genres. It's frightening how many people don't bother to read the guidelines or the publication and still expect to be published in *Crescent Blues*." Subject: All aspects of literature, entertainment, and the arts. "Our motto is 'All genres, all the time." Frequency: Bimonthly with weekly updates. Format: Web magazine/zine. Est. October 1, 1998. Circ. Unknown, but we average about 100,000 hits/month. 50% freelance written. Pays on acceptance. Kill fee: None. (If a piece/graphic is not published within 24 months of acceptance, all rights revert to the author.) Rights: First-time electronic rights. Byline given. Submit seasonal material 3 months in advance. Queries: E-mail. Reports in 1-2 weeks on queries. Reports in 1-2 weeks on mss. Lead time: Varies. Mss published average of 1 month after acceptance. Sample: Free on Web site. Guidelines: www.crescentblues.com/constantpages/abou tus.shtml#submission. COLUMNS: Book Views: New book reviews; Movie Views: New movie reviews; Video Views: Reviews of currently available videos; Theater Views: Reviews of current plays, etc.; Music Views: Reviews of new CDs; Average length: 300-500 wds for all single-item reviews. Pays: $2.50. Mss bought/yr: 100.

How to submit: Send complete ms. NONFICTION: General interest, interview/ profile, photo feature, travel. Pays: Minimum $2.50. (*Crescent Blues* pays ½¢/wd for articles, and $1/photo or graphic.) Mss bought/yr: 100-130. Length: 300 wds minimum. Maximum varies based on the nature of the article. Reviews limited to 500 wds. How to submit: Query. Does NOT want: "Fiction." Other: Reviews of all media (book, CD, video, movies, games, theater, ballet, exhibits, etc.). TIPS: "Reviews should be submitted without query. Include 'Review' or 'Submission' in the subject line. All other items should be queried."

Cyber Age Adventures—www.cyberageadventures.com

The weekly magazine of superhero fiction. 2403 NW 27th Ave., Boynton Beach, FL 33436. Frank Fradella, Editor (Editor@cyberageadventures.com). "*Cyber Age Adventures* is the next evolutionary step in the superhero genre. Our stories are for more mature readers, appealing more to those who feel they may have outgrown the comic book format; after all, the comic book readers of yesterday are the book readers of today. Our philosophy is simple: Tell stories about people. They may be people with powers, but they're people nevertheless." Subject: Serialized and short superhero fiction. Frequency: Weekly. Format: Web magazine/zine, e-mail newsletter. Est. November 1998 (first issue January 1, 1999). Circ. Several hundred and growing rapidly. 50% freelance written. Pays on publication. Rights: One-time electronic rights/one-time print rights. Byline given. Accepts simultaneous submissions and previously published material. Submit seasonal material 3 months in advance. Queries: E-mail. Reports in 1 week on queries. Reports in 4 weeks on mss. Mss published average of 2 months after acceptance. Sample: Free on Web site or free by e-mail. Guidelines: On Web site or e-mail Submissions@cyberageadve ntures.com. FICTION: Pays: 2-5¢/wd. Mss bought/yr: 30. Length: 3,000 wds maximum (in the case of serials, the story may contain no more than 3 parts, with each part containing no more than 3,000 wds). How to submit: Send complete ms. Other tips: "We publish cutting-edge superhero fiction, which may contain elements of adventure, science fiction, romance, mystery, or any other element needed to further the story." TIPS: "We're looking for exceptional fiction that pushes the envelope of the superhero genre. We don't publish parodies, or stories that only serve to mock the superhero conventions that have existed for time out of mind."

Cyber Oasis—www.sunoasis.com

David Eide, Editor/Publisher (eide491@earthlink.net). "Monthly electronic magazine dedicated to the literary world." Rights: FNASR. First electronic byline given. Accepts previously published material. Reports in 6 weeks on queries. Guidelines: www.sunoasis.com/submit.html. FICTION: Pays: $20. Length: 2,000 wds (longer accepted if exceptional). NONFICTION: Pays: $20. Length: 2,000 wds (longer accepted if exceptional). POETRY: Pays: $10 for poems (not hard and fast, work out with editor). TIPS: "We need literary work (poems and stories), personal essays (evocative, personalist, 'think Thoreau'), articles (well written and factual, should deal with problems writers encounter), and commentary ('take something in the real world and deal with it')." To submit: Send with e-mail as plain-text ASCII attachment, with "submission/oasis" as the subject line. "I'm looking for the best literary material I can find for an audience that thinks, as well as material that helps writers become more resourceful in their endeavors." No simultaneous submissions.

d'Work Zone—www.d-workzone.com

Resources to Build Your Business. DigitalWork, 230 W. Monroe, Chicago, IL 60606. Fax: (312)261-4010. Dave Glines, Editor (editor@digitalwork.com). "*d'Work Zone* offers its readers practical advice on growing revenue and working more efficiently. All stories focus on a specific business service or task, don't have quotes, include supporting stats, and usually focus on working online." Subject: For small business owners and managers across the world. Frequency: Biweekly. Format: Web magazine/zine, e-mail newsletter. Est. March 1999. 90% freelance written. Pays on acceptance. Rights: All rights. Byline given. Accepts simultaneous submissions. Queries: E-mail. Lead time: 2-3 months. Mss published average of 2-3 months after acceptance. Sample: Free on Web site. NONFICTION: How-to. Pays: Assigned articles $150-250; unsolicited articles $150-250. Mss bought/yr: 24. Length: 500-700 wds. How to submit: Send published clips. Does NOT want: "Motivational fluff." TIPS: "Catch us with your e-mail. Chances are that if you send an e-mail saying, 'Please send me your guidelines,' it's not going to be read. Our writers are usually small business owners themselves with a focus in one of our departments (can be viewed on the site). In terms of receiving assignments, freelancers need to show us in their e-mails and their samples that they are creative, can support their ideas with facts and can provide accurate, up-to-date advice."

Dark Matter Chronicles—www.eggplant-productions.com/darkmatter

Eggplant Productions, P.O. Box 2248, Schiller Park, IL 60176. Raechel Henderson, Editor (darkmatter@eggplant-productions.com). "*Dark Matter Chronicles* seeks out and reviews Web sites, e-zines and other electronic media devoted to speculative fiction. Our goal is to show surfers what is out there for speculative fiction in the wide, wide Web." Subject: Speculative fiction Web sites, e-zines, and other electronic media. Frequency: Biweekly. Format: E-mail newsletter. Est. February 1999. Circ. 260. 100% freelance written. Pays on publication. "Review Magazine" Rights: One-time electronic rights. Byline given. Accepts simultaneous submissions and previously published material. Submit seasonal material 6 months in advance. Queries: E-mail. Reports in 4 weeks on queries. Reports in 4 weeks on mss. Lead time: 6 months. Mss published average of 1 month after acceptance. Sample: Free by e-mail. Guidelines: On Web site. FICTION: Fantasy, horror, science fiction. Pays: $1.25-$7.50. Mss bought/yr: 26. Length: 500-3,000 wds. How to submit: Send complete ms. Does NOT want: "Anything that doesn't fall under the umbrella of speculative fiction." NONFICTION: Pays: $5 for assigned or unsolicited articles. Mss bought/yr: 78. Length: 500-750 wds. How to submit: Send complete ms. Other: Reviews.

Deep Outside—www.clocktowerfiction.com/Outside

Clocktower Fiction, 6549 Mission Gorge Rd., P.O. Box 260, San Diego, CA 92120. Editor (outside@clocktowerfiction.com). "*Outside* is a paying professional magazine of SF and dark imaginative fiction, aimed at people who love to read well-plotted, character-driven genre fiction. We are interested in fiction that transcends the limitations and ventures outside the stereotypes of genre fiction." Subject: Science fiction, horror, and darkly imaginative fiction. Pays on acceptance. Rights: First serial rights for one year. Byline given. Queries: Post. Reports in 6 weeks on mss. Sample: Free on Web site. Guidelines: www.clocktowerfiction.com/Outside/Main/guidelines.shtml. FICTION: Horror, science fiction. Pays: 3¢/wd. Length: 1,500-4,000 wds. Does NOT want: "Sword & Sorcery, pornography, or excessive violence and gore, derivative works (e.g., emulating TV shows and movies)." Other tips: "Dark fantasy." TIPS: "We strive to be both writer friendly and reader friendly. We eagerly look forward to receiving top-quality, professional material from you."

Desktop Engineering Magazine—www.deskeng.com

The Complete Computer Resource for Engineers. Helmers Publishing Inc., 174 Concord St., P.O. Box 874, Peterborough, NH 03458-0874. Tel: (603)924-9631. Fax: (603)924-4004. Anthony J. Lockwood, Editor (de-editors@helmers.com). "Computer hardware and software for hands-on design, electrical/electronic, and mechanical engineers in the process/manufacturing industries. Topics of interest include analysis, data acquisition, CAD, CAM, CFD/FEA, EDM/PDM, graphics, T&M, workstations, and components." Frequency: Monthly. Format: Hardcopy controlled circulation with Web ancillary. Est. September 1995. Circ. 65,000. 90-95% freelance written. Pays on publication. Kill fee: Case-by-case basis. Rights: All rights. Byline given. Submit seasonal material 2 months in advance. Queries: Post, e-mail. Reports in 2 weeks on queries. Reports in 5-6 weeks on mss. Lead time: News item—27 days; major feature—2 months; review—6 weeks or less. Mss published average of 2 months after acceptance. Sample: Free on Web site. Guidelines: on Web site. COLUMNS: Reviews (hardware, software, books) 700-1,200 wds; New Products 50-150 wds. Pays: Negotiated on a case-by-case basis. Mss bought/yr: 30-40. How to submit: Query, send published clips. NONFICTION: New product, technical. Pays: Rates negotiated on a per article basis. Mss bought/yr: 60. Length: 75-2,000 wds. How to submit: Query, send published clips. Does NOT want: "Case studies."

DIMSUM—www.dimsum.com.hk

The Journal of Good Reading. Chameleon Press, 1902, Hing Wai Centre, 7, Tin Wan Praya Rd., Aberdeen, Hong Kong SAR, China. Fax: (852)2873-6807. Nury Vittachi, Editor (editor@dimsum.com.hk). "*Dimsum*, founded in early 1999, aims to be a world-class literary journal. It appears on a quarterly basis in hardcopy format and has been well received so far. Sample stories, forums workshop. Material must relate to Asia or Asians in some way." Subject: Stories and writers with an Asian connection. Frequency: Quarterly. Format: Web magazine/zine. Est. 1999. Circ. 2,000. 100% freelance written. Pays on publication. "We publish only completed stories." Rights: All rights. Byline given. Accepts simultaneous submissions and previously published material. Queries: E-mail, post. Lead time: 4 months. Mss published average of 4 months after acceptance. Guidelines: On Web site. FICTION: Pays: $250-1,000. Mss bought/yr: 24. Length: 1,000-7,000 wds. How to submit: Query. POETRY: Avant-garde, free verse, haiku, light verse, traditional. Pays: Negotiated. Mss bought/yr: 8. Maximum line length: Flexible. TIPS: "Go to the Web site, join in with the online debates, read others' submissions, critique them, submit your stories, subscribe to the magazine and get a feel for the Asian perspective. We run an online workshop, and unsolicited submissions are made that way. You must conform to the rules of the workshop. We buy stories that we consider suit our web site and may ask to see more if your contributions to the workshop are interesting."

Discovery Channel Online—www.discovery.com

Discovery Communications, Inc., 700 Wisconsin Ave., Bethesda, MD 20814. Andrew Cary, Managing Editor; Randy Rieland, Editor. Subject: Core subjects include science, space, nature, technology, history, culture. Frequency: Daily updates, weekly/montly features. Format: Web magazine/zine, online directory, company Web site, and e-mail newsletter. 20% freelance written. Pays on acceptance. Kill fee: 20%. Rights: One-time electronic rights and exclusive electronic rights, and second serial (reprint) electronic rights, or all rights, or makes work-for-hire assignments. Byline given. Accepts simultaneous submissions. Submit seasonal material 1 month in advance. Queries: Post. Reports in 2 weeks on queries. Reports in 1 month on mss. Lead time: 1-2 months. Mss published average of 1 month after acceptance. Sample: Free on Web site. NONFICTION: General interest, historical/nostalgic, how-to, photo feature, travel. Pays: Negotiated. Mss bought/yr: 20. Length: 600-800 wds; news briefs, 300-400 wds. How to submit: Send complete ms. Does NOT want: "Political news, opinion pieces (note: there can be opinion in first-person accounts but not as main topic)" TIPS: "Watch Discovery Channel, TLC, Animal Planet, and Travel Channel."

Dragonlaugh—www.freeyellow.com/members6/dragonlaugh

Possum Press, 191 Azalea Circle, Madison, MS 39110. Mark W. Johnson, Editor (possumpress@iName.com). Subject: Humorous swords and sorcery fiction and art. Frequency: Published 3 times/yr. Format: Web magazine/zine. Est. January 1999 (first issue was April 1999). Circ. 300-400 hits. 100% freelance written. Pays on acceptance. Rights: First-time electronic rights and one-time nonexclusive print anthology rights. Byline given. Accepts simultaneous submissions and previously published material. Submit seasonal material 1 month in advance. Queries: E-mail, post. Reports in 3 weeks on mss. Lead time: Less than 1 month. Mss published average of 2 months after acceptance. Sample: Free on Web site. Guidelines: On Web site. FICTION: Humorous. Pays: $3 (flat rate). Mss bought/yr: 12-20. Length: Maximum 6,000 wds. How to submit: Send complete ms. Does NOT want: "Pornography, R-rated material, poetry." Other tips: "Swords and sorcery ONLY." TIPS: "E-mail submissions are preferred, and should be embedded in the e-mail or sent as an attached ASCII file. Preferred length is about 1,000-3,000 words. Most of all, read the guidelines. We ONLY accept funny prose and artwork that fits within the swords and sorcery subgenre of fantasy."

Earthmaven—www.earthmaven.com

Baywave Media, 2859 St. Anthony Dr., Green Bay, WI 54311. Michelle Kennedy Hogan, Editor (editor@earthmaven.com). "Seeking pro-environment pieces, everything from the spiritual to hard news." Subject: Ecology and conservation. Frequency: Weekly. Format: Web magazine/zine, online directory, e-mail newsletter. Est. December 1999. Circ. 30,000. 50% freelance written. Pays on publication. Rights: One-time electronic rights. Byline given. Accepts previously published material. Submit seasonal material 3 months in advance. Queries: Post, e-mail. Reports in 2 weeks on queries. Reports in 2 weeks on mss. Lead time: 1-2 months. Mss published average of 1 month after acceptance. Sample: Free on Web site or free by e-mail. Guidelines: E-mail write@baywave.com. COLUMNS: Inspirations: Mainly poetry about nature, wildlife, etc.; Adventure Mavens: Firsthand descriptions of adventures taken, generally in the wild, 2,000 wds; In Your Backyard: Things you can do to incorporate nature and an ecologically healthy attitude into your own backyard, how-to projects, classes, crafts, etc., 500-700 wds; Journeys to Make: Eco-tourism, 800-1,500 wds; Natural Health: Aromatherapy, herbs, Feng Shui, you name it, 800-1,500 wds; Ecokidz.com: Games, stories, how-to, fun stuff just for kids, 500-1,000 wds. Pays: Minimum $10. Mss bought/yr: 75. How to submit: Query, send published clips, send complete ms. FICTION: Adventure, humorous, novel excerpts, slice-of-life vignettes. Pays: Minimum $20. Mss bought/yr: 20. How to submit: Send published clips, send complete ms. NONFICTION: Book excerpts, essays, exposé, general interest, historical/nostalgic, how-to, humor, inspirational, interview/profile, new product, personal experience, opinion. Pays: $10-50 for assigned or unsolicited articles. Mss bought/yr: 100 minimum. Length: 500-

2,000 wds. How to submit: Query, send published clips, send complete ms. POETRY: Free verse, haiku, light verse, traditional. Pays: $10-25. Mss bought/yr: 12. Maximum poems/submission: 5. Does NOT want: "Trendy poetry." FILLERS: Anecdotes, facts, newsbreaks, short humor. Pays: $10-20. Mss bought/yr: 25. TIPS: "Write about what you are interested in. That always comes through . . . we need writers who are passionate about getting their message across . . . so that readers will want to take action in their own communities."

El Sitio.com—www.elsitio.com

El Sitio, 311 Lincoln Rd., Ste 204, Miami Beach, FL 33139. Tel: (305)535-1112, ext. 117. Fernando Battaglia, Editor; Fernando Gonzalez, Managing Editor; Patricia Maldonado, Assignment Editor (pmaldonado@elsitioinc.net). "Target audience: U.S. Latinos and Latin American Internet users." Subject: Latino issues in North America. Frequency: Daily. Format: Web magazine. Est. 1995. 10% freelance written. Pays on publication. Kill fee: none. Rights: All rights, also makes available a 90-day exclusive rights that allows the author to republish elsewhere. Byline given. Accepts previously published material. Queries: E-mail, phone. Mss published average of 1 month after acceptance. Guidelines: E-mail pmaldonado@elsitioinc.net. COLUMNS: Hometown: Local news from NY, LA, Chicago, Miami, San Antonio, Houston, San Juan, San Francisco/San Jose; News; Sports; Technology; Romance; Entertainment. Contact: Patricia Maldonado. Pays: $100. How to submit: Query. NONFICTION: Book excerpts, essays, general interest, historical/nostalgic, humor, interview/profile, new product, opinion, personal experience, photo feature, religious. Pays: $100 for assigned articles. Length: 500-800 wds. How to submit: Query. Other: Sports, romance. New product must be computer related TIPS: "Try to tap into the Latino community either where you live or in the country. Get to know who the leaders are, find out the issues, and understand the group's history, politics, and culture."

Electric Wine—www.electricwine.com

An Online Magazine of Science Fiction, Fantasy, and Horror. PMB #182, 2500 Dallas Hwy., Suite 202, Marietta, GA 30064. Diana Sharples and James Rasmussen, Editors (electricwine@netscape.net). "We publish fiction, poetry, articles, and artwork related to the genres of science fiction, fantasy, and horror." Frequency: Bimonthly. Format: Web magazine/zine. Est. October 31, 1999. Circ. Published on World Wide Web, available worldwide. 90-100% freelance written. Pays on return of signed contract by author. "No attachments; submissions must be pasted into the body of the e-mail. Surface mail submissions may result in a delay since they are forwarded to our co-editor in South Africa." Kill fee: None. (Rights revert to author if manuscript has not been published within 18 months of acceptance.) Rights: First-time, one-time, second serial (reprint) electronic rights. Will consider reprints provided rights have reverted to author and work does not currently appear online. All rights revert back to author after issue in which piece appears is removed from the Internet. We do not maintain an online archive. Byline given. Accepts previously published material. Submit seasonal material 2 months in advance. Queries: Post, e-mail. Reports in 1 week on queries. Reports in 3-6 weeks on mss. Lead time: 6 months. Mss published average of 2-6 months after acceptance. Sample: Free on Web site. Guidelines: On Web site or e-mail electricwine@netscape.net. COLUMNS: Book Reviews; Movie Reviews; Convention Reports. Average lengths: 300-2,000 wds. Pays: $5-20. Mss bought/yr: 6-12. How to submit: Query. FICTION: Fantasy, horror, science fiction. Pays: $5-150 (1¢/wd for fiction and articles, with a $5 minimum. Mss bought/yr: 36. Length: 500-5,000 wds. We do accept 6 novella-length stories/yr, 10,000-15,000 wds. How to submit: Send complete ms. Does NOT want: "Material based on media (e.g., *Star Trek, Xena*), role-playing creations, existing worlds, anthology themes (e.g., *Thieves World*)." NONFICTION: Essays, general interest, historical/nostalgic, interview/profile, new product. Pays: $5-20 for assigned or unsolicited articles. Mss bought/yr: 6-12. Length: 300-2,000 wds. How to submit: Query. Other: Convention reports, market essays, writer's tips. POETRY: Avant-garde, free verse, haiku, light verse, traditional. Contact: James Rasmussen. Pays: $5-25. Mss bought/yr: 12-15. Maximum poems/submission: 4. Line length: 4-60. TIPS: "SF/Fantasy/Horror tropes are fine, but uniqueness in the approach to established character types or themes is highly recommended. Vivid imagery and artistry in the writing is a plus."

Energy Insight—www.einsight.com

Financial Times Energy, 1320 Pearl St., #300, Boulder, CO 80302. Tel: (303)444-7788. David Wagman, Director (dwagman@ftenergy.com); Ann de Rouffignac, Senior Writer (aderouff@ftenergy.com); Rick Stouffer, Senior Writer (rstouffer@fte nergy.com). "Objectivity, analytical skills, business angle." Subject: North American energy industry. Frequency: Daily. Format: Web magazine/zine. Est. June 1997. Circ. 5,500 worldwide. 1% freelance written. Pays on publication. Rights: All rights. Byline given. Queries: Post, e-mail, phone. Lead time: Daily. Sample: Free on Web site.

Eternity—www.pulpeternity.com

The Online Journal. P.O. Box 930068, Norcross, GA 30003. Editor (pulpeternity@hotmail.com). "Our creed: (1) I don't know what I like until I like it. (2) If it fits nowhere else, it's probably an *Eternity* story. (3) If you can think of a better market first, it's probably not an *Eternity* story." Subject: Cross-genre fiction. "First issue due in 2001." Rights: First electronic rights (12-month electronic exclusivity) and the nonexclusive audio rights on publication. We will also hold a nonexclusive anthology right for possible print publication. Byline given. Accepts simultaneous submissions. Queries: Post, e-mail. Reports in 1-2 months on queries. Reports in 1-2 months on mss. Guidelines: On Web site. FICTION: Science fiction, historical, adventure, fantasy, horror. Pays: 5¢/wd. Length: Maximum 3,000 wds. Does NOT want: "Underage sex, child molestation/abuse, bestiality, incest, or suicide stories." Other tips: "We like cross-genre stories, sly, sexy, or cerebral humor, strong female protagonists, exploratory fiction that defies genre boundaries, feminist SF/F/H, controversial pieces, and stories that other genre publications are afraid to publish." TIPS: "Cut and paste your submission into the body of an e-mail only. Due to the large number of viruses attaching themselves to attached files, all submissions sent as attached documents will be returned unread. Remember to always include personal information on all e-mail submissions. A good list of hints is available on the guidelines page of the Web site, www.pulpeternity.com/gl/eol.htm."

etown.com—www.etown.com

The Consumer Electronics Source. Collaborative Media Inc., 75 Maiden Lane, 7th Floor, New York, NY 10038. Tel: (212)373-7111. Fax: (212)363-3424. Larry Henchey, Executive Editor (larry@etown.com); Brent Butterworth, Editor-in-Chief (brent@etown.com). "We write for the general consumer—not trade pub. We are 'that knowledgeable friend' who takes you out shopping and explains the technology without the hype or hard sell." Subject: Consumer electronics: Television, video, audio, telecom, portables, accessories. Frequency: Daily. Format: Web magazine. Est. October 1995. Circ. 750,000 hits/month. 25% freelance written. Pays on acceptance. Kill fee: 50%. Rights: First-time electronic rights for 120 days exclusively, and reuse indefinitely thereafter, nonexclusively. Byline given. Submit seasonal material 1 month in advance. Queries: E-mail. Reports in 1 week on queries. Lead time: "We can publish a story the same day it's submitted if we want to." Mss published average of 2 weeks after acceptance. Sample: Free on Web site. Guidelines: "Editors will make our full guidelines available to writers when giving assignments." COLUMNS: "Our columns are by people who write for us regularly, though we will accept an occasional one-shot feature." Pays: 25-50¢/wd. Mss bought/yr: 150. How to submit: Query, send published clips. NONFICTION: How-to, interview/profile, new product, technical. Pays: 25¢-$1/wd for assigned articles; the average is 50¢. "We don't use or pay for unsolicited material." Mss bought/yr: hundreds. Length: 500-1,000 wds. How to submit: Query, send published clips. Other: "'We buy mainly reviews and columns, with occasional news stories or feature material." TIPS: "We encourage queries and clips/URLs but cannot promise personal responses to unsolicited manuscripts. Send a query to one of the editors with a brief summary, 300 words or less, of a well-fleshed-out idea. Provide a résumé or a description of your background. Include clippings or URLs of previously published work. E-mail is best, but if the published versions of your clips are not online, faxing or U.S. mail is acceptable. Your query may be answered by Larry or Brent, or they may forward it to other editors in particular areas of specialty."

fabjob.com—www.fabjob.com

Editors (editor@fabjob.com). "*Fabjob.com* is an online publisher of career guides. Our guides give consumers practical step-by-step information on how to break into and succeed at 'fab' jobs. We invite you to consider becoming an author of one of our fabjob career guides. A fabjob is the kind of job that people dream about having. The kind of fabjobs we publish guides about are those that people would love to break into but typically have no idea where to get started. For example, many thousands of people would like to become professional actors but have no idea how to get an agent, where to find out about auditions, what to do at an audition, and so on." Subject: Career guides. Rights: Purchases all rights for the term of the contract (until the guide is permanently removed from the Web site). Byline given. Queries: E-mail. NONFICTION: Pays: " 'Signing bonus' of U.S.$300. That's cash in your pocket. It is not an advance against royalties. You will earn royalties on top of your signing bonus. In addition to your signing bonus, you can earn up to 50% of the guide's sale price in royalties and commissions. See Web site for details." TIPS: "See online guidelines for complete details and submission format."

Fables—www.fables.org.

M3IP (The Meredith Miller Memorial Internet Project, Inc.), 30 Silver Lake Terrace #47, Morton, PA 19070. Megan Powell, Editor (mpowell@fables.org). "*Fables* publishes speculative fiction, retellings of traditional folktales (all cultures welcome), audio recordings of selected works, and related artwork. Original fiction should fall into the genres of science fiction, fantasy, horror, or one of the innumerable related subgenres. In each issue, I want a variety of stories with different themes, POVs, settings, and 'feels.' " Subject: Speculative fiction, folktales. Frequency: Quarterly. Format: Web magazine/zine. Est. Winter 1999. 90% freelance written. Pays on publication. Rights: First-time electronic rights, second serial (reprint) electronic rights, and nonexclusive archive. Copyright remains with authors. Byline given. Accepts simultaneous submissions and previously published material. Submit seasonal material 1-3 months in advance. Queries: Post, e-mail. Reports in 1 week on queries. Reports in 4 weeks on mss. Lead time: 3 months. Mss published average of 3-6 months after acceptance. Sample: Free on Web site. Guidelines: On Web site. FICTION: Fantasy, horror, novel excerpts, science fiction, serialized novels. Contact: Megan Powell, Editor (mpowell@fables.org). Pays: Flat rates: $5 for reprints and folktales, $10 for original fiction; serialized pieces and other exceptions (e.g. collections of short-shorts) negotiated on a case-by-case basis. Mss bought/yr: 50. Length: No limit. How to submit: Send complete ms. Other tips: "Retellings of folktales, other subgenres of speculative fiction." TIPS: "So far, nonfiction has been written by staff, but this may change in the future. E-mail submissions preferred for reasons of speed, and attachments tend to look prettier than pasted text. New twists on traditional themes are appreciated. I like character-driven stories, but I also don't simply want an issue full of introspection; I want some action for balance. It's great if that balance exists in the story; if it doesn't, I'll look for different stories that complement each other. We're willing to serialize longer stories, but mostly concentrate on short fiction (short-shorts to 1,000 words, short stories to 7,500, novelettes to 17,500)."

FamilyClick—www.familyclick.com

2877 Guardian Lane, Virginia Beach, VA 23452. Tel: (757)459-6056. Fax: (757)459-6422. Linda Stewart, Editor (articles@familyclick.net). "*FamilyClick* is dedicated to providing families with an online experience that is safe (through the use of our advanced filtering technology) and delivers top-quality content. We want material that is engaging and hopefully even compelling. We want to empower our subscribers with knowledge and useful tools. What will set us apart is our attention to these ideals and an unwavering focus on the family." Frequency: Weekly. Format: Web magazine. Est. November 1999. 80% freelance written. Pays on acceptance. Rights: First-time electronic rights, exclusive electronic rights, second serial (reprint) electronic rights, all rights; makes work-for-hire assignments. Byline given. Accepts previously published material. Submit seasonal material 1-2 months in advance. Queries: E-mail. Reports in 1 week on queries. Reports in 1-2 weeks on mss. Lead time: 1 month. Mss published average of 1-2 months after acceptance. Guidelines: E-mail articles@familyclick.net. FICTION: Adventure, historical, humorous, mainstream, mystery, religious, science fiction, suspense. Pays: 10¢/wd. Mss bought/yr: 50. Length: 200-2,000 wds. How to submit: Query. NONFICTION: General interest, historical/nostalgic, how-to, humor, inspirational, personal experience, religious, travel. Pays: 10¢/wd for assigned or unsolicited articles. Mss bought/yr: 200. Length: 200-2,000 wds. How to submit: Query. Other: Educational, family entertainment must be family appropriate (G or PG rated). FILLERS: Facts, tips. TIPS: "Any material that would be considered R-rated would be inappropriate—we are not interested in articles discussing sex, gambling, or alternate lifestyles."

FamilyFun—www.familyfun.com

Disney Corp., 244 Main St., Northampton, MA 01060. Ann Hallock, Editor; Jon Adolph, Executive Editor; Ann Hallock, Editor. "We are a national service magazine for parents of children ages 3 to 12, and we cover all the great things families can do together: educational projects, holiday celebrations, crafts, travel, cooking, and more." Subject: Parenting/family life. Frequency: Monthly. Format: Web magazine/zine. Est. 1991. Byline given. Reports in 4-8 weeks on queries. Reports in 4-8 weeks on mss. Sample: Free on Web site. Guidelines: On Web site. COLUMNS: Family Almanac—Cindy Littlefield, Associate Editor: Simple, quick, practical, inexpensive ideas and projects (outings, crafts, games, nature activities, learning projects, and cooking with children), 200-600 wds, 50¢/wd, also pays $75 for ideas in the event a staff writer is used; Family Traveler—Deb Geigis Berry, Travel Editor: Brief, newsy items about family travel—what's new, what's great, and especially, what's a good deal, 100-125 wds, $100, also pays $50 for ideas in the event a staff writer is used; Family Ties—Ann Hallock, Editor: A first-person column that spotlights some aspect of family life that is humorous, inspirational, or interesting, 1,500 wds, pays $1,500; My Great Idea—Greg Lauzon, Staff Writer: Fun and inventive ideas that have worked for a writer's own family, 800-1,000 wds, $750/column. In addition, letters 100-150 wds are also published and pay $25 upon publication. How to submit: Query, send published clips, send complete ms.

Fantasy Folklore & Fairytales (FF&F)—www.fantasytoday.com

Chaos Manor Enterprises, Ltd., P.O. Box 753, Sioux City, IA 51102-0753. Tel: (712)258-2655. Fax: (712)258-3635. Kathleen Hill, Editor; Lea Docken, Managing Editor; Kathleen Hill, Submissions (submissions@fantasytoday.com). "We are interested in publishing quality fiction, nonfiction, and art with a fantasy, folklore, and/or fairytale background." Frequency: Monthly. Format: Web magazine. Est. September 1999. 90% freelance written. Pays on publication. Kill fee: None. Rights: Varies, but usually first-time electronic rights. Byline given. Accepts simultaneous submissions and previously published material. Submit seasonal material 3 months in advance. Queries: Post, e-mail, fax. Reports in 2 weeks on queries. Reports in 4-6 weeks on mss. Lead time: 6 weeks. Mss published average of 1 month after acceptance. Sample: Free on Web site. Guidelines: On Web site. COLUMNS: Articles and Reviews, maximum 1,500 wds; Mother Goose Archives, which is politically incorrect, fractured, and taking the old and making it new fairytales, 1,500-7,500 wds. Contact: Lea Docken (Mother Goose Archives) (publisher@fantasytoday.com). Pays: $5-15. Mss bought/yr: 50. How to submit: Query. FICTION: Fantasy, historical, horror, mystery, novel excerpts, romance, science fiction. Contact: Kathleen Hill, Editor (submissions@fantasytoday.com). Pays: $5-20. Mss bought/yr: 150. Length: 750-7,500 wds. How to submit: Query. Other tips: "Mythology, folklore, dark fantasy." NONFICTION: Historical/nostalgic, interview/profile, new product. Contact: Kathleen Hill (submissions@fantasytoday.com). Pays: $5-15 for assigned and unsolicited articles. Mss bought/yr: 25 maximum. How to submit: Query. POETRY: Contact: Kathleen Hill, Editor (submissions@fantasytod ay.com). Pays: $3/poem. Mss bought/yr: 100. Maximum poems/submission: 3. Maximum line length: Varies. Does NOT want: "Epic poetry." FILLERS: Query first. Contact: Kathleen Hill, Editor (submissions@fantasytoday.com). TIPS: "Check monthly themes. Submissions: First page should contain theme written for, name, and contact info. A good way to get into *FF&F* is to enter the Strange Picture Contest for Writers and the Strange Story Contest for Artists found on the Fantasy Today Web site."

fastfiction.com—www.fastfiction.com

Spincycle Media, Inc., 2 Clarendon Dr., Darby, PA 19023. Fax: (610)534-4217. Joe Taylor Jr., Editor/Managing Editor (joetaylor@fastfiction.com). "We're looking for compelling, short fiction (under 2,000 words) that takes advantage of the online medium. Writing should leap right off the page without sounding terse or crammed." Frequency: Weekly. Format: Web magazine/zine. Est. June 1999. 80% freelance written. Pays on publication. Kill fee: 50% (only on work that is commissioned). Rights: "First-time publications receive higher compensation and better placement, but we also accept previously published works." Byline given. Accepts simultaneous submissions and previously published material. Queries: Post, e-mail, fax. Reports in 2 weeks on queries. Reports in 6 weeks on mss. Lead time: 2 months. Mss published average of 2 months after acceptance. Sample: Free on Web site. Guidelines: On Web site. FICTION: Adventure, confession, ethnic, experimental, fantasy, historical, humorous, mainstream, mystery, religious, romance, science fiction, slice-of-life vignettes, suspense, western. Pays: $10-25. Mss bought/yr: 250. Length: 2,000 maximum. How to submit: Send complete ms. Does NOT want: " 'Fan fiction' or works containing characters to which the author does not fully own the rights." TIPS: "Freelancers can submit and track submissions on our site. We're looking for authors with vibrant voices. Don't be afraid to express your own style!"

Fiction Fix Newsletter—www.fictionfix.com

Coffeehouse for Writers, 910 S. Westover St., Oconomowoc, WI 53066. Karen A. Hertzberg, Managing Editor (karen@coffeehouse4writers.com). "*Fiction Fix* exists to help writers discover the craft. (We're about WRITING fiction—we don't PUBLISH fiction.) Our readership spans the novice writer wannabe to the professional." Frequency: Monthly. Format: E-mail newsletter and Webzine. Est. December 1997.

Circ. 2,500. 80% freelance written. Pays on publication. Rights: First-time electronic rights. Byline given. Accepts simultaneous submissions. Submit seasonal material 3 months in advance. Queries: E-mail. Lead time: 3 months. Mss published average of 2 months after acceptance. Sample: Free on Web site or free by e-mail. Guidelines: On Web site. NONFICTION: Essays, interview/profile, how-to, personal experience. Pays: $10-20. Mss bought/yr: 12-15. Length: 800-1,200 wds. How to submit: Query. Does NOT want: "Fiction of any kind. We don't pay for articles other than our monthly features, which must be how-to or educational personal experience articles." Other: Essays: "We sponsor a monthly essay contest." Prizes are awarded. Writers are not otherwise compensated for essays. Information is available at www.fictionfix.com/contest. How-to: Fiction-writing techniques interview/profile (by assignment only. Mostly staff personal experience: Personal experience pieces should have educational value for fiction writers). TIPS: "We assume a certain level of intelligence in our readers and look for smart, descriptive how-to articles. We prefer a light, humorous tone over a dry, clinical one. Keep it fun! Write as though you're talking to a group of writer friends and saying, 'Hey, look at this! I've learned some interesting things that have helped me become a better writer. Let me share them with you.' "

The Fiction Writer—www.thefictionwriter.com

Online Literary Magazine. P.O. Box 20142, Canton, OH 44701. Joyce Siedler, Submissions Editor (submissions@thefictionwriter.com). Frequency: Monthly. Format: Web magazine/zine. Est. August 1999. 98% freelance written. Pays on publication. Rights: First-time electronic rights and exclusive electronic rights. Byline given. Queries: E-mail. Mss published average of 1-3 months after acceptance. Sample: Free on Web site. Guidelines: On Web site. FICTION: Adventure, experimental, fantasy, historical, horror, humorous, mainstream, mystery, novel excerpts, religious, romance, science fiction, serialized novels, slice-of-life vignettes, suspense, western. Pays: $50. Mss bought/yr: 12. Length: 1,500-5,000 wds (variable). How to submit: Send complete ms. Other tips: "Must query for serialized novels." NONFICTION: Book excerpts, essays, general interest, historical/nostalgic, how-to, humor, inspirational, interview/profile, personal experience, photo feature, religious, technical, travel. Pays: $50. Mss bought/yr: 12 minimum. Length: 1,000-3,500 wds. How to submit: Send complete ms. Does NOT want: "Opinion and political commentary." Other: How-to; general interest and writing related; interview/profile: with authors, editors, or any person related to writing; technical: related to writers and the Web. FILLERS: Anecdotes, facts, gags to be illustrated by cartoonist ("I would love to find a person who could do this"), newsbreaks, short humor. Pays: $5-15. Mss bought/yr: 6 minimum. Length: 50-800 wds.

Fitness Management—www.fitnessworld.com

Issues and Solutions in Fitness Services. Leisure Publications, Inc., 4160 Wilshire Blvd., Los Angeles, CA 90010. Tel: (323)964-4800. Fax: (323)964-4840. Ronale Tucker, Editor (rtucker@fitnessmanagement.com); Anne McDonnell, Associate Editor; Ronale Tucker, Submissions. "*Fitness Management* is a professionally written magazine for owners and operators of physical fitness centers. Articles should emphasize ideas for responsibly and profitably managing those centers." Subject: Health/fitness centers. Frequency: Monthly. Format: Company Web site. Est. March 1985. Circ. 26,000. 30% freelance written. Pays on publication. Kill fee: 50%. Rights: All rights. Byline given. Accepts simultaneous submissions. Queries: Post, e-mail, fax. Reports in 3 weeks on queries. Reports in 3 weeks on mss. Lead time: 3 months. Mss published average of 6 months after acceptance. Sample: Free on Web site. Guidelines: E-mail. NONFICTION: Book excerpts, general interest, how-to, new product, opinion, technical. Contact: Ronale Tucker. Pays: 12-25¢/ wd. Mss bought/yr: 12-15. Length: 1,500-3,000 wds. How to submit: Send published clips. Does NOT want: "Success stories or interviews." FILLERS: Facts and Newsbreaks. Contact: Ronale Tucker. Pays: 12-25¢/wd. Mss bought/yr: 5-10. Length: 200-700 wds.

Folks Online—www.folksonline.com

Editor (Editor@FolksOnline.com). Byline given. Guidelines: www.folksonline.com/ folks/sd/contrib.htm. COLUMNS: True Stories: Tell us about how the use of computers or the Web has benefited your life, 900-1,200 wds, $100; Look Ma, I Did Something Useful on the Web Today: Write an advice article on how to go about using the Web for a practical project that would be of interest to the general consumer public, for example, have you ever used the Web as a resource for a major project that would be helpful for others to know? 900-1200 wds, $100; Cyberfolks Web Tours: Compile a list of recommended sites revolving around 1 or 2 of your favorite subject areas, 600-700 wds, $50; Promoting My Business/Interest on the

Web: Help others learn from your experience of how you market your product or service on the Web. ("We welcome your guidance regardless of whether your product/service is house-sitting pet snakes or selling restored mainframe computers. Here are some general guidelines: please develop your own theme just as long as the article is a useful how-to for someone considering or starting to market her product on the Web"), 900-1,200 wds, $100; Folks Family Trees: Features how people and families have successfully used computers, e-mail, or the worldwide Web to trace their genealogical roots, 900-1,200 wds, $100.

Freelance Success—www.freelancesuccess.com

Marketing and Managing Guide for Nonfiction Writers. 801 NE 70th St., Miami, FL 33138. Teresa Mears, Editor (editor@freelancesuccess.com). "*Freelance Success* content is tailored to experienced nonfiction writers." Subject: Nonfiction writers' markets. Frequency: Weekly. Format: E-mail newsletter. Est. 1993. 100% freelance written. Pays on acceptance. Rights: First-time electronic rights or one-time electronic rights. Byline given. Accepts previously published material. Submit seasonal material 2 months in advance. Queries: E-mail. Reports in 1 week on queries. Lead time: 1 month. Mss published average of 1 month after acceptance. Sample: Free on Web site. Guidelines: On Web site or e-mail editor@freelancesuccess.com. COLUMNS: Market Guides: Interviews with editors at publications that pay 50¢/wd or more, 600-700 wds; Editor Interviews: Interviews with editors at prestigious consumer magazines, 1,000 wds; Writer's Voice: How the writer solved a problem common to experienced writers, 700 wds; Biz Basics: The nuts and bolts of running a freelance business, 700 wds. Pays: $100-200. Mss bought/yr: 75. How to submit: Query. NONFICTION: Book excerpts, essays, how-to, interview/profile. Pays: $100-500/assigned article, $100 maximum for unsolicited. Length: 700-2,000 wds. How to submit: Query. Does NOT want: "Generic how-to's, without marketing leads, articles on how to break into writing, other material not aimed at experienced writers."

Freelance Writer's Report Online—www.writers-editors.com

CNW Publishing, Editing & Promotion, Inc., P.O. Box A, North Stratford, NH 03590. Dana K. Cassell, Editor (danakcnw@ncia.net). "*FWR* covers the marketing and business/office management aspect of running a freelance writing/editorial business. Articles are geared to the established freelancer, not the beginner." Subject:

Freelance writing. Frequency: Monthly. Format: Web magazine and e-mail newsletter. Est. March 1982. Circ. 500. 25% freelance written. Pays on publication. Kill fee: None. Rights: One-time electronic rights. Byline given. Accepts simultaneous submissions and previously published material. Submit seasonal material 1 year in advance. Queries: E-mail. Reports in 1 week on queries. Reports in 1 week on mss. Lead time: 1 month. Mss published average of 6 months after acceptance. Sample: Free with SASE and 55¢ postage for US; 67¢ to Canada; $1.40 to International. Guidelines: On Web site. NONFICTION: Book excerpts, how-to, personal experience. Pays: 10¢/published wd. Mss bought/yr: 40-50. Length: Maximum 500 wds. How to submit: Send complete ms. Does NOT want: "Basics for beginners." Other: How to make more money or save time/money as a freelance writer/editor, personal experience doing same.

Freshwater Seas—www.freshwaterseas.com

Serving All Who Sail in Great Lakes Waters. 2401 Colony Court, Ann Arbor, MI 48104. Tel: (734)975-0925. Fax: (734)975-0925. Robert Bethune, Editor (editor-@freshwaterseas.com). Subject: Sailing in the Great Lakes. Frequency: "We publish material as we generate it." Format: Web magazine/zine. Est. January 1998. Circ. 5,000/month. 20% freelance written. Pays on acceptance. Byline given. Accepts simultaneous submissions and previously published material. Submit seasonal material 1 month in advance. Queries: E-mail. Reports in 1 week on queries. Reports in 1 week on mss. Lead time: 1 month. Mss published average of 1 month after acceptance. Sample: Free on Web site. Guidelines: www.freshwaterseas.com/Recur/ Guidelines.htm. COLUMNS: The Spyglass: Shorter items that profile or review something of interest to sailors: equipment, books, software, music, etc.; The Crow's Nest: Short items that highlight an issue, an event, or some other newsworthy material; Emergencies: Accounts of situations in which life or property is at risk that arise in connection with sailing in the Great Lakes. Pays: $25. Mss bought/ yr: 5-10. How to submit: Query. FICTION: Adventure, historical, humorous, mainstream, mystery, novel excerpts, slice-of-life vignettes. Pays: $75-150. Mss bought/yr: 3-6. How to submit: Query. Other tips: "Each October around Halloween, we plan on running 2 or 3 ghost stories that have Great Lakes sailing themes." NONFICTION: Essays, exposé, historical/nostalgic, interview/profile, new product, opinion, personal experience, photo feature, technical, travel. Pays: $75-150 for assigned articles; $0-150 for unsolicited articles (see guidelines for payment polices). Mss bought/yr: 6-12. How to submit: Query. Other: Essays: On material of interest to people who sail in the Great Lakes; Exposé: On material of interest to people who sail in the Great Lakes; Historical/nostalgic: Tall ships and history of sailing in the Great Lakes; Interview/Profile: Interesting sailing vessels or people who sail the Great Lakes; Technical: must be sailing related. POETRY: Free verse, light verse, traditional. Pays: $25-50. Mss bought/yr: 2-3. Maximum poems/submission: 6. FILLERS: Anecdotes, facts, newsbreaks, short humor. Pays: $25. Mss bought/yr: 6-10. TIPS: "In a nutshell: solidly researched, thoroughly developed, personably readable text, usually with a minimum of 2 illustrations. Our first priority is to publish material that directly relates to Great Lakes sailing."

Fringe Golf—www.fringegolf.com

Alternative Golf Press Magazine. Pays up to $1/wd for original feature and lifestyle contributions. Target audience is 18-39. Query with story idea, bio, background. E-mail: editor@fringegolf.com. Women's content: women@fringegolf.com.

Gamasutra—www.gamasutra.com

The Art & Science of Making Games. CMP Media, 600 Harrison St., San Francisco, CA 94107. Brad Kane, Editor (brad@gamasutra.com). "By game developers, for game developers. We place high importance on the credentials of our authors because our readers want firsthand information from experienced professionals." Subject: Designing, developing, and producing interactive entertainment for the PC, console, and arcade. Frequency: Daily. Format: Web magazine/online directory. Est. June 1997. Circ. 65,000. 80% freelance written. Pays on publication. Kill fee: 25%. Rights: First-time and second serial (reprint) electronic rights. Byline given. Accepts simultaneous submissions and previously published material. Submit seasonal material 2 months in advance. Queries: E-mail. Reports in 2 weeks on queries. Reports in 3 weeks on mss. Lead time: 1 month. Mss published average of 1 month after acceptance. Sample: Free on Web site. Guidelines: On Web site. NONFICTION: Book excerpts, essays, exposé, historical/nostalgic, how-to, interview/profile, personal experience, technical. Contact: Brad Kane, Editor (brad@gamasutra.com). Pays: $200 for assigned or unsolicited articles. Mss bought/yr: 100. Length: 3,000-5,000 wds. How to submit: Send complete ms. Does NOT want: "Game reviews. We let the consumer publications handle that." TIPS: "We're looking for experienced game developers to impart advice to other professional game developers. If you've developed a video game before, and you'd like to write about the experience or technology you used, get in touch with us."

GardenGuides—www.gardenguides.com

2509 Dare St., Burlington, NC 27217. Fax: (770)216-1756. Jackie Carroll, Managing Editor (GardenGuides@gardenguides.com). "*GardenGuides* is seeking informative and entertaining gardening articles on subjects related to growing flowers, herbs, and vegetables, and insect control. Though we do advocate the use of chemicals in the garden in extreme circumstances when necessary to save a crop from total destruction, we focus primarily on organic techniques." Subject: Gardening. Frequency: Weekly. Format: Web magazine/zine, e-mail newsletter. Est. October 1996. Circ. 101,000 subscribers; 1,000,000 Web site. 75% freelance written. Pays on publication. Rights: First-time electronic rights, second serial (reprint) electronic rights. Byline given. Accepts simultaneous submissions and previously published material. Submit seasonal material 2 months in advance. Queries: Post, e-mail, fax. Reports in 1-2 weeks on queries. Reports in 1-2 weeks on mss. Lead time: 1-2 months. Mss published average of 1 month after acceptance. Sample: Free on Web site or by e-mail. Guidelines: E-mail gardenguides@yahoo.com. NONFICTION: Book excerpts, essays, how-to, personal experience, photo feature. Pays: $45. Mss bought/yr: 258. How to submit: Query, send complete ms. Other: Essays (gardening); how-to (gardening, lawn maintenance, cooking from the garden). FILLERS: Anecdotes, facts. TIPS: "Many of the articles published at *GardenGuides* are simultaneously published in international publications. We give preference to writers who respect our international audience by using brand names and slang terms sparingly, if at all."

genrEZONE—www.genrezone.com

P.O. Box 0536, Bogart, GA 30622-0536. G. Woodrum, Editor-in-Chief (editor@genrezone.com). Subject: Genre fiction and articles of interest to readers and authors of genre fiction. Frequency: Quarterly. Format: Web magazine. Est. March 1999. Circ. 3,000-4,500/issue. 100% freelance written. Pays on publication. Rights: First North American or second serial rights (in the case of reprints). Byline given. Accepts previously published material. Submit seasonal material 3-6 months in advance. Queries: Post, e-mail. Reports in 1 week on queries. Reports in 1-5 months on mss. Lead time: 1-12 months. Mss published average of 2 weeks after acceptance. Sample: Free on Web site. Guidelines: On Web site. COLUMNS: *genrEZONE* Book Reviews: Reviews of genre books, magazines, and more. 100-500 wds. Actively seeking freelancers willing to review e-books. Contact: Michael Barnette, Senior Reviewer (mbarnette2@genrezone.com). Pays: $2/review. Mss bought/yr: No limit. How to submit: Send complete ms, query. FICTION: Adventure, experimental, fantasy, historical, horror, mystery, romance, science fiction, serialized novels, suspense, western. Contact: G. Woodrum, Editor-in-Chief (submit@genrezone.com). Pays: $1-25. Mss bought/yr: 40. Length: 100 wds minimum, no maximum. How to submit: Send complete ms. Does NOT want: "Religious material disguised as a story." Other tips: "Prefer cross-genre (e.g., Sf/Romance, western/fantasy, etc.) to straight-up one genre tale." NONFICTION: Personal experience, interview/profile, essays. Contact: Michael Barnette, Editor (mbarnette2@genrezone.com). Pays: $1-5 for unsolicited articles. Mss bought/yr: 12-20. Length: 100-5,000 wds. How to submit: Send complete ms. POETRY: Free verse, haiku, traditional. Contact: G. Woodrum, Editor-in-Chief (editor@genrezone.com). Pays: $1/poem, $5 for the Featured Poet of the issue. Mss bought/yr: 40. Maximum poems/submission: 5. Maximum line length: 50. Does NOT want: "Mainstream, horror, poetry about being a writer." TIPS: "All material must be genre related. Please check the Hot List for our current needs, overstocked material, etc. Guidelines change frequently. We also publish electronic anthologies; please see guidelines for reading periods."

GettingIt—gettingit.com

What You Want. Web Power, 153 Kearny St., San Francisco, CA 94108. Fax: (415)956-2498. Allyson Quibell, Managing Editor (aquibell@gettingit.com); Cara Burns, Senior Editor (cara@gettingit.com); Matt Honan, Senior Editor (mat@gettingit.com). "*GettingIt* stories are carved from willful sensationalism with trace elements of gonzo and guerrilla journalism. *GettingIt* concentrates its twisted vision on 'news of the weird, celebrities, subcultures, extreme tabloid fantasy, tabloid news parody, politics, entertainment, sports and pop culture.'" Subject: News of the weird, sex, subcultures, politics. Frequency: Other. Format: Web magazine/zine. Est. July 1999. Circ. 15,000 unique visitors/day. 75% freelance written. Pays on acceptance. Kill fee: 30%. Rights: First-time electronic rights. Byline given. Queries: E-mail, fax. Reports in 1 week on queries. Reports in 2 weeks on mss. Lead time:

2 weeks. Mss published average of 2 weeks after acceptance. Sample: Free on Web site. Guidelines: E-mail guidelines@gettingit.com with subject "Writer's Guidelines." COLUMNS: Sections are Scope: Culture and Consumption; Dirt: Scandal and Celebrity; Crave: High-Tech and Hormones (Sex); Whoa: Oddities and Diversions. Average lengths for all departments: 500 wds. Contact: Allyson Quibell. Pays: approximately 40¢/wd. Mss bought/yr: 1,000. How to submit: Query, send published clips, send complete ms. FICTION: Erotica. Contact: Cara Burns. Pays: 40¢/wd. Mss bought/yr: 25. Length: 250-750 wds. How to submit: Query, send published clips, send complete ms. Does NOT want: "Anything that isn't erotica." NONFICTION: Book excerpts, essays, exposé, general interest, historical/nostalgic, how-to, humor, interview/profile, new product, opinion, personal experience, photo feature, technical, travel. Contact: Allyson Quibell. Pays: average 40¢/wd. Mss bought/yr: Very few. Length: 200-750 wds. How to submit: Query, send published clips, send complete ms. Does NOT want: "Hard technology, poetry, serious dry politics." FILLERS: Anecdotes, facts, gags to be illustrated by cartoonist, newsbreaks, short humor. Contact: Matt Honan. Pays: 40¢/wd. Mss bought/yr: 150. Length: 150-600 wds. TIPS: "Get around. Read subculture zines, news magazines, humor magazines and be aware of what good writing is."

Girlfriends Magazine—www.gfriends.com

3415 Cesar Chavez St., Suite 101, San Francisco, CA 94110. Managing Editor (editorial@gfriends.com). "Our mission is to provide entertaining, visually pleasing coverage of culture, politics, and entertainment—all from an informed and critical lesbian perspective." Subject: National monthly magazine for gay women. Byline given. Reports in 6-8 weeks on mss. Guidelines: www.gfriends.com/write.htm. COLUMNS: Lead Book Review: In-depth review and analysis of 1 or 2 signifigant recent lesbian releases, 850 wds; Music Review: A critical review of 1 or 2 recent albums, interviews, 550 wds; Film Review: "While we have a regular film reviewer, we have a guest writer 1-2 times/yr," 650 wds; Video Review: Focuses on 1 recent release, discussing 5-6 other videos that tie into its theme or genre, 900 wds. How to submit: Query, send complete ms. NONFICTION: Pays: 10¢/wd. How to submit: Query. Other: Feature-length articles: 2,500-3,500 wds. "Investigative features or human-interest stories that explore in depth an area of interest to our readers." Topics should be directly related to lesbian culture, politics, or entertainment. Celebrity Interviews: 2,000-3,000 wds. "Interview with a celebrity or well-known public figure, usually in Q&A format, which covers topics that are specifically relevant to our lesbian readers. Please query our staff only if you actually have already done or are able to get an interview with a celebrity." Travel: 600 wds. Focuses on 1 vacation spot, featuring a local event or being seasonally relevant, which includes specific advice and information for lesbian travelers. Humor: 550 wds. Short piece that takes a humorous look at lesbian culture or relationships, or that pokes fun at mainstream culture from a lesbian perspective. TIPS: "Please query the editorial staff with clips of previous work before submiting nonfiction material, and indicate the availability of artwork for your piece. Prefer to receive articles in electronic format, either through e-mail or on disk, formatted in MS Word for the Mac. All first time work is done on spec."

Global Competition News—www.voyagemag.lookscool.com

Regent Publications, 14 Honor Ave., Goldthorn Park, Wolverhampton WV4 5HH United Kingdom. Tel: (440)01902652999. Fax: (440)01902652999. John Dunne, Editor (voyagemag@zyworld.com). "For competition newbies and addicts alike, *GCN* brings together news of and guidelines for all the competitions we can find from around the world, as well as features, hints, tips, and feedback from previous entrants." Frequency: Monthly. Format: Web magazine/e-mail newsletter. Est. January 2000. Circ. 600. 100% freelance written. Pays on publication. Rights: One-time electronic rights. Byline given. Accepts simultaneous submissions. Submit seasonal material 6 months in advance. Queries: Post, e-mail, fax. Reports in 1 week on queries. Reports in 3 weeks on mss. Lead time: 1 month. Mss published average of 1-3 months after acceptance. Sample: Free on Web site or by e-mail. Guidelines: E-mail voyagemag@zyworld.com, subject "GCN_Guidelines." NON-FICTION: How-to, inspirational, interview/profile. Pays: $10-35 for unsolicited articles. Mss bought/yr: 100. Length: 150 wds minimum for news items, 800-1,500 standard one-off features. How to submit: Query, send complete ms. TIPS: "We accept but do not pay for press releases or competition rules put out by organizers—we get those sent to us directly. To get paid, your news item or feature about a specific competition needs some insight not normally available to entrants, comments from previous entrants, an interview with the organizer, an ex-judge, editor, or a recent past winner. Some competitions produce special anthologies of the best entrants—we might be interested in a review of last year's anthology providing you check to make sure nothing has changed in this year's rules. We also need features and news about awards (e.g., the year's best SF)."

GORP—www.gorp.com

Great Outdoor Recreation Pages. 22 W. 19th St., 8th Floor, New York, NY 10011. Fax: (212)675-8114. Robert Andrejewski, Editorial Dept. (randrejewski@gorp.com). "*GORP* delivers an informative, entertaining, and interactive encyclopedia of places to go and things to do around the world. Our editorial mission is to enrich people's outdoor experiences. We strive to enable all walks of life to get the most out of their adventures, from weekend strolls to round-the-world journeys." Subject: Outdoor recreation and active travel. Format: Web magazine. Length indeterminate but author is free to sell work elsewhere. Byline given. Accepts previously published material. Queries: Fax, e-mail, post. Sample: Free on Web site. Guidelines: On Web site www.gorp.com/gorp/freelance/guide.htm#pay. COLUMNS: Activities: Can include a roundup of activities or trips in a specific region, skill-building tips and other how-to articles, adventurous travel to exotic climes, etc.; Regional Attractions: "If you have knowledge of an area in which our coverage is lacking, we'd especially like to hear from you;" Regional Roundups: A summary of the adventure and weekend getaway opportunities in or near major cities or destinations; Off-the-Beaten-Track Adventures; Gear/How to Buy: *GORP* needs experts in outdoor pursuits to review gear, report on new products, and offer advice on purchasing equipment—ideal candidates will have access to gear from a wide range of manufacturers (work in an outdoor retail store?) and will possess a strong knowledge of technical and design concepts. "Because of the specialized knowledge required for these kinds of articles, we have a higher pay schedule for experienced gear writers." Please contact the editor for more information. How to submit: Query, send published clips. NONFICTION: Travel. Pays: $100-300 or more for assigned articles. How to submit: Send published clips, query, send complete ms.

Gothic.Net—http://gothic.net

c/o Editor, 431 Holloway, San Francisco, CA 94112. Darren P. Mckeeman, Publisher/Editor-in-Chief (weasel@gothic.net); Seth Lindberg, Fiction Editor (ghost@gothic.net); Mehitobel Wilson, Nonfiction (sighs@gothic.net). "*Gothic.net* is a market for horror and dark fantasy fiction that strives to be intelligent, macabre, interesting, and truly weird. We publish stories to entertain our readership, and the readership we target is smart, hip, urbane, acerbic, and any other adjective like that. And maybe they spend money on the Internet. We buy fiction primarily to please that target audience: We want to build such a reputation that like the stories or no, they'll come back next month just to see what weirdness we might pull out." Subject: Horror and dark fantasy fiction, and related nonfiction and reviews. Format: Web magazine. Pays on publication. Byline given. Accepts previously published material. Queries: Post, e-mail. Sample: Free on Web site. Guidelines: On Web site. FICTION: Experimental, fantasy, horror. Pays: 4¢/wd for original material; 1¢/wd for previously published material; preference is for original material. Length: 5,000 wds maximum. How to submit: Send complete ms. Does NOT want: "SF or high fantasy." NONFICTION: Essays, interview/profile. Pays: Articles, interviews, and movie reviews 3¢/wd for original material, 1¢/wd for previously published material; preference is for original material. $10/review. How to submit: Query, send complete ms. Does NOT want: "SF or high fantasy." Other: Reviews.

GOWANUS—www.gowanusbooks.com

An International Online Journal of Idea & Observation. Thomas J. Hubschman, Editor (tom@gowanusbooks.com). "The purpose of the magazine is to showcase writers from the so-called 'Third World.' The emphasis is on good writing—essay, short story, review." Subject: Third World writing (Asia, Africa, the Caribbean, e.g.). Frequency: Quarterly. Format: Web magazine/zine. Est. June 1997. 75% freelance written. Pays on publication. Rights: Electronic and archival plus one-time print rights. Byline given. Accepts simultaneous submissions and previously published material. Queries: E-mail. Reports in 1 week on queries. Reports in 1-8 weeks on mss. Mss published average of 2 months after acceptance. Sample: Free on Web site. Guidelines: On Web site. COLUMNS: Book and periodical reviews (local). Pays: $15-25. Mss bought/yr: 3-5. Length: 1,000-4,000 wds. How to submit: Query. FICTION: Mainstream, novel excerpts. Pays: $15-25. Mss bought/yr: 8. Length: 1,000-5,000 wds. How to submit: Send complete ms. NONFICTION: Book excerpts, essays, general interest, interview/profile. Pays: $15-25. Mss bought/yr: 8-10. Length: 1,000-5,000 wds. How to submit: Query. Other: Essays—political, personal, local culture. TIPS: "This is a publication primarily for writers from Third World nations. We do not require that an author's English be perfect—

that's what editors are for. We are looking for writing rooted in a particular place. We publish well-established writers as well as newcomers."

HappyCampers.Net—www.happycampers.net

Paginas World Wide Web, 1111 Tenth St. #175, Alamogordo, NM 88310. David Keeney, Managing Editor. "The World Wide Web is awash in data." Subject: Travel in the American Southwest and northern Mexico. "We write about the reader's *prospective* experience. Imagine what the reader and prospective traveler will experience. Travelogues are not wanted. We have a strong preference for topic sites that are not currently described well on the Web." Frequency: Daily. Format: Web magazine/online directory. Est. 1996. Circ. 30,000 visits/month. 4% freelance written. Rights: Exclusive electronic rights. Byline given. Queries: Accepted by surface mail and e-mail. Reports in 3 weeks on queries. Reports in 8 weeks on mss. Lead time: 2-3 months. Sample: Free on Web site. Guidelines: On Web site www.happycampers.net/admin/policy.html. NONFICTION: Personal experience, photo feature, travel. Pays: 5¢/wd on average, $50-100. Length: 800-1,500 wds. How to submit: Query, send complete ms. TIPS: "Choose locations that are new to *Happy Campers* and relatively undescribed on the Web (do a search to verify). Have photographs to support work, or be willing to obtain such images. Queries are preferable to manuscripts, though including a 3- to 4-paragraph excerpt from the manuscript can be very helpful. Provide references to your writing published on the Web, if at all possible. Have patience, but follow up diplomatically if necessary, a few weeks after submitting."

Healthy Living Series Webzines—www.healthgate.com

Healthy Woman, Healthy Man, Healthy Parenting, Healthy Eating, Healthy Sexuality, Healthy Mind, Healthy Athlete, Alternative Medicine, Healthy Over 50, Healthy Traveler, and *Healthy Rx.* HealthGate, 25 Corporate Dr., Burlington, MA 01803. Michelle Badash, Editor (mbadash@healthgate.com); Laurie Brown, Managing Editor; Jill Shuman, Consulting Editor. "The *Healthy Living Webzines* are designed to provide interesting, highly accurate health and medical information to consumers on the Internet. The topics are drawn from the latest in medical research, health news, and health-related lifestyle issues. Articles need to be well researched, include quotes from experts in the field, and must provide a balanced view of the subject." Subject: Health and medicine. Frequency: Weekly. Format: Web magazine/zine.

Est. 1996. 90% freelance written. Pays on acceptance. Kill fee: $250. Rights: First-time electronic rights. Byline given. Accepts previously published material. Submit seasonal material 5 months in advance. Queries: E-mail. Reports in 3 weeks on queries. Lead time: 3 months. Mss published average of 1-2 months after acceptance. Sample: Free on Web site. Guidelines: E-mail. NONFICTION: General interest, interview/profile. Pays: $450-650 for assigned articles; unsolicited articles not accepted. Length: 1,000-1,500 wds. Other: General interest (ONLY regarding health and medical topics). TIPS: "There are a total of 11 individual Webzines: *Healthy Woman, Healthy Man, Healthy Parenting, Healthy Eating, Healthy Sexuality, Healthy Mind, Healthy Athlete, Alternative Medicine, Healthy Over 50, Healthy Traveler,* and *Healthy Rx.*"

Hello Heaven—www.helloheaven.org

Catholic Digest Publications, 2115 Summit Ave., St. Paul, MN 55105-1081. Michael McCarthy, Associate Editor (CDigest@stthomas.edu). "We favor the anecdotal approach. Stories submitted must be strongly focused on a definitive topic. This topic is to be illustrated for the reader by way of a well-developed series of true-life, interconnected vignettes." Subject: Catholicism, religion, spirituality. Frequency: Monthly. Format: Web magazine/zine. Est. 1996. Circ. 30,000 page views per month. 30% freelance written. Pays on publication. Rights: First-time electronic rights and one-time electronic rights. Byline given. Accepts previously published material. Submit seasonal material 4-6 months in advance. Reports in 3-6 months on mss. Lead time: 2 months. Mss published average of 6 months after acceptance. Sample: Free on Web site. Guidelines: On Web site. NONFICTION: Book excerpts, essays, general interest, historical/nostalgic, how-to, humor, inspirational, interview/profile, personal experience, religious, travel. Pays: $100-400 for unsolicited articles. Mss bought/yr: 12-24. Length: 500-3,000 wds. How to submit: Send complete ms. FILLERS: Anecdotes, facts, gags to be illustrated by cartoonist, short humor. Pays: $100 maximum. Mss bought/yr: 300.

Hint Fashion Magazine—www.hintmag.com

240 W. 15th St. #4, New York NY 10011. Fax: (212)675-6514. Lee Carter, Editor (leecarter@hintmag.com). "*Hint* is the Web's leading independent fashion magazine. The magazine takes a nonmainstream approach to fashion journalism, catering to thinking people interested in intelligent fashion commentary." Subject: Fashion.

Frequency: Weekly. Format: Web magazine/zine. Est. April 1998. Circ. 700,000 monthly impressions, 8,000 daily viewers. 50% freelance written. Pays on publication. Rights: Writer keeps copyright. Byline given. Accepts simultaneous submissions and previously published material. Queries: E-mail, fax. Lead time: 2 weeks. Mss published average of 1 month after acceptance. Sample: Free on Web site. Guidelines: E-mail. NONFICTION: Book excerpts, essays, exposé, new product, opinion, interview/profile, humor, photo feature, general interest. Contact: Lee Carter, Editor-in-Chief (leecarter@hintmag.com). Pays: 25-75¢/wd. Mss bought/ yr: 5. Length: 400-800 wds. How to submit: Send published clips. Does NOT want: "Writing about fashion trends." TIPS: "*Hint* is interested in irreverent, colorful, and 'sassy' writing only."

iAgora—www.iagora.com

Connecting Internationals. 594 Broadway, Suite 310, New York, NY 10012. Fax: (212)625-1991. Rebecca Finkel, Community Content Developer (rebecca@iagora .net). "Our purpose is to foster a sense of community, so the writing should be personal and aimed at people from all over the world (generally 18-35) who are not living in their countries of nationality. Submissions are accepted in French, Spanish, and English, and all pieces are published in the 3 languages. We do not aim for a politically correct Web site, but one where open and honest discussions of cultural differences can take place in an intelligent manner." Subject: People who live abroad. Frequency: Web site updated several times/day. Format: Web magazine/zine community for internationals. Est. November 1998. 60% freelance written. Pays on acceptance. Byline given. Accepts simultaneous submissions and previously published material. Submit seasonal material 3 months in advance. Queries: E-mail. Reports in 2 weeks on queries. Reports in 4 weeks on mss. Lead time: 2-3 wks. Mss published average of 2 months after acceptance. Sample: Free on Web site. Guidelines: On Web site. COLUMNS: Global Gourmet International food history column, humorous and personal, 750 wds; Only in New York: Gen. humorous tidbits on life in NYC, 800 wds, (interested in expanding section with columns from other cities); City of the Week: Highlights insider view of a popular city by providing descriptions and specific places to see, eat, and stay 500 wds, (include list of 10 dos and don'ts about the customs of the city; provide 3-4 links in tourism, places to stay, food & drink, arts & entertainment, shopping, and excursions). No e-mail attachments, please . . . include submission in the body of your e-mail. Subject header should state which part of the site you are submitting to. Pays: $20-$50. Mss bought/yr: 150. How to submit: Send complete ms. TIPS: "We ask that all of our writers become members of iAgora, because the whole purpose of the site is to create a sense of community online. Someone who understands the experience of living or traveling abroad and the kinds of people who the site would attract will have a much better sense of what we are looking for."

Independent and Self-Publishers News—www.voyagemag.lookscool.com

Regent Publications, 14 Honor Ave., Goldthorn Park, Wolverhampton WV4 5HH UK. Tel: (440)01902652999. Fax: (440)01902652999. John Dunne, Editor (voyag emag@zyworld.com). "This publication helps independent and self publishers of all levels of experience share knowledge and resources, and increase networking." Frequency: Monthly. Format: Web magazine/e-mail newsletter. Est. April 2000. Circ. 400. 100% freelance written. Pays on publication. Rights: One-time electronic rights. Byline given. Accepts simultaneous submissions. Submit seasonal material 6 months in advance. Queries: Post, e-mail, fax. Reports in 1 week on queries. Reports in 3 weeks on mss. Lead time: 1 month. Mss published average of 1-3 months after acceptance. Sample: Free on Web site or by e-mail. Guidelines: E-mail voyagemag@ zyworld.com, subject "ISPN_Guidelines." NONFICTION: Book excerpts, how-to, inspirational, interview/profile, new product, personal experience, technical. Pays: $10-35 for unsolicited articles. Mss bought/yr: 100. Length: 150 wds minimum for news items, 800-1,500 standard one-off features. How to submit: Query, send complete ms. TIPS: "We're looking for inspirational success stories within the trade, as well as report of failures that can help our readers avoid pitfalls. All feature-length material should provide e-mail or Web site addresses where the reader can follow up for more information."

The Ink Blotter—www.inkspot.com/inkblot

A Writer's Sanity Break. Inkspot.com, 67 Mowat Ave., Suite 239, Toronto, Ontario M6K 3E3 Canada. Christopher Donner, Editor (chris@inkspot.com). "*The Ink Blotter* is a source of inspiration and humor for writers of all kinds." Subject: Writing and humor. Frequency: Biweekly. Format: Web magazine. Est. June 1999. Circ. 7,000 monthly. 90% freelance written. Pays on publication. Rights: Nonexclusive worldwide first publication rights. Byline given. Queries: E-mail. Reports in 2-3 weeks on queries. Reports in 2-3 weeks on mss. Mss published average of 2-3 months after acceptance. Sample: Free on Web site. Guidelines: On Web site, or e-mail guidelinesblotter@inkspot.com. FICTION: Humorous. Contact: Chris Donner, Editor (chris@inkspot.com). Pays: $20 for prose pieces. Mss bought/yr: 15-20. Length: 500 wds maximum. How to submit: Send complete ms. Other tips: "Inspirational vignettes and essays." NONFICTION: Humor, inspirational, personal experience. Contact: Chris Donner, Editor (chris@inkspot.com). Pays: $20 for short prose. Mss bought/yr: 15-20. Length: 500 wds maximum. How to submit: Send complete ms. POETRY: Avant-garde, free verse, haiku, light verse, traditional. Contact: Chris Donner, Editor (chris@inkspot.com). Pays: $10/poem. Mss bought/yr: 50-100. Maximum poems/submission: 3. Maximum line length: 20 (4-8 preferred). TIPS: "The site intends to encourage and entertain writers. Pieces should be relatively short and should deal with the subject of writing in some way. Submissions should be by e-mail, with the text in the body of the e-mail; no attachments please, they will not be opened."

Inklings—www.inkspot.com/inklings

Inkspot's Newsletter for Writers on the Net. Inkspot, 67 Mowat Ave., Suite 239, Toronto, Ontario M5J 2S9 Canada. Debbie Ridpath Ohi, Editor-in-Chief (ohi@inkspot.com); Moira Allen, Managing Editor (submissions) (moira@inkspot.com). "*Inklings* is a free, biweekly electronic newsletter for writers. Focus is on the craft and business of writing. Highlights useful resources, market information, how-to tips for writers. Q&A columns by professionals in the fields of publishing and writing." Subject: Business and craft of writing. Frequency: Biweekly. Format: Electronic newsletter. Est. September 1995. Circ. 45,000 minimum. 75% freelance written. Pays on publication. Rights: First-time one-time electronic rights, plus archival rights (back issues of newsletter are kept online). Byline given. Submit seasonal material 2 months in advance. Queries: E-mail. Reports in 2 weeks on queries. Reports in 1-2 months on mss. Mss published average of 2 months after acceptance. Sample: Free on Web site. Guidelines: www.inkspot.com/inklings/guidelines.html. NONFICTION: How-to, interview/profile. Contact: Moira Allen. Pays: 6¢/wd. Mss bought/yr: 25. Length: 500-1,000 wds, 800 preferred. How to submit: Query, send published clips. Does NOT want: "First-person essays, 'How I Got Published,' general inspirational, fiction, poetry." TIPS: "We're looking for a specific type of journalistic style . . . please look at back issues before submitting queries. Articles should be well researched, specific rather than general, supported with quotes and statistics. It's helpful to include pointers to other online resources at the end of your article. For full guidelines, please see the Web site." Queries and submissions accepted only by e-mail.

Inscriptions—www.inscriptionsmagazine.com

The Weekly E-zine for Professional Writers. Attn: Jade Walker, 1120 Sixth Ave., 6th Floor, New York, NY 10036. Fax: (815)346-1770. Jade Walker, Editor and Editorial Contact (submissions) (editor@inscriptionsmagazine.com). "*Inscriptions* is the weekly e-zine for professional writers. We cover the publishing industry for working, freelancing, and telecommuting writers, editors, and publishers." Subject: Publishing, both print and electronic. Frequency: Weekly. Format: Web magazine/zine, e-mail newsletter. Est. August 1998. Circ. 4,000 minimum weekly and 24,500 people to our Web site/month. 100% freelance written. Pays on publication. "Text attachments OK; prefers material to be pasted directly into the body of an e-mail. Other formats will be deleted. Style: Single-spaced, 2 spaces between paragraphs (don't indent). Include your full name, pen name (if preferred), mailing address, phone number, and e-mail address with each submission." Rights: One-time electronic rights. Byline given. Accepts simultaneous submissions and previously published material. Submit seasonal material 2-3 months in advance. Queries: E-mail. Reports in 2 weeks on queries. Reports in 2 weeks on mss. Lead time: 1-3 months. Mss published average of 1-3 months after acceptance. Sample: Free on Web site or by e-mail. Guidelines: E-mail Inscriptions@sendfree.com. COLUMNS: Book reviews: Honest and critical reviews, 300-500 wds. Pays: $5, plus a free book. Mss bought/yr: 250. How to submit: Query. NONFICTION: Book excerpts, how-to, interview/profile. Pays: $40 for assigned unsolicited articles. Mss bought/yr: 80. Length: 500-1,500 wds. How to submit: Query. FILLERS: Short humor. Pays: $5. Mss bought/yr: 50. Length: 250-1,000. TIPS: "We prefer to work with experienced and published writers and editors. To subscribe: Send an e-mail to Inscriptions-subscribe@egroups.com."

iParenting.com.—www.iparenting.com

P.O. Box 1724, Evanston, IL 60204. Jessica Williams, Associate Editor (info@iparenting.com). Pays on publication. Rights: All rights. Byline given. NONFICTION: Essays, interview/profile, humor. Contact: Elisa Ast All, Editor-in-Chief (elisa@ipar enting.com). Pays: Minimum $25/article. Length: 500-1,200 wds. How to submit: Query, send published clips. TIPS: "*iParenting* is an award-winning network of family-oriented Web sites. We publish a number of parenting-related e-publications on the WWW. These include, but are not limited to, *Preconception.com, Pregnancy Today, Breastfeed.com, Babies Today, Toddlers Today, Preschoolers Today, Children Today, Preteenagers Today, Teenagers Today,* and *Recipes Today.* Our tone is friendly, personal, and helpful without being preachy. Our articles are easy to read and full of information, expert sources and anecdotes. We pride ourselves on offering material from parents who have 'been there, done that.' "

IRR Romancer—www.iReadRomance.com/romancer

E-zine for Romance Readers. Red Merle, Ltd., Pinegrove P.O. Box 64004, Oakville, Ontario L6K 2C0 Canada. Tel: (905)337-2188. Fax: (905)337-0999. Maralyn Ellis, Editor (email@iReadRomance.com); Stacey Doherty, Managing Editor. "The *iRR Romancer* publishes articles and stories of interest to romance readers, based on seasonal or issue themes." Subject: Romance fiction. Frequency: Bimonthly. Format: Web magazine/zine. Est. February 14, 1997. Circ. 25,000. 50% freelance written. Pays on acceptance. Kill fee: $25. Rights: Exclusive electronic rights. Byline given. Submit seasonal material 4 months in advance. Queries: Post. Reports in 8 weeks on queries. Reports in 8 weeks on mss. Lead time: 4 months. Mss published average of 3 months after acceptance. Sample: Free on Web site. Guidelines: E-mail Editor@iReadRomance.com. COLUMNS: Movie Reviews, Book Reviews, Profiles, Historical Couples, eRomance. Contact: Stacey Doherty, Managing Editor. Pays: $25 maximum. Mss bought/yr: 12. How to submit: Send published clips, query. FICTION: Erotica, romance, slice-of-life vignettes. Contact: Lynn Fraser. Pays: $25 maximum. Mss bought/yr: 12. Length: 2,500 wds maximum. How to submit: Send published clips, query. NONFICTION: Essays, general interest, historical/nostalgic, humor, interview/profile, new product, opinion, personal experience, photo feature, technical, travel. Contact: Stacey Doherty. Pays: Individual maximum for assigned articles. $25 maximum for unsolicited articles. Mss bought/ yr: 12-24. Length: 500-2,000 wds. How to submit: Send published clips, query. Does NOT want: " 'How to write a romance' pieces."

Jackhammer E-zine—www.eggplant-productions.com

Eggplant Productions, P.O. Box 2248, Schiller Park, IL 60176. Raechel Henderson,

President and Editor-in-Chief. E-mail: submissions@eggplant-productions.com. Electronic speculative fiction publication. Stories are posted on the Web site for as long as readers vote for the story (no less than a month and no longer than a year). Frequency: As necessary (possibly daily). Circ: 1,500. Needs: Speculative fiction stories. Length: 3,000 wds maximum. This is a firm limit. Guidelines: "Stories should be submitted as plain-text e-mail to submissions@eggplant-productions.com in the body of the message. No attachments. No surface mail submissions. Please include all pertinent information in the submission (see E-mail Submission Standards for Eggplant Productions for more information). Please make sure that your e-mail address is correct. Simultaneous submissions are accepted as long as they are disclosed as such in the submission. No reprints. "If the story has appeared anywhere in print, on the Web, on a newsgroup, or an e-mailed e-zine, it is considered a reprint. The one exception I make is e-mail-based critique groups (such as Critters). If the story has appeared on your Web page (even if the only person who looked at it was your mother), I will still consider it a reprint." Rights: First electronic worldwide. 1 yr maximum. Pays: Per story: "Payment is an initial U.S.$25 (upon return of signed and dated contract) and U.S.50¢ for each day the story is posted on the Web site after an initial one month period." Reports in 2-4 weeks average. TIPS: "My key criterion in evaluating a story is whether or not the story moves me in some way. I want to care about the characters, their stories, and the world you've created. I have a broad definition of what is speculative fiction, but stories should have an element of speculation or the fantastic to them." Also: "Taboos: These are stories that either I flat out won't accept or have seen too much of—child molestation; stories with excessive gore; stories involving God and the Devil; stories based on the idea that humans developed from aliens crash landing millions of years ago; writer stories; excerpts from novels unless they are self-contained episodes." Last: "Since *Jackhammer E-zine* is available free on the Web, I want to keep the stories PG-13. Adult language isn't a problem as long as it is in keeping with the story and characters." Submission Standards: www.eggplant-productions.com/standards. Guidelines: www.eggplant-productions.com/j2guidelines.asp.

JaneZine—www.janesguide.com

HLSG, Inc., 2275 Lake Whatcom Blvd., PMB123, Bellingham, WA 98226. Jane

Duvall, Editor (jane@janesguide.com); Adrienne Benedicks, Fiction Editor (adrienn e@erotica-readers.com). "Sex-positive is the one true guideline. We appreciate sexuality in all its consensual forms. Our publication especially appeals to women and couples, and we like to focus on women actively participating in and enjoying sexuality." Subject: Erotica and sexuality. Frequency: Biweekly. Format: Web magazine/zine. Est. March 1998. Circ. 30,000. 100% freelance written. Pays on first of the month for all writing to be run that month. Kill fee: 100%. Rights: For erotic fiction we ask for first-time, one-time only (2-week) rights. We buy second serial rights occasionally, but only for nonelectronically published works. Byline given. Accepts previously published material. Submit seasonal material 4 months in advance. Queries: Post, e-mail. Reports in 1 week on queries. Reports in 1 month on mss. Mss published average of 4-8 months after acceptance. Sample: Free by e-mail (ask for current entrance password). Guidelines: On Web site: (www.erotica-readers. com) or e-mail jane@janesguide.com. FICTION: Erotica, experimental, fantasy, historical, humorous, slice-of-life vignettes. Pays: $25—our fiction is a very modest rate, but we also publish bylines that include links to the writer's Web site and/or e-mail address. Mss bought/yr: 55. Length: 1,000-4,000 wds. How to submit: Send complete ms. Does NOT want: "Flowery romance, nonconsensual sexual portrayals, tired scenarios. I don't want negative portrayals of women. Know the difference between explicit and crude. Most importantly, no straight 'stroke' fiction—there has to be some story line to interest us." Other tips: "All with erotic/ adult themes."

January Magazine—www.januarymagazine.com

For People Who Like to Read. January Publishing, Inc., #101-1001 W. Broadway, Suite 192, Vancouver, British Columbia V6H 4E4 Canada. Linda Richards, Editor (editor@januarymagazine.com). "All of our writers have a great deal of passion for the subject at hand. If you don't care a great deal about books and the people who make them, this isn't a market for you. Also, read the magazine. Our tone is fresh and the writing is sharp." Subject: Books—Book reviews and author interviews and profiles. Frequency: Daily. Format: Web magazine/zine. Est. November 1997. Circ. 5,000/day. 20% freelance written. Pays on publication. Kill fee: 50%. Rights: Electronic rights: *January* is self-archiving and material stays on the site "forever." However, writers retain copyright. Byline given. Accepts simultaneous submissions.

Submit seasonal material 3 months in advance. Queries: E-mail. Reports in 4 weeks on queries. Reports in 4 weeks on mss. Mss published average of 1 month after acceptance. Sample: Free on Web site. NONFICTION: Interview/profile. Pays: Negotiated. Mss bought/yr: 20-50. Length: 450 wds minimum. How to submit: Query. Other: Book reviews.

JavaWorld—www.javaworld.com

Fueling Innovation. ITworld.com, an IDG company, 501 Second St., San Francisco, CA 94107. Tel: (415)243-4188. Fax: (415)267-1732. Carolyn Wong, Editor (Carolyn_Wong@itworld.com). "Articles are very 'how-to,' technical in nature, for the advanced Java developer." Frequency: Weekly. Format: Web magazine. Est. February 1996. Circ. 150,000 minimum. 80% freelance written. Pays on acceptance. Kill fee: 20%. Rights: First-time electronic rights. Byline given. Submit seasonal material 1 month in advance. Queries: E-mail. Reports in 1 week on queries. Lead time: 1 month. Mss published average of 2 months after acceptance. Sample: Free on Web site. Guidelines: www.javaworld.com/javaworld/common/jw-guidelines.html. NONFICTION: How-to, new product, technical. Pays: Varies. Length: Varies. How to submit: Query.

John Hewitt's Writer's Resource Center—www.poewar.com

Poet Warrior Press, P.O. Box 65989, Tucson, AZ 85728. John Hewitt, Editor (poewar @azstarnet.com). "*WRC* publishes articles about the craft and the business of writing. *WRC* looks for articles that are educational in nature and benefit the writing community." Subject: Writing. Frequency: Daily. Format: Web magazine. Est. January 1993. Circ. 500 readers daily. 50% freelance written. Pays on publication. Rights: One-time electronic rights. Byline given. Accepts simultaneous submissions and previously published material. Submit seasonal material 2 months in advance. Queries: E-mail. Reports in 2 weeks on queries. Reports in 2 weeks on mss. Sample: Free on Web site. Guidelines: On Web site. TIPS: "Freelancers seeking publication in *WRC* should be ready to provide solid, helpful information for fellow writers. Articles about the craft of writing are the most likely to be published with articles about the business of writing a close second. An interview with a successful writer is another excellent area for submissions. 'Inspirational' articles without educational information about the craft or business of writing will not be considered. My advice is to write what you know best. If you feel you have mastered or are very knowledgeable about a particular area of writing, then that is what you should write about for *WRC*. Also, try and find areas you feel haven't been covered well enough by *WRC*—chances are that I will agree with you. *WRC* is aimed at a very wide writing audience, and is open to queries about a wide range of writing topics, including genre-specific articles."

Kafenio—www.kafeniocom.com

Meier & Jacobson Editorial Services, Box 142, GR-85700, Karpathos, Greece. Tel: (+30)24531716. Roberta Beach Jacobson, Editor (editor@kafeniocom.com). "*Kafenio* is a dynamic monthly e-zine offering intelligent features, photos, columns, and insider tips on European life and culture. Check us out at www.kafeni ocom.com. There is nothing to join and no way to subscribe, so 'Klick on Kafenio' to discover what's going on around Europe." Frequency: Monthly. Format: E-zine. Est. March 2000. Pays on acceptance. Rights: One-time, one-month electronic rights are purchased, running from the first to last days of the month of publication. Then the column is yours again to do with as you please. *Kafenio*'s archives will consist only of titles of articles with authors' names, so be assured your work will never be posted beyond "your" month. Byline given. Accepts previously published material. COLUMNS: Writers worldwide are invited to submit columns for Speakers' Table, a regular department of *Kafenio*. Each issue will include 4 columns. Never preachy, they offer a witty, sometimes humorous approach to the surprises of life in Europe. Pays: Payment of U.S.$100 or euro 100 (check of your choice) is made upon acceptance of a Speakers' Table item. How to submit: Send complete ms. TIPS: "No queries please! Simply e-mail your best shot (without photos) to essay@kafeniocom.com. Editorial response time is a few days. Competition is keen and often editors must select from among top-quality submissions. If you don't have luck the first time, just try us again. Editors strive to cover a variety of European destinations in each issue of *Kafenio*. Please note that, other than the above, no features, photos, or queries will be accepted from freelance writers."

Keystrokes—www.writelinks.com/keystrokes

Writelinks.com, P.O. Box 142002, Fayetteville, GA 30214. Kate Johnston, Managing Editor (Editor@WriteLinks.com). "*Keystrokes* content is intended to assist published as well as new writers improve their writing skills and find paying markets for their work." Subject: Writing, getting published. Frequency: Monthly. Format: Web magazine/zine. Est. October 1997. Circ. 5,000 subscribers to notification list; unknown number of readers. 100% freelance written. Pays on publication. Rights: First-time or reprint rights. Byline given. Accepts simultaneous submissions and previously published material. Submit seasonal material 2-3 months in advance. Queries: E-mail. Reports in 1-2 months on queries. Reports in 1-2 months on mss. Lead time: 1 month. Mss published average of 1-2 months after acceptance. Sample: Free on Web site. Guidelines: On Web site. NONFICTION: How-to, humor, inspirational, interview/profile, personal experience, technical. Pays: $25 maximum for assigned or unsolicited articles. Mss bought/yr: 84. Length: 5,000 wds maximum. How to submit: Query, send complete ms. Does NOT want: "Book reviews (I already have a book reviewer)." TIPS: "I prefer full articles to queries, but do accept queries. I want articles that take a slightly different slant. I don't want articles on topics all the other writing magazines are publishing this month or last month."

Kids' Highway—home.att.net/~kidshighway

The Literary Magazine for Kids and Their Grown-ups. P.O. Box 6275, Bryan, TX 77805-6275. Hector Cole Garza, Fiction Editor (kidshighway@att.net); Miranda Garza, Poetry & Nonfiction Editor (kidshighway@att.net). "*Kids' Highway* is a literary magazine for kids and their grown-ups. For fiction and nonfiction, payment is as follows: $5 and writers receive one copy with cash payment. Payment for columns is negotiated from writer to writer. No cash payment for pieces shorter than 400 words; they receive one copy in which work appears." Subject: Family-oriented content. Frequency: Publishes 5 times/yr. Format: Web magazine/zine. Est. July 1999. Circ. 50. 75% freelance written. Pays on publication. "With submissions, include your name, address, correct e-mail address, word count, and a brief bio. Students should include their age. If submitting a reprint or simultaneous submission, please let us know." Rights: One-time electronic rights and one-time print rights. Byline given. Accepts simultaneous submissions and previously published material. Queries: Post, e-mail. Reports in 2-4 weeks on queries. Reports in 2-5 weeks on mss. Lead time: 2-8 months. Mss published average of 2-8 months after acceptance. Sample: Send check or money order for $3 payable to Kids Highway. Guidelines: home.att.net/~kidshighway/submissionsheet.html. COLUMNS: Career Watch: Ongoing series of articles that inform kids on different career prospects, 500 wds maximum; Grown-ups' Tear-out Pages: Fiction and nonfiction by and for adults—good mysteries are ALWAYS welcome, 2,200 wds; Video Reviews: No PG-13 or R movies. 150-250 wds. Pays: Varies. Contact: Hector Cole Garza. Book Reviews: No reviews on books where first loves, horror, coming-of-age or death of a loved one is the main theme, 150-250 wds. Pays: Varies. Contact: Miranda Garza. Mss bought/yr: 20-30. How to submit: Query, send complete ms. FICTION: Adventure, humorous, mainstream, mystery, novel excerpts, science fiction, suspense, western. Contact: Hector Cole Garza. Mss bought/yr: 20-30. Length: Children's fiction: 1,500 wds maximum. Adult fiction: 2,200 wds maximum. Will consider longer lengths. NONFICTION: Book excerpts, how-to, humor, new product, technical, travel. Contact: Miranda Garza. Mss bought/yr: 10-15. How to submit: Query, send complete ms. Does NOT want: "Ghosts, depressing themes, and holidays." POETRY: Free verse, haiku, light verse, traditional. Contact: Miranda Garza. Pays: $2 maximum. Mss bought/yr: 20-25. Maximum poems/submission: No limit. Maximum line length: 20. FILLERS: Anecdotes, facts, short humor, jokes, riddles, tips, and puzzles. Contact: Hector Cole Garza. Pays: Pays in copies for fillers. Mss bought/yr: 10-20. Length: 400 wds maximum. TIPS: "Be original and fun when writing for us. Make us smile with your work. Avoid clichés and come up with something fresh and different."

Kung Fu Online—www.kungfuonline.com

P.O. Box 330, Helena, AL 35080. Fax: (530)884-4653. Steve Creel, Editor (editor@kungfuonline.com). "Electronic-only publication promoting and preserving the arts of the traditional Chinese martial systems." Subject: Kung Fu, Tai Chi, and the Martial Arts. Frequency: Daily. Format: Web magazine. Circ. 800,000 hits/month. Pays on publication. Rights: First world rights and reprint rights. Byline given. Queries: E-mail. Reports in 1 week on queries. Reports in 1 week on mss. Guidelines: www.kungfuonline.com/guidelines.html. COLUMNS: Book reviews, columns related to Kung Fu, Tai Chi, and the Martial Arts, 1,500 wds maximum; also accepting fitness, health and entertainment articles related to martial arts, 1,500 wds maximum. Pays: $25/page minimum (query for more info). How to submit: Query. NONFICTION: Essays, interview/profile. Pays: $25/page minimum (query for more info). Length: 10,000 wds maximum. Other: Also accepting fitness, health, and entertainment articles related to martial arts. TIPS: "*Kung Fu Online* is accessible to persons of varied backgrounds, ages, and occupations. For this reason, articles are written in a clear style for those who may not be totally familiar with the subject and its particular vocabulary. Queries should state qualifications, provide a clear outline of intended article, and state whether illustrations are available. For submissions, cut and paste directly into e-mail and send in ASCII format (only photos and illustrations should be sent as an attachment)."

LesbiaNation—www.LesbiaNation.com

Outonthenet.com, Inc., 2800 Biscayne Blvd., 8th Floor, Miami, FL 33137. Fax: (305)572-0902. Claudia Miller, Managing Editor (cmiller@ootn.com). "*LesbiaNation* provides a mix of features that includes everything from humor to activism to entertainment highlighting the voices of the lesbian community. Our features are often edgy with a twinge of ironic humor and always cutting-edge." Subject: The lesbian and bisexual community. Frequency: Daily. Format: Web magazine. Est. 1997. 100% freelance written. Pays 1 month after publication. "Simultaneous if it is in a print publication only and previously published if it was either in print or a noncompeting Web site." Kill fee: 50%. Rights: First-time electronic rights for 30 days after publication and archival rights. Byline given. Accepts simultaneous submissions and previously published material. Submit seasonal material 1 month in advance. Queries: E-mail. Reports in 1 week on queries. Mss published average of 1 month after acceptance. Sample: Free on Web site. Guidelines: E-mail. NONFICTION: Book excerpts, essays, exposé, general interest, historical/nostalgic, how-to, humor, interview/profile, opinion, personal experience, religious, travel. Contact: Claudia Miller, Managing Editor (cmiller@ootn.com). Pays: $100 minimum for assigned articles. Mss bought/yr: 400. Length: 800-1,000 words. How to submit: Query, send published clips. Other: Politics and activism; all must relate to lesbians or bisexual women.

Literary Traveler—www.literarytraveler.com

The Guide for the Literary Traveler. The Nomad Group, 289 Summer St. #1, Somerville, MA 02144. Francis McGovern, Editor (francis@literarytraveler.com). "Each one of our articles is about someone who creates, or a place that inspires. If you write well and can find the story behind a writer or a place, then we are interested in hearing it. We feature first-person travel pieces as well as meditative pieces and objective pieces that just report the facts. We can also use short articles about interesting literary events and book reviews about writers and places." Subject: We are an online magazine dedicated to exploring the literary imagination and the link between literature and travel. We publish nonfiction articles about writers, artists, and places. Frequency: Quarterly. Format: Web magazine/zine. Est. March 1998. Circ. 20,000 monthly. 50% freelance written. Pays on publication. Rights: Exclusive electronic rights for 6 months and right to archive on the site. Byline given. Accepts simultaneous submissions and previously published material. Submit seasonal material 3 months in advance. Queries: Post, e-mail. Reports in 1-3 weeks on queries. Reports in 1-4 weeks on mss. Lead time: 3 months. Mss published average of 3 months after acceptance. Sample: Free on Web site. Guidelines: On Web site. COLUMNS: Articles about writers and places, literary road trips, visits to graves of prominent literary figures and stories of how they died, sunrises and sunsets at inspiring literary sites; 500-1,500 wds. We also use relevant book reviews and coverage of interesting literary events; 500 wds. NONFICTION: Essays, travel, historical/nostalgic. Pays: $25/article; $5 for short pieces such as reviews. Length: 500-2,000 wds. How to submit: Query, send complete ms. Does NOT want: "Any fiction or poetry. Articles that are just travel pieces that don't connect with literature or an artist in some way."

Lodging.com—www.lodging.com

InterNetwork Publishing Corp., 5455 N. Federal Hwy., Suite O, Boca Raton, FL 33487. Fax: (801)720-9997. Bill Marbach, Editor; Wendy Maxey, Managing Editor (wmaxey@lodging.com). "Lodging.com is a comprehensive travel Web site that focuses on lodging and lodging reservations. Our audience is in the market for a hotel room(s), so the content is geared specifically toward business travelers and leisure travelers based on where they plan to stay." Subject: Travel and lodging. Frequency: Daily. Format: Web magazine/zine, company Web site, and e-mail newsletter. Est. 1994. Circ. 25,000 daily. 70% freelance written. Pays on acceptance. Rights: Exclusive electronic rights and makes work-for-hire assignments. Byline given. Submit seasonal material 2 months in advance. Queries: Post, e-mail. Lead time: 2 months. Mss published average of 1 month after acceptance. Sample: Free on Web site. NONFICTION: Travel. Pays: $50-200 for assigned articles. Mss bought/yr: 130. Length: 400-1,000 wds. How to submit: Query, send published clips. Does NOT want: "A day in the life of a traveling freelancer. Also, not big on area attractions as much as the meat on hotels/b&bs/inns/resorts."

Marryingman.com—www.marryingman.com

9363 Wilshire Blvd. #217, Beverly Hills, CA 90210. Tel: (310)271-7297. Fax: (310)271-4582. Dino Londis, Editor (editors@ungroomd.com). Subject: Men's perspective on marriage. Frequency: Weekly. Format: Web magazine/zine. Est. February 17, 1996. 90% freelance written. Pays on publication. Rights: One-time electronic rights. Byline given. Accepts previously published material. Submit seasonal material 1 month in advance. Queries: E-mail. Reports in 1 week on queries. Lead time: 1 month. Mss published average of 1 month after acceptance. Sample: Free on Web site. Guidelines: On Web site. COLUMNS: Contact: Brian Kahn, Co-Editor (brian@marryingman.com). Pays: 5¢/wd. Mss bought/yr: 50. How to submit: Send published clips. NONFICTION: Essays, how-to, humor. Pays: 5¢/wd. Length: 300-800 wds. How to submit: Send published clips. Does NOT want: "Material not related to marriage or relationships."

Mastering 3D Graphics—www.mastering3dgraphics.com

306 NW El Norte Pkwy., Suite 408, Escondido, CA 92026. Richard Foster, Editor (xtx74@dial.pipex.com). "Guiding principle: to provide the reader with the very best in tutorial and general interest material. This must serve not only to explain precisely the subject of the article, but also to act as inspiration for users to explore further their technical and artistic skills. An article should guide a new user each step of the way and appeal to experienced users alerting them to other ways of doing things. Whilst an article may well be specific to a particular 3D program, some thought should be given to readers who may be following your ideas and attempting to apply the techniques described in another 3D package." Subject: 3D graphics, software. Frequency: Monthly. Byline given. Queries: E-mail. NONFICTION: How-to. Pays: $500/tutorial. Length: 3,600 wds (10 pages). Lower pay for shorter pieces. How to submit: Query. TIPS: "Although we have a core of writers, we are always looking for new contributors with fresh ideas. *Mastering 3D Graphics* is a monthly magazine, alternating between issues with a specific theme (see below) and those devoted to more general 3D matters. The bimonthly issues with a specific theme should be at least 3,600 words with references to 25-30 relevant figures. Query first. Submission/style pointers on Web site."

Millennium Science Fiction & Fantasy Magazine—www.jopoppub.com

JoPop Publications, P.O. Box 8118, Roswell, NM 88202-8118. Diana R. Moreland,

Editor/Managing Editor (submissions@jopoppub.com); S. Joan Popek, Senior/Review and Poetry Editor. "We publish almost all types of SF and fantasy, but in the horror category, we prefer mostly the psychological type (we do not do slash and gash or gore). We cater to an audience from young adult to senior citizens and appeal to the imaginative spirit who believes that mankind can overcome evil." Subject: Speculative fiction. Frequency: Monthly. Format: Web magazine/zine. Est. 1993. Circ. 1,000. 95% freelance written. Pays on acceptance. Rights: One-time electronic rights (option to include one time in the annual hard copy if chosen by our readers as a Best of the Month). Byline given. Accepts previously published material. Submit seasonal material 6 months in advance. Queries: Post, e-mail. Reports in 2-4 weeks on queries. Reports in 2-8 weeks on mss. Lead time: 1-3 months. Mss published average of 2-6 months after acceptance. Sample: Free on Web site. Guidelines: www.jopoppub.com/Guidelines.htm. FICTION: Fantasy, horror, science fiction. Contact: Diana R. Moreland, Fiction Editor (tsuki@iname.com). Pays: 1¢/wd, $20 maximum. Mss bought/yr: 40-50. Length: 50-2,500 wds. How to submit: Send complete ms. Other tips: "Short-shorts and flash fiction." NONFICTION: Contact: S. Joan Popek, Review and Poetry Editor (jopoppub@jopoppub.com). Pays: Nothing (publication and copy of hard copy if it is chosen for the annual). How to submit: Send complete ms. Other: Reviews. POETRY: Free verse, light verse, traditional. Contact: S. Joan Popek, Review and Poetry Editor (jopoppub@jopoppub.com). Pays: Nothing (publication and copy of hard copy if it is chosen for the annual). Mss bought/yr: 20-30. Maximum poems/submission: 3. Maximum line length: 40. Does NOT want: "Prose poetry or haiku."

Millennium Shift—www.millenniumshift.com

Hawkeye Studios, 75 Bernard Dr. NW, Calgary, Alberta T3K 2B5 Canada. Tel: (403)295-3556. Ken J. Davies, Editor (kjd1@millenniumshift.com). "*Millennium Shift* endeavors to be true to its name: that is, it offers content that, individually and collectively, presents the readership with bold, distinct perspective and style, no matter what the subject or genre." Subject: Eclectic subject matter. Frequency: Weekly. Format: Web magazine/zine. Est. January 2000. 80% freelance written. Pays on publication. Kill fee: Full fee paid if accepted for publication. Rights: Nonexclusive right to publish online with minimum 30-day exposure; either *MS* or writer may "pull" the piece after 30 days' exposure. Byline given. Accepts simultaneous submissions and previously published material. Submit seasonal material 1 month in advance. Queries: Post, e-mail, phone. Lead time: 1 month. Mss published average of 1 month after acceptance. Sample: Free on Web site. Guidelines: On Web site. COLUMNS: Feature; Life; Death; Love; Hate; Sex. Pays: U.S.$10 minimum. Mss bought/yr: No limit. How to submit: Send complete ms. FICTION: Adventure, condensed novels, confession, erotica, experimental, fantasy, historical, horror, humorous, mainstream, mystery, novel excerpts, religious, science fiction, serialized novels, slice-of-life vignettes, suspense, western. Pays: U.S.$10 minimum. Mss bought/yr: No set limit. Length: 600 wds maximum. How to submit: Send complete ms. Does NOT want: " 'Formula' romance." Other tips: "I do not publish erotica, per se, but material may contain an erotic element." NONFICTION: Book excerpts, exposé, general interest, historical/nostalgic, humor, inspirational, interview/profile, opinion, personal experience, religious, travel. Pays: U.S.$10 minimum for assigned or unsolicited articles. Mss bought/yr: 12-15. Length: 1,000 wds maximum. How to submit: Send published clips, query. POETRY: Avant-garde, free verse, haiku, light verse, traditional. Pays: U.S.$10 minimum. Mss bought/yr: No set limit. Maximum poems/submission: 3. Maximum line length: 1,000 wds maximum. FILLERS: Anecdotes, facts, newsbreaks (biased and witty commentary only), short humor. Pays: U.S.$10 minimum. Mss bought/yr: No set limit. Length: 1,000 wds maximum. TIPS: "Looking for writing that, though it may appeal to the mainstream reader, is not something that would readily be found in the 'mainstream' magazines or journals."

Mocha Memoirs E-zine of Short Fiction and Poetry—www.mochamemoirs.com

Mocha Memoirs, Inc., 3125 W. Berteau #3, Chicago, IL 60618. Nicole L. Givens, Editor-in-Chief (nicgivens@worldnet.att.net). "*Mocha Memoirs* is geared toward the Internet reader; we strive to offer short stories of 1,000 words or less and poetry of 25 lines or less. *Mocha Memoirs* does not sacrifice plot or characters; each story should be complete within itself. We also offer a workshop and book recommendations to assist writers." Frequency: Monthly. Format: Web magazine/zine. Est. July 1998. Circ. 130 subscribers. 100% freelance written. Pays on acceptance. Rights: *Mocha Memoirs* accepts first-time electronic rights or one-time electronic rights or second serial (reprint) electronic rights. Byline given. Accepts simultaneous submissions. Submit seasonal material 5 months in advance. Queries: Post, e-mail. Reports in 1 week on queries. Reports in 3 weeks on mss. Lead time: 2 months. Mss published average of 2 months after acceptance. Sample: Free on Web site. Guidelines: On Web site or by e-mail. FICTION: Adventure, confession, ethnic, experimental, fantasy, historical, horror, humorous, mainstream, mystery, romance, science fiction, slice-of-life vignettes, suspense. Contact: Lara Kenney, Senior Editor (larakenney@yahoo.com). Pays: $5. Mss bought/yr: 48. Length: 1,000 wds maximum. How to submit: Send complete ms, query. Does NOT want: "Gore (no blood-and-guts type of horror. Prefer psychological horror to gore)." POETRY: Avant-garde, free verse, haiku, light verse, traditional. Contact: Courtney Boland, Poetry Editor (CBoland134@aol.com). Pays: $0. Maximum poems/submission: 10. Maximum line length: 25. Does NOT want: "Poetry that rhymes for the sake of rhyming or poetry that only the poet can interpret."

The MoJo Wire—www.motherjones.com

Mother Jones Online. Foundation for National Progress, 731 Market St., Suite 600, San Francisco, CA 94103. Tel: (415)665-6637. Brooke Biggs, Editor; Vince Beiser, Senior Editor (freelance@motherjones.com). "We are a progressive news magazine, with an international readership. No local stories. No product, book, or movie reviews." Subject: Overlooked and undercovered news stories, especially having to do with criminal justice, the environment, gay/lesbian issues, international issues, corporate wrongdoing and political influence-mongering. Frequency: Weekly. Format: Web magazine. Est. 1993. Circ. 40,000 hits/day. 60% freelance written. Pays on publication. "Does not send reports on manuscripts." Rights: First-time electronic rights. Byline given. Queries: Post, e-mail. Reports in 4 weeks on queries. Lead time: Depends. Mss published average of 1 month after acceptance. Sample: Free on Web site. Guidelines: On Web site. NONFICTION: Essays, exposé, interview/profile, opinion. Pays: $100-750 for assigned articles. Mss bought/yr: 25. Length: 500-2,500 wds. How to submit: Send published clips. Does NOT want: "Product, book, or movie reviews; travel pieces; political screeds; fiction or poetry. Anything already covered heavily in the major U.S. media." Other: News features.

Mountainfreak On-Line Magazine—www.mountainfreak.com/index.html

P.O. Box 4149, Telluride, CO 81435. Tel: (970)728-9731. Fax: (970)728-9821. Suzanne Cheavens, Editor (editor@mountainfreak.com). "*Mountainfreak On-Line* is 'for a growing number of readers dedicated to helping shift the world's consciousness toward better stewardship of the Earth, social, cultural, religious, and racial tolerance, alternative healing, and having a darn good time (and spiritual communion) in the temple that is the natural world.' " Subject: Those interested in mountain living, sports, culture, art, music, politics, alternative health, and sustainable living. Frequency: Quarterly. Format: Web magazine/zine. Pays on publication. Kill fee: Only for assigned pieces. Rights: First North American serial rights. Byline given. Accepts simultaneous submissions and previously published material. Submit seasonal material 1 month in advance. Queries: E-mail. Lead time: 1 month. Sample: Free on Web site. Guidelines: On Web site. COLUMNS: Feature: An epic adventure, spiritual journey, or in-depth investigation into the human experience; Smoke Signals: Political and environmental news from the extended Mountain Community, 50-1,500 wds; Touch the Earth: Sustainable building and product information, herbal remedies, and organic gardening, 250-1,500 wds; query Associate Editor Cameron Brooks for this section (cameron@mountainfilm.org); Yummy Grub: Tasty and healthy recipes; Good Biz: Profiles of companies that successfully produce quality products while maintaining conscientious business ethics, 500-1,000 wds; Playground: Seasonal guides for cool spots and treading lightly while there, 100-2,000 wds. Pays: 10-25¢/published wd. FICTION: Pays: 10-25¢/published wd with a $500 maximum. Length: 1,000-4,000 wds. How to submit: Query. NONFICTION: Pays: 10-25¢/wd for department pieces. Length: 2,000-3,000 wds. POETRY: Haiku, traditional, avant-garde, free verse, light verse. Pays: $25 for poetry. TIPS: "We are eclectic and decidedly nonmainstream."

Moveo Angelus—www.moveoangelus.com

Literary Arts. Submissions, 31450 NE Bell Rd., Sherwood, OR 97140. Editor (editor@ moveoangelus.com). Subject: *Moveo Angelus* is looking for poetry, prose, and short fiction. We are open to all forms and subjects. Frequency: Biannual. Format: Web magazine and print. Pays on publication. Rights: First-time electronic rights and first print. Byline given. Queries: Post, e-mail. Reports in 2 months on queries. Sample: Free on Web site. Guidelines: www.moveoangelus.com/submission.html. FICTION: Pays: $50. How to submit: Send complete ms. POETRY: Pays: $25.

Moviebytes.com—www.moviebytes.com

Screenwriting Contests & Markets Online. Frederick Mensch Multimedia, 254 S. Greenwood Ave., Palatine, IL 60067. Frederick Mensch, Editor (fmensch@moviebytes.com). "We publish on the Web continuously; our e-mail newsletter is distributed biweekly." Subject: Screenplay MARKETING issues. Frequency: Other. Format: Online directory and e-mail newsletter. Est. July 1997. Circ. 8,000 minimum. 10% freelance written. Pays on publication. Rights: Exclusive electronic rights. We'll also publish electronic reprints of articles published elsewhere, but these are published for promotional consideration only; no cash payment. Byline given. Accepts previously published material. Queries: E-mail. Reports in 1 week on queries. Reports in 1 week on mss. Lead time: 1 month. Mss published average of 1 month after acceptance. Sample: Free by e-mail. Guidelines: Visit Web site for sample articles. NON-FICTION: How-to, interview/profile, personal experience. Pays: $50. Mss bought/yr: 10-15. Length: 500 wds minimum. How to submit: query. Does NOT want: "Articles about the craft of writing, book reviews, opinion pieces." TIPS: "We're interested in marketing issues exclusively: how to bring a screenplay to market."

Myria Media Publications—www.myria.com

Myria, ePregnancy, Interactive Parent. Myria Media, Inc., P.O. Box 29, Kingston, OH 45644. Tel: (925)947-6667. Nancy Price, Editor (feedback@myria.com); Betsy Gartrell-Judd, Managing Editor. "*Myria:* For women who are mothers. Travel, arts, fashion, health, craft/hobbies, home, work, time for you. *ePregnancy:* Topics related to preconception, pregnancy, and postpartum. *Interactive Parent:* Parenting issues. Especially seeking articles dealing with children over the age of 5, particularly teens." Frequency: Weekly. Format: Web magazine/zine. Est. *Myria* November 1998, *ePregnancy* April 1999, *IP* November 1999. 50% freelance written. Pays on acceptance. Kill fee: 20%. Rights: First-time electronic rights. We buy first online rights, exclusive for 3 months, and pay on publication (generally anytime between 1 week to 2 months). Additional details will be discussed with individual writers. Byline given. Accepts previously published material. Submit seasonal material 3 months in advance. Queries: E-mail. Reports in 1-3 weeks on queries. Reports in 1-3 weeks on mss. Mss published average of 1 month after acceptance. Sample: Free on Web site. Guidelines: www.myria.com/submissions.htm. NONFICTION: Book excerpts, essays, general interest, historical/nostalgic, how-to, humor, inspirational, opinion, photo feature, travel. Contact: Nancy Price. Pays: $10-25 for assigned articles. Mss bought/yr: 100. Length: 500-2,500 wds (depending on subject and on a case-by-case basis, may be serialized). How to submit: Query, send published clips. Does NOT want: "Personal essays or opinion pieces at this time." Other:

Also reviews. TIPS: "We are looking for information from experts in a variety of fields as well as features written by journalists and others with appropriate writing skills and style. Our sites are primarily freelance written. We like articles based on research and interviews, presented with a friendly, accessible approach, and written for our audience. We work with some previously unpublished writers. If you're interested in writing for us, please e-mail us at feedback@myria.com. If you are interested in article assignments, please e-mail us your query and a list of links to published clips. If you are writing as an expert, please detail your relevant experience. Spec work: You may include your article for review, but please paste the article in the body of your e-mail message; do not send it as an attachment. Please also include a brief bio with your submission."

National Neighborhood News—www.neighborhoodamerica.com

Hot Issues. Neighborhood America, 4380 Gulf Shore Blvd. N., Suite 808, Naples, FL 34103. Fax: (941)403-4835. Christina Morrow, Content Coordinator (hotissues@neighborhoodamerica.com). Subject: Land use planning/environmental—related to neighborhoods. Frequency: Weekly. Format: Web magazine/zine. Est. May 1999. 75% freelance written. Pays on acceptance. "Send complete contact information, a bio, sample of writing, and query." Rights: Archival. Accepts simultaneous submissions. Submit seasonal material 1 month in advance. Queries: E-mail. Reports in 1 month on queries. Lead time: 1 month. Mss published average of 1-2 months after acceptance. Sample: Free on Web site. Guidelines: On Web site or e-mail. NONFICTION: Interview/profile. Pays: $300 for assigned or unsolicited articles. Length: 500-1,000 wds. How to submit: Query, send published clips. Does NOT want: "Fiction, opinion." Other: Land use planning/environmental issues in local neighborhoods.

netauthor.org—www.netauthor.org

An Educational Opportunity for Writers on the Internet. Net Author, P.O. Box 79765, Houston, TX 77279-9765. Rhonna J. Robbins-Sponaas, Managing Editor; Robert Marcom, Publisher (moderator@netauthor.org). "Our perspective on the writing process: Writing is a lifelong process that takes place in a cultural context, and has its own conventions and rules. Relationships count—the world of writing is populated by people: readers, other writers, editors and publishers, to name a few. Grammar and punctuation count—these are the primary tools of the craft. Without a firm command of each, no writer can hope to be taken seriously."

Subject: E-publishing. Nonprofit, unincorporated. Frequency: Updated as new material is available, weekly, minimum. Format: Web magazine/zine. Est. September 1999. Circ. 3,500 hits/month. 50% freelance written. Pays on acceptance. Rights: Author retains all rights. We ask for permission to maintain the article for as long as our readers find it useful (as judged by hits in the article). Byline given. Accepts simultaneous submissions. Queries: E-mail. Reports in 1 week on queries. Reports in 4 weeks on mss. Lead time: 1 month. Mss published average of 1-2 months after acceptance. Sample: Free on Web site. Guidelines: On Web site. NONFICTION: Pays: $5. Mss bought/yr: 42. How to submit: Query. Other: Essays on the craft of writing, literary philosophy.

Neverworlds Unique Fiction—neverworlds.com

Neverworlds Press. Dr. Jonathon Sullivan, Editor (jsulliva@med.wayne.edu); Marilyn K. Fuller, Managing Editor; Mr. Kevin McPherson, Editor-in-Chief (editor@neverworlds.com). Subject: Science fiction, horror, fantasy, slipstream, magical realism, speculative poetry. Frequency: Quarterly. Format: Web magazine/zine. Est. April 1998. Circ. Unknown—Webzine, free distribution. 90% freelance written. Pays on publication. Kill fee: 50% or $10. Rights: First-time electronic rights. Byline given. Accepts previously published material. Submit seasonal material 4 months in advance. Queries: E-mail. Reports in 1-2 weeks on queries. Reports in 6-8 weeks on mss. Lead time: 4 months. Mss published average of 3-4 months after acceptance. Sample: Free on Web site. Guidelines: On Web site. FICTION: Experimental, fantasy, horror, science fiction. Pays: $5-25. Mss bought/yr: 20-30. Length: 25,000 maximum. How to submit: Send complete ms. Does NOT want: "Fantasy creatures, Adam and Eve stories, shared/media universes (e.g., Star Trek)." POETRY: Avant-garde, haiku, free verse, light verse, traditional. Pays: $5-10. Mss bought/yr: 8-10. Maximum poems/submission: 5. Does NOT want: "No traditional subjects—we want daring poetry that plumbs the depths and extremes of human experience, that uses as its subject matter the horrible, the terrifying, the mind-blowing, the awesome. If you can write haikus about genetic engineering, free verse about quantum chromatics, couplets about succubi, and sonnets about space travel, you're our kind of poet." TIPS: "We want thoughtful, literate, mind-provoking speculative fiction and horror with fresh approaches, complex and interesting characters, and mature prose. If you don't read SF, you can't write SF."

On the Bright Side—www.onthebrightside.com

3120 Kerry Lane, Costa Mesa, CA 92626. Tel: (714)545-6044. Sheryl L. Cooley, Editor-in-Chief (feedback@onthebrightside.com). "*On the Bright Side* highlights nonfiction stories (and some poetry) of common man (including men, women, children, and groups) doing uncommon things, stories/poetry that illustrate strength of character and/or describe instances of people making a difference in others' lives. Stories should remind readers that, despite the horror that we read about in the papers and see on the news daily, there are millions of people out there making our world a better place, through either their commitment, self-sacrifice, or personal triumphs. This magazine is the place to read about them." Frequency: Every 6 weeks. Format: Web magazine. Est. January 2000. Circ. expect 10,000 by year end. 70% freelance written. Pays on acceptance. Kill fee: 100%. Rights: One-time electronic rights. Byline given. Accepts simultaneous submissions. Submit seasonal material 3 months in advance. Queries: Post, e-mail. Reports in 2 weeks on queries. Reports in 3 weeks on mss. Lead time: 3 months. Mss published average of 3 months after acceptance. Sample: Free on Web site. Guidelines: On Web site. COLUMNS: Book Review—Slants: Nonfictional, positive experience(s) or advice mixed with experience. Length: 750 wds. Pays: $25. Mss bought/yr: 8. How to submit: Query. NONFICTION: General interest, humor, inspirational. Pays: $35 for unsolicited articles. Mss bought/yr: 60. Length: 750-2,100 wds. How to submit: Query, send complete ms. Does NOT want: "Religious testimonials." Other: Stories of survival, success, personal strength/character, reaching out to help others, good deeds, unsung heros. POETRY: Free verse, haiku, light verse, traditional. Contact: Sheryl Cooley, Editor-in-Chief (feedback@onthebrightside.com). Pays: $25. Mss bought/yr: 8. Maximum poems/submission: 4. Line length: 5-20. Does NOT want: "Fictional poetry. Poem must reflect a real-life experience." TIPS: "Looking for well-researched, well-written manuscripts. Writers should note that these should be nonfiction stories, not fictionalized versions of fact. Poems, on the other hand, will, by nature, probably be fictionalized versions of fact. Keep in mind the upbeat nature of the magazine."

Orato—www.orato.com

Tel: (604)608-1070. Fax: (604)605-8262. Editor (editor@orato.com). "Electronic publication providing a place for newsmakers and ordinary people to tell their own stories.

First-person stories that will inspire, anger, and delight readers while lending perspective to issues of the day. Can be based on writer's own experience, or writer can help someone else tell their story." Pays 30 days prior to publication. Rights: Exclusive publication rights for 60 days from our date of publication in *Orato*, and the right to license or syndicate your work. Unless otherwise agreed upon, we'll pay you 25% of any such payments we receive. Byline given. Accepts simultaneous submissions. Queries: E-mail. Guidelines: On Web site. NONFICTION: Interview/profile, personal experience. Pays: $100-400/article. How to submit: Query. TIPS: "We aren't interested in traditional feature stories. Our writers help people tell their own stories by transcribing their interviews and composing tight narratives, purely from those words. Edit for brevity, focus, and structure. Make the story sing, but don't paraphrase or add color in the main body of the story. Respect the integrity of your subject's message but don't lose focus. *Orato*'s first issue will go online Winter 2000. If accepted, ensure final piece is edited for brevity, vitality, and libel. Include sidebar info and provide balanced background information (50-200 wds) on story subjects and issues with which they are involved. Written permission from story subjects a must."

OrpheusRomance—www.OrpheusRomance.com

> Greater Love Stories. Orpheus Romance (A division of Red Merle, Ltd.), Pinegrove P.O. Box 64004, Oakville, Ontario L6K 2C0 Canada. Marybeth O'Halloran, Editor; Maralyn Ellis, Managing Editor (publisher@orpheusromance.com); Stacey Doherty, Submissions Editor. "*Orpheus Romance* publishes love stories that often do not fit the conventional 'formula.' " Subject: Romance fiction. Frequency: Weekly. Format: Web magazine/zine, e-books (PDF and RocketEdition). Est. October 1996. Circ. 25,000. Pays advance on acceptance. Kill fee: Advance. Rights: Individually negotiated. Byline given. Accepts simultaneous submissions and previously published material. Submit seasonal material 4 months in advance. Queries: Phone, post, e-mail, fax. Reports in 1 month on queries. Reports in 2-3 months on mss. Lead time: 2 months. Mss published average of 6-18 months after acceptance. Sample: Free on Web site. Guidelines: On Web site or by e-mail. FICTION: Romance. Contact: Maralyn Ellis, Publisher (publisher@orpheusromance.com). Pays: $25 plus royalties. Mss bought/yr: 20 minimum. Length: 5,000-75,000 wds. How to submit: Query, send published clips. Does NOT want: "Nonromance." Other tips: "Sensual romance; new light romance."

Outdoor Nova Scotia—www.outdoorns.com

P.O. Box 1883, Liverpool, Novia Scotia B0T 1K0 Canada. Fax: (902)354-2624. Vaughn Mullen, Editor (info@outdoorns.com). Subject: Outdoor activities. Frequency: Monthly. Format: Web magazine, online directory, and company Web site. Est. June 1995. Circ. 60,000/month. 90% freelance written. Pays on publication. Rights: First-time electronic rights. Byline given. Submit seasonal material 2 months in advance. Queries: post, e-mail. Lead time: 1 month. Mss published average of 1 month after acceptance. NONFICTION: Book excerpts, essays, exposé, general interest, historical/nostalgic, how-to, interview/profile, new product, opinion, personal experience, photo feature, travel. Pays: $40-220. Mss bought/yr: 30. Length: 600-1,200 wds. How to submit: Query.

Pantarbe.com—www.pantarbe.com

Your Muse's Creative Domain for Art, Myth, and Alchemy. BAM Works/Webcraft, P.O. Box 21809, Seattle, WA 98111-3809. Tel: (206)283-8090, box 1. Benjamin A Miller, Editor and Domain Administrator (editor@pantarbe.com). "*Pantarbe.com* is ultimately about living as a creative person in an ever-changing world." Frequency: Bimonthly. Format: Web magazine/zine, online directory, e-mail newsletter. Est. September 2000. Circ. 500 hits/month. 90% freelance written. Pays on acceptance. Kill fee: 25%. Rights: First-time electronic rights or second serial electronic rights. Byline given. Accepts simultaneous submissions and previously published material. Submit seasonal material 6 months in advance. Queries: Post, e-mail, phone. Reports in 6 weeks on queries. Reports in 3 months on mss. Lead time: 6 months. Mss published average of 6 months after acceptance. Sample: On Web site; 2 months free access for contributors during initial posting; public trial membership is 1 month. Guidelines: www.pantarbe.com/info/submit/index.htm or e-mail submit@pantarbe.com. COLUMNS: The Arts; Creative Processes; Mythic Images; Mythopoesis; Health; Prosperity. Pays: $25-100. Mss bought/yr: 54. How to submit: Query. FICTION: Adventure, confession, erotica, ethnic, experimental, fantasy, historical, horror, humorous, mainstream, mystery, novel excerpts, religious, romance, science fiction, slice-of-life vignettes, suspense, western. Pays: $25-100. Mss bought/yr: 6. How to submit: Query. Other tips: "Erotica: Must be tasteful and appropriate to this site." NONFICTION: Book excerpts, essays, exposé, historical/nostalgic, how-to, humor, inspirational, interview/profile, new product, opinion, personal experience, photo feature, technical. Pays: $25-100. Mss bought/yr: 12. How to submit: Query. Other: News, announcements, reviews. POETRY: Pays: $5-25. Mss bought/yr: 60. Maximum poems/submission: 3. Other tips: "I look for poems with good use of figurative language and imagery, and that explore human issues meaningful to the poet and his/her culture—or personal mythology." FILLERS: Queries considered: Anecdotes, facts, gags to be illustrated by in-house, cartoonist, newsbreaks, short humor. Pays: $5-15. Mss bought/yr: 60. TIPS: "Length of pieces: Maximum 20 double-spaced pages with size 10 font; 50KB file of unformatted ASCII text. We also accept scripts for stage, screen, or radio. Short one-act plays or self-contained excerpts from larger scripts. Looking for exploration of human issues through character interaction and development, and drama from change with creative resolutions. Buys 12/yr. $25-100/script."

Parenting Today's Teen—www.parentingteens.com

P.O. Box 11864, Olympia, WA 98508. Tel: (360)753-2965. Fax: (360)753-2965. Diana Kathrein, Publisher/Editor (editor@parentingteens.com). "We prefer our editorial to be down-to-earth, not preachy or clinical. The majority of our readers are parents, and we like to communicate to them parent-to-parent." Subject: Parenting teenagers. Frequency: Biweekly. Format: Web magazine/zine. Est. September 1996. 80% freelance written. Pays on publication. Rights: One-time electronic rights and second serial (reprint) electronic rights and makes work-for-hire assignments. Byline given. Accepts simultaneous submissions and previously published material. Submit seasonal material 2 months in advance. Queries: Post, e-mail, fax. Reports in 1 month on queries. Reports in 1 month on mss. Lead time: 2-3 months. Mss published average of 1-3 months after acceptance. Sample: Free on Web site. Guidelines: On Web site. COLUMNS: Communication: Advice for Parents on communicating better with their teen, 450-700 wds; Education: Advice for parents about education and their teen, 450-700 words; Teen Voices: Written by teens as a conduit to bridge the parent/teen communication gap, 450-700 wds; Single Parenting: Advice and support for single parents and their unique parenting issues, 450-750 wds; Feature Articles: Open topics dealing with parenting a teenager; Editorial: Open topics dealing with parenting a teenager. Pays: $10-25 reprints. Mss bought/yr: 6-12. How to submit: Query. NONFICTION: Book excerpts, essays, general interest, how-to, humor, inspirational, interview/profile, opinion, personal experience, religious. Pays: $25 for assigned articles; $10-25 for reprints or unsolicited articles. Mss bought/yr: 12. Length: 450-1,000 wds. How to submit: Query. Does NOT want: "Poetry, fiction, anything that duplicates our columnists' topics." Other: Book excerpts: Nonpaying; How-to: Anything pertaining to the parent/teen relationship. TIPS: "Query first. We are easy to approach and work frequently with new, unpublished writers."

Peridot Books—www.peridotbooks.com

Online Magazine of Sci/Fi, Fantasy & Horror. Peridot Consulting, Inc., 32 Pennsylvania Ave., Stratford, NJ 08084. Ty Drago, Editor (submissions@peridotbooks.com). "*Peridot Books* is an e-zine for writers. It offers articles geared toward published and unpublished authors, as well as links and resources for writers." Subject: Science fiction, fantasy, and horror as well as nonfiction articles on the art of writing. Frequency: Quarterly. Format: Web magazine/zine. Est. June 1, 1998. 75% freelance written. Pays on publication. Kill fee: 25%. Rights: One-time electronic rights. Byline given. Accepts simultaneous submissions and previously published material. Submit seasonal material 3 months in advance. Queries: E-mail. Reports in 1 week on queries. Reports in 4 weeks on mss. Lead time: 3 months. Mss published average of 2 months after acceptance. Sample: Free on Web site. Guidelines: On Web site. FICTION: Adventure, fantasy, horror, science fiction. Pays: 5¢/wd, $25 maximum. Mss bought/yr: 24. Length: 10,000 wds maximum. How to submit: Send complete ms. NONFICTION: How-to, inspirational. Pays: 5¢/wd. Mss bought/yr: 10 maximum. Length: 2,000 wds maximum. How to submit: Send complete ms. TIPS: "We look for solid characterization, clever plots, often with little twists at the end. Avoid old ideas and hackneyed plotlines. Be original, readable, and entertaining!"

Pif Magazine—www.pifmagazine.com

The Starting Point for the Literary e-Press. Pif, LLC, PMB #248, 4820 Yelm Hwy. SE, Suite B, Lacey, WA 98503-4903. Camille Renshaw, Senior Editor of Content Development (camille@pifmagazine.com); Richard Luck, Managing Editor of Technical Development. "We're looking for high-quality writing that uses hyperlinks. We want our articles and literature to truly serve as a 'starting point' to anyone interested in literature on the Web." Subject: Writing and literature, literary focus. Frequency: Monthly. Format: Web magazine/zine. Est. October 1995. Circ. 100,000 original readers/month; roughly a million impressions/month. 95% freelance written. Pays on publication. Rights: First-time electronic rights (and these are exclusive for 60 days). Byline given. Accepts simultaneous submissions. Submit seasonal material 3 months in advance. Queries: E-mail. Reports in 2-4 weeks on queries. Reports in 4 weeks on mss. Lead time: 1-2 months. Mss published average of 2 months after acceptance. Sample: Free on Web site. Guidelines: On Web site. COLUMNS: One-on-One: Interviews with authors, poets, editors, 1,500-4,000 wds; Book Lovers: Literary book reviews, 1,000-2,500 wds; Zine-o-Rama: Zine/literary Web site reviews, 500-1,300 wds. Contact: Michael E. Burgin, Commentary Editor (michael@pifmagazine.com). Pays: $5-100. Mss bought/yr: 100. How to submit: Send published clips, send complete ms. FICTION: Erotica, experimental, novel excerpts. Contact: Jen Bergmark, Fiction Editor (jen@pifmagazine.com). Pays: $50 for micro fiction; $200 for all other fiction. Mss bought/yr: 30. Length: 4,000 wds maximum. How to submit: Send complete ms. Other tips: "Micro fiction, prose poems, hyperfictions, and other literary or fine fiction." NONFICTION: Book excerpts, essays, how-to, interview/profile, opinion. Contact: Michael E. Burgin, Commentary Editor (michael@pifmagazine.com). Pays: $5-100. Mss bought/yr: 100. Length: 250-4,000 wds. How to submit: Send published clips, send complete ms. POETRY: Avant-garde, free verse, haiku, traditional. Contact: Anne Doolittle, Poetry Editor (anne@pifmagazine.com). Pays: $50/poem. Mss bought/yr: 60. Maximum poems/submission: 5. TIPS: "Submit using our submissions page at www.pifmagazine.com/rules.shtml. Editorial contact (submissions): Submissions should be sent directly to editors of specific depts. Columns and nonfiction are known as the 'Commentary Department' at Pif."

Planet Relish E-Zine—www.planetrelish.com

The Web's First Speculative Humor Magazine. You Can't Be Serious Publications. Mark Rapacioli, Publisher/Editor (editor@planetrelish.com). "*Planet Relish E-Zine* publishes only short stories of speculative humor (humorous science fiction, fantasy, or horror)." Frequency: Monthly. Format: Web magazine/zine. Est. April 1999. 100% freelance written. Pays on publication. Rights: One-time exclusive Web rights (other electronic rights held by writer). Byline given. Accepts simultaneous submissions and previously published material. Submit seasonal material 4 months in advance. Queries: E-mail. Reports in 1 week maximum on queries. Reports in 1-3 weeks on mss. Lead time: 3 months. Mss published average of 10 weeks after

acceptance. Sample: Free on Web site. Guidelines: www.planetrelish.com/submissio
n.html or e-mail editor@planetrelish.com. FICTION: Fantasy, horror, humorous,
novel excerpts, science fiction. Pays: $5 plus free banner ad for 30 days. Mss bought/
yr: 60. Length: 5,280 wds maximum for fiction; 1,000 wds maximum for "Fegh-
oots." How to submit: Send complete ms. Does NOT want: "Commentary on
politicians and sex, ethnic humor, rape scenes, violence against animals (except
cockroaches, who deserve to be squished so hard that their guts skitter across the
floor), and Mike the Headless Chicken poems." TIPS: "The First Rule of Relish:
MAKE ME LAUGH! All other rules are secondary. Published works must be of a
literary, speculative nature. Your writing style should grab the reader's attention. It
isn't enough to toss a few funny jokes together and call it a story. 'Feghoot' stories
(limit 1,000 words, but the shorter the better) must end in a very bad, groan-
worthy pun. Other stories (limit 5,280 words; again, shorter is better) may have
any type of humor, including slapstick, black comedy, light humor, biting satire,
parody, etc. Preferred submission format is in the body of an e-mail, single-spaced,
but double-spaced between paragraphs. E-mail attachments (MS Word, text, or
RTF files) are also acceptable."

Plot Line Foyer—home.att.net/~plotlinefoyer

Seeks any subject/genre except children's, religious, occult, gay/lesbian. Pays $10 for
fiction on acceptance, $5 for nonfiction and poetry. Guidelines: home.att.net/~plotl
inefoyer/submit.html.

The Quill Magazine Quarterly—www.thequill.com

The Quarterly E-Zine for Beginning Writers. Austin Aerospace, Ltd., 2900 Warden
Ave., P.O. Box 92207, Toronto, Ontario M1W 3Y9 Canada. Tel: (416)410-0277.
Fax: (416)293-6148. Charlotte Austin, Editor/Managing Editor (austin@thequill.c
om); Sue Elliot, Assistant Editor (sueelliot@thequill.com). "For beginning and established writers. Use a concise, jounalistic style. Feature articles should answer the
particular concerns of beginning writers. No first-person accounts, essays, poetry,
or personal experience. The magazine exists to provide timely information and
assistance to writers starting out on the arduous road to publishing." Frequency:
Quarterly. Format: Online directory, PDF format. Est. August 1, 1998. Circ. 2,700.
100% freelance written. Pays on acceptance. Rights: First-time electronic rights.
Byline given. Queries: E-mail. Reports in 1 week on queries. Reports in 2 weeks

on mss. Lead time: 3 months. Mss published average of 2 months after acceptance. Sample: Free on Web site. Guidelines: On Web site. COLUMNS: The Craft of Writing: Technical, 500-1,200 wds; Book Review: Reviews, 350-450 wds. Contact: Sue Elliot. Pays: $25-30/column, $5/review. Mss bought/yr: 36-70. How to submit: Query. FICTION: Mainstream. Contact: Charlotte Austin. Pays: $25-30. Mss bought/yr: 20. Length: 800-1,200 wds. How to submit: Send complete ms. Does NOT want: "Experimental fiction, science fiction, or mystery." NONFICTION: How-to, interview/profile, technical, travel. Contact: Charlotte Austin. Pays: $50-60/article. Mss bought/yr: 30-40. Length: 800-1,200 wds. How to submit: Query first. Does NOT want: "Personal experience, humor, opinion, essays, 'how I sold my first novel/article.' " TIPS: "Available in .pdf format by paid subscription. Query letters should propose a well-thought-out article with a specific slant, not simply a topic to explore. Beginning writers are knowledgeable and make up a demanding market. We strive to present timely information, good fiction from new writers, and technical columns on the use of language. Through the magazine, we try to promote and teach writing excellence."

Realtor Magazine Online—www.realtormag.com

The online business tool for real estate professionals. National Association of REALTORS®, 430 N. Michigan Ave., Chicago, IL 60611-4087. Fax: (312)670-2962. Christina Hoffmann Spira, Managing Editor (Choffmann@realtors.org). "Yes, our audience are real estate professionals, NOT consumers. They're interested in trends and how-to information that affect their business practice. They want tips they can use today." Subject: Real estate: Commercial, residential, business practice, selling and marketing, technology. Frequency: Weekly. Format: Web magazine. Est. Late 1997. 40% freelance written. Pays 45 days after acceptance. Kill fee: 20%. Rights: All rights. Byline given. Accepts simultaneous submissions. Submit seasonal material 2-3 months in advance. Queries: Post, e-mail, fax. Lead time: 2-3 months. Mss published average of 3 months after acceptance. Sample: Free on Web site. Guidelines: E-mail. NONFICTION: How-to, interview/profile. Pays: Depends on wd count; assign a range, such as $700-900. Writer receives $900 for stellar piece. Wd count is 900 in this case. Mss bought/yr: 5. Length: 500-1,000 wds. How to submit: Query, send published clips. Other: News and trends. TIPS: "Understand the market."

RecursiveAngel—www.RecursiveAngel.com

An excursion into the poetics of the mind. Aslan Enterprises, 25 Acacia Dr., Hopewell, NY 12533. David Hunter Sutherland, Managing Editor (dsutherland@calldei.com); Gene Doty or Arianna Fischer, Poetry Editors; Paul Kloppenborg, Fiction Editor; Cindy Duhe, Art Editor; Anita Gonzalez, Editorial Assistant. "*RA* looks for the subtle and often subconscious motivations behind a writer's work. This can include the metaphysical, philosophical, abstract, and experimental. Extra consideration is given to works that integrate technology and the ever growing communications medium." Subject: Poetry, fiction, art. Frequency: 3 times/year. Format: Web magazine/zine. Est. March 1991. Circ. 10,000 monthly. 90% freelance written. Pays on publication. Kill fee: $40 (on art). Rights: First-time electronic rights. Submit seasonal material 6 months in advance. Queries: E-mail. Reports in 1 week on queries. Reports in 4 weeks on mss. Lead time: 3 months. Mss published average of 3 months after acceptance. Sample: Free on Web site. Guidelines: www.RecursiveAngel.com/policy.htm. FICTION: Experimental. Contact: Paul Kloppenborg, Fiction Editor (paul.kloppenborg@rmit.edu.au). Pays: $15. Mss bought/yr: 6-8. Length: 1,000-1,500 wds. How to submit: Send complete ms. POETRY: Avant-garde. Contact: Gene Doty or Arianna Fischer, Poetry Editors. Pays: $10. Mss bought/yr: 30-40. Maximum poems/submission: 5. Does NOT want: "Light verse." Other tips: Experimental.

Reunions magazine—www.reunionsmag.com

Reunions magazine, Inc., P.O. Box 11727, Milwaukee, WI 53211-0727. Fax: (414)263-6331. Edith Wagner, Editor (reunions@execpc.com). "*Reunions* magazine is the only periodical devoted to reunion organizers—individuals who are committed to their family, class, or military group. Our goal is to capture, share, and, when necessary, create information about reunions to help our readers make informed decisions." Subject: Family, class, and military reunions. Frequency: Quarterly. Format: Web magazine/zine. 75% freelance written. "I'm swamped, overwhelmed, and unable to respond sometimes for a year, BUT I do get back to everyone and read everything we receive. When I was submitting stuff, my biggest frustration was hearing nothing, so I'm committed to at least acknowledging everything we receive." Byline given. Accepts simultaneous submissions and previously published material. Submit seasonal material 6-12 months in advance. Queries:

Post, e-mail, fax. Lead time: 9-24 months. Sample: Free on Web or $2 by mail. Guidelines: On Web site or send SASE. NONFICTION: Book excerpts, general interest, historical/nostalgic, how-to, humor, inspirational, interview/profile, new product, personal experience, photo feature, technical, travel. Pays: $25-40. Mss bought/yr: 25-30. Length: 2,000-2,500 wds is often too long. How to submit: Query, send published clips, send complete ms. FILLERS: Anecdotes, facts, newsbreaks, short humor. Must be primarily about family, class, or military reunions. Pays: $5. Mss bought/yr: 30. TIPS: "Just keep our specific subject matter in mind. We prefer tight, well-written pieces to lengthy ones."

Robb Report—theluxurysource.com

Magazine for the Luxury Lifestyle. Luxury Media, One Acton Place, Acton, MA 01720. Tel: (978)795-3000. Steven Castle, Editor; Larry Bean, Managing Editor; Samantha Poste, Editorial Assistant (samanthap@luxurymedia.com). "Knowledge of the luxury lifestyle." Subject: Luxury lifestyle. Frequency: Monthly. Format: Web magazine/zine. Circ. 100,000 minimum. 60% freelance written. Pays on publication. Kill fee: 50%. Rights: All rights. Byline given. Submit seasonal material 5 months in advance. Queries: Post. Reports in 1-2 months on queries. Reports in 2 months on mss. Lead time: 4 months. Mss published average of 4-6 months after acceptance. COLUMNS: Travel, sport, investments, golf, food, wine and spirits, cigars, fashion, jewelry, watches, and more. Contact: Steven Castle, Editor. Pays: $1/wd maximum. How to submit: Query, send published clips. NONFICTION: General interest, how-to, interview/profile, new product, technical, travel. Contact: Steven Castle. Pays: $1/wd maximum for assigned or unsolicited articles. Mss bought/yr: Varies. Length: 200-1,500 wds. How to submit: Query, send published clips. Other: Automobiles, airplanes, golf, fashion, food, and wine, etc. Anything dealing with luxury lifestyle.

Romancer—www.iReadRomance.com/Romancer

Romance Reader Online 'zine. iRR—iReadRomance (Division of Red Merle, Ltd.), Pinegrove P.O. Box 64004, Oakville, Ontario L6K 2C0 Canada. Tel: (905)337-2188. Fax: (905)337-0999. Lynn Fraser, Editor; Stacey Doherty, Submissions Editor; Maralyn Ellis, Publisher (publisher@ireadromance.com). "Friendly, upbeat information of interest to romance readers." Frequency: Monthly. Format: Web magazine/zine. Est. December 1996. Circ. 25,000. Pays on publication. Kill fee:

Advance. Rights: Individually negotiated. Byline given. Accepts simultaneous submissions and previously published material. Submit seasonal material 4 months in advance. Queries: Phone, e-mail, post, fax. Reports in 2 months on queries. Reports in 4 months on mss. Lead time: 2 months. Mss published average of 4 months after acceptance. Sample: Free on Web site. Guidelines: On Web site or e-mail. COLUMNS: eRomance: Romance fiction online news, average 300 wds; In Review: Reviews of print/e-books/movies/etc., average 300 wds. Contact: Maralyn Ellis. Pays: $10-25. Mss bought/yr: 10. How to submit: Send complete ms, send published clips. FICTION: Condensed novels, romance. Contact: Maralyn Ellis. Pays: $25-125. Mss bought/yr: 12. Length: 1,000-2,500 wds. How to submit: Send published clips, send complete ms. NONFICTION: Book excerpts, general interest, how-to, humor, interview/profile, new product, opinion, personal experience, photo feature. Contact: Maralyn Ellis. Pays: $15-50 assigned; $10-45 unsolicited. Mss bought/yr: 10. How to submit: Send published clips, send complete ms. Does NOT want: "Highly controversial topics; items not of interest to romance readers." FILLERS: Anecdotes, facts, gags to be illustrated by cartoonist, newsbreaks, short humor. Contact: Maralyn Ellis. Pays: $10-25. Mss bought/yr: 10. Length: 100-500 wds.

The Romantic Bower E-Zine—www.theromanticbower.com

Enchantment Unlimited, Inc., P.O. Box 429, Sanger, TX 76266. Tel: (940)637-2727. Fax: (940)637-2726. Chris Bossert, Managing Editor (trbchris@aol.com); Marcia Kiser, Senior Aquisitions Editor (trbmarcia@aol.com). "For readers 14-100." Frequency: Monthly. Format: Web magazine/e-mail newsletter. Est. February 1997. Circ. 40,000 monthly. 95% freelance written. Pays 2-3 months after publication. Kill fee: 25% or $50. Rights: First-time electronic rights (one-fourth the stated payment), second serial (reprint) electronic rights (one-fourth the stated payment), all rights for 1 year (full payment). Also makes work-for-hire assignments. Byline given. Accepts previously published material. Submit seasonal material 6 months in advance. Queries: Post, e-mail, fax, phone. Lead time: 6-12 months. Sample: Send U.S.$1, Can.$1.50, or $3 Int'l postage. Guidelines: On Web site. COLUMNS: Books; movie, video, actor, actress interviews contracted; Table for Two. Contact: Chris Bossert (trbchris@aol.com). Pays: Contracted and negotiated. Mss bought/yr: 50 minimum. How to submit: Query. FICTION: Adventure, condensed novels, confession, ethnic, fantasy, historical, horror, humorous, mainstream, mystery, novel excerpts, romance, science fiction, slice-of-life vignettes, serialized novels, suspense, western. Contact: Marcia Kiser (trbmarcia@aol.com). Pays: $50-500. Mss bought/yr: 200 minimum. Length: 500-5,000 wds. How to submit: Query, send published clips, send complete ms. Does NOT want: "Erotica, bondage. No excessive profanity." Other tips: "Inspirational. Romance or women's fiction only with the above elements." NONFICTION: Book excerpts, essays, exposé, general interest, historical/nostalgic, how-to, humor, inspirational, personal experience, opinion, new product, interview/profile, photo feature, travel. Contact: Marcia Kiser (trbmarcia@aol.com). Pays: $25-50 for assigned and unsolicited articles (plus stock). Mss bought/yr: 50 minimum. Length: 500-1,000 wds. POETRY: Avant-garde, free verse, haiku, light verse, traditional. Contact: Tabatha D'Agata (trbtabatha@aol.com). Pays: Current issue of print magazine. Mss bought/yr: 100 minimum. Maximum poems/submission: 5. Maximum line length: 20. FILLERS: Anecdotes, facts, gags to be illustrated by cartoonist, newsbreaks, short humor. Contact: Chris Bossert (trbsec@aol.com). Pays: Negotiable. Mss bought/yr: No set limit. Length: Negotiable. TIPS: "Be professional. Know your market. Write ledgibly. Provide return envelopes. Introduction letter with all correspondence."

Salon—www.salon.com

22 Fourth St., 16th Floor, San Francisco, CA 94103. Editors (salon@salon.com). "Frequently updated throughout the day, Salon.com exploits the medium with topical, informative, entertaining, and thought-provoking content that ignites an impassioned interplay among devoted readers." Frequency: Daily. Est. 1995. Byline given. Queries: E-mail. Guidelines: www.salon.com/contact/submissions. TIPS: "We ask that you please send the text of your query or submission in plain text in the body of your e-mail, rather than as an attached file, as we may not be able to read the format of your file. If you wish to contribute, please spend some time familiarizing yourself with *Salon*'s various sites and features. If you think you know which site you want to submit your story or article pitch to, you can find the appropriate editor's name on our *Salon*'s Staff page and send your inquiry to our main editorial mailbox at salon@salon.com—we'll route it for you. Please put the words 'Editorial Submissions' along with the name of the editor you wish to contact in the subject line of the e-mail. And please tell us a little about yourself—your

experience and background as a writer and qualifications for writing a particular story. If you have clips you can send us via e-mail, or Web addresses of pages that contain your work, please send us a representative sampling (no more than 3 or 4, please). We do our best to respond to all inquiries, but be aware that we are sometimes inundated. If you have not heard back from us after 3 weeks, please assume that we will not be able to use your idea or submission. Also please note that *Salon* does not solicit fiction or poetry submissions and will not be able to respond to such submissions."

Service911.com—www.service911.com

5875 Castle Creek Pkwy. N. Dr., Suite 495, Indianapolis, IN 46250. Fax: (317)842-0656. Karen Reinisch, Chief Content Officer; Aaron Harlett, Director of Content Development; Dave Henthorn, Director of Content Acquisition (dhenthorn@service911.com). Subject: Consumer technology. Frequency: Other. Format: Online directory. Est. June 1999. Pays on acceptance. Rights: Exclusive electronic rights. Accepts simultaneous submissions. Sample: Free by e-mail. Guidelines: E-mail. NONFICTION: How-to, new product, technical. Contact: Dave Henthorn. How to submit: Query. Does NOT want: "Anything that does NOT fall into the following categories: On the Web, handheld computing, MP3s and digital multimedia, Linux, software applications, hardware and operating systems."

ShesGotBaby.com—www.shesgotbaby.com

ShesGotNetwork. Kim Lane, Editor (STSEditor@aol.com). "We prefer work that reflects an unusual twist on our role as mothers, be it a controversial approach to mothering, a new insight or outlook derived from motherhood, a reflective daughter's perspective, etc., but will consider all submissions on the merit of their content. Queries and ideas for future essays welcome." Format: Web magazine/ezine. Est. March 2000. Pays after publication. Rights: *She'sGotBaby* purchases one-time World Wide Web rights and unlimited archiving rights. All other rights remain with the author. Byline given. Accepts previously published material. Sample: Free on Web site after August 2000. NONFICTION: Pays: $125 for original work; $50 for reprints. Length: 800-1,500 wds. TIPS: "Currently seeking high-quality, personal essays pertaining to any and all facets of mothering for a new area of *ShesGotBaby.com*. Please do not send attached files. Instead, paste your submission into the body of an e-mail with a short bio and links to online clips if available."

ShesGotNetwork.com—www.shesgotnetwork.com

Includes ShesGotItTogether.com, ShesGotSports.com, ShesGotMoney.com, ShesGot Email.com, ShesGotBaby.com (*ShesGotBaby* has a separate listing above). c/o 369 FM 2104, Smithville, TX 78957. Deb Nyberg, Director of Community Development. "*ShesGotNetwork* is a portal of women's Web sites of many different topics. Articles are needed for each one of those Web sites on a weekly basis. It is difficult to list a specific topic listing for you because of the diversity of our network. Please advise your users to visit the Web site at www.shesgotnetwork.com to see what types of articles we are publishing at the time of their interest." Subject: Women's topics. Frequency: Weekly. Format: Web magazine/e-zine. Byline given. Queries: E-mail. COLUMNS: "If after I have had an opportunity to review a sample article from a writer, and we decide to offer the writer a position, we would set a column up with their picture and bio, and a direct link from their column to their Website. All columnists expected to have weekly articles in by the Wednesday of each week." NONFICTION: Pays: $40 ("We do not pay for reprints unless we agree in advance, in writing, to use a previously written article.").

Shyflower—www.shyflowersgarden.com

Linda Paquette, Editor (shy@flowersgarden.com); Carol Lee Doeden, Assistant Editor. Rights: Your work will be displayed for approximately 30 days. Writer retains copyright of work. Byline given. Queries: E-mail. FICTION: Erotica, humorous, mainstream. Pays: 4¢/wd for fiction and essay, $50 maximum. How to submit: Query. NONFICTION: Travel, how-to, inspirational, humor, new product, opinion, personal experience. Pays: 5¢/wd for articles, $75 maximum. Please query all articles before submitting. How to submit: Query. POETRY: Traditional, light verse, free verse. Pays: $1/line, $25 maximum. TIPS: "Send the URL (link) and the name of your personal Web site in the body of the e-mail. Also include a short bio of yourself if you desire. If the work is titled, be sure to include the title and your 'handle' and/or name. Please see guidelines at shyflowersgarden.homestead .com/files/WriterGuidelines.htm for other details."

SpaceWays Weekly—spaceways.mirror.org

The E-mail Magazine of Science Fiction and Fantasy. London Application Solutions, Inc., 148 York St., London, Ontario N6B 1B4 Canada. Rigel D. Chiokis, Editor (spaceways@mirror.org). "No special slant or philosophy. Must be well crafted, with strong characterization and intelligent plot." Subject: Science fiction, fantasy, and sword and sorcery short stories. Frequency: Weekly. Format: E-mail magazine. Est. September 1997. Circ. 280. 100% freelance written. Pays on acceptance. Rights: First world electronic. Byline given. Reports in 1 week on queries. Reports in 4 weeks on mss. Lead time: 3 months. Mss published average of 3 months after acceptance. Sample: Free on Web site. Guidelines: On Web site. FICTION: Fantasy, science fiction. Pays: Can.1¢/wd. Mss bought/yr: 52. Length: 1,000-5,000 wds. How to submit: Send complete ms. Does NOT want: "Horror, religious, or historical." Other tips: "Sword and sorcery." TIPS: "Your story must meet 4 criteria: (1) strong characterization; (2) intelligent, well-designed plot; (3) as a rule have an upbeat/positive ending (but don't force it); (4) must meet all other criteria listed in the guidelines."

S-2 Report—www.seidata.com/~dlatham/index.html

VA Compensation and PTSD. Latham Publishing, P.O. Box 105, Guilford, IN 47022. Tel: (812)487-2990. Fax: (812)487-2990. Dennis Latham, Publisher (dlatham@seidata.com). "Mostly how-to subjects on VA Compensation and new legislation for veterans and claim procedure. This is a specialized niche market, not for general readers. Most subscribers are in the VA claim system or just starting claims." Subject: VA Compensation, primarily dealing with combat stress (PTSD) and benefits and treatment. Frequency: Bimonthly. Format: Newsletter on Web site. Est. January 1994. Circ. 200 paid; approximately 4,000 total. 10-50% freelance written. Pays on acceptance. Rights: One-time print and electronic. Writer may resell. Byline given. Accepts simultaneous submissions and previously published material. Queries: Post, e-mail, fax, phone. Reports in 1 week on queries. Reports in 1 week on mss. Mss published average of 1 month after acceptance. Sample: Free on Web site. Guidelines: E-mail dlatham@seidata.com. COLUMNS: Short Fillers. VA legislation and Treatment for PTSD. Length: 50-100 wds. Contact: Dennis Latham, Publisher (dlatham@seidata.com). Pays: $5. Mss bought/yr: Varies. How to submit: Send complete ms. NONFICTION: Exposé, how-to, humor, opinion. Length: 250-500 wds. Contact: Dennis Latham, Publisher (dlatham@seidata.com). Pays: $15 for unsolicited articles. Mss bought/yr: Varies. How to submit: Query, send complete ms. Does NOT want: "Personal experience." Other: Opinion pieces are mostly from VA lawyers. FILLERS: Newsbreaks, short humor. Length: 50-100 wds. Pays: $5. Mss bought/yr: Varies. TIPS: "Anyone with knowledge in the field I cover will be published if the article is timely and relevant. I prefer standard submission format with SASE (#10). Prefer to dispose of manuscripts not used. I've been doing this by myself for 6 years, and my resubscribe rate is about 98%. The newsletter is 4 pages crammed with information. Veterans like it because they can read it fast and not have to wade through tons of statistics like the major service organization magazines put out. Also, I try to keep it on a personal level."

Suite 101—www.suite101.com/join.cfm/54099

i5vie.com, 1122 Mainland St., Suite 390, Vancouver, British Columbia V6B 5L1 Canada. Jason Pamer, Editor-in-Chief (jason@suite101.com). "Access to the Internet's most comprehensive Web directories with more than 20,000 links in over 890 unique topics, from ancient Egypt to Lhasa apsos to daffodils." Frequency: Weekly. Format: Online directory, online community. 100% freelance written. Pays weekly, biweekly, or monthly. Rights: Author keeps all rights. Byline given. Queries: E-mail. Mss published immediately after acceptance. Sample: Free on Web site. Guidelines: On Web site. COLUMNS: Pays: $15. Mss bought/yr: 9,924. How to submit: Send complete ms. NONFICTION: General interest, historical/ nostalgic, how-to, humor, inspirational, interview/profile, new product, opinion, personal experience, religious, technical, travel. Pays: $15. Length: 450-700 wds. How to submit: Send complete ms. Does NOT want: "Those not rated PG." TIPS: "You need to register as a member prior to sending Contributing Editor Application form reserved only for members. Site to register: www.suite101.com/join.cfm/ 54099. Contact Jennie S. Bev at penpusher@suite101.com for more info."

The Tales' Realm—http://pages.prodigy.net/dengar/index3.htm

Editor (Dengar@prodigy.net). Subject: Science fiction and fantasy. Frequency: Monthly. Format: Web magazine. Pays on acceptance. Rights: First North American serial rights or reprint rights. Byline given. Accepts previously published material. Queries: E-mail. Sample: Free on Web site. Guidelines: pages.prodigy.net/dengar/column/guide.htm. FICTION: Fantasy, science fiction. Pays: ¼¢/wd for first rights; ⅒¢/wd for reprints. Length: 500-10,000 wds. How to submit: Query. Other tips: "Hint: I just love a story with an exotic setting." POETRY: Avant-garde, free verse, haiku, light verse, traditional. Pays: ¼¢/wd for first rights; ⅒¢/wd for reprints. TIPS: "Submission guidelines are at pages.prodigy.net/dengar/index3.htm."

Teenwire.com—www.teenwire.com

Planned Parenthood Federation of America, 810 Seventh Ave., New York, NY 10019. Fax: (212)261-4565. Kim Jack Riley, Content Editor (kim.jack.riley@ppfa.org). Subject: Teen issues, sexual health, relationships. Frequency: Weekly. Format: Web magazine/zine. Est. February 1999. 100% freelance written. Pays on acceptance. Kill fee: 25%. Byline given. Accepts previously published material. Submit seasonal material 2 months in advance. Queries: E-mail, fax. Reports in 6 weeks on queries. Lead time: 1 month. Mss published average of 1 month after acceptance. Sample: Free on Web site. Guidelines: E-mail adrienne_carlish@ppfa.org. COLUMNS: World Views covers international issues related to sexuality, population, and the environment; In Focus covers news, current events, and issues of social impact on a domestic U.S. level, includes pop culture; Hothouse is a teenzine written for, by, and about teens—articles, essays, and poetry; Taking Action is grassroots public policy. These are stories about everyday teens in communities around the country who are involved with direct service, volunteerism, peer counseling, or activism. Also includes profiles of young people who have turned their lives around. How to submit: Query. NONFICTION: Interview/profile, personal experience. Pays: $250 maximum for assigned articles (50¢/wd). Length: 500 wds maximum. How to submit: Query. TIPS: "Story ideas should be submitted to Editor-in-Chief/teenwire .com, PPFA, 810 Seventh Ave., 12th Floor, New York, NY 10019."

This Way Up: Speculative Fiction Online—www.wayup.co.uk

Willowsoft Communications, P.O. Box 243, Portsmouth PO6 1EB United Kingdom. E-mail: editor@wayup.co.uk. Published every 4 months. "Each issue will contain about 6 short stories and 1 or 2 nonfiction articles, with perhaps a review, readers' letters (when we get any!), and an editorial." FICTION: 1,000-6,000 wds. Looking for strong stories of engaging characters in unusual situations. NONFICTION: Topics should concern the field of written speculative fiction. Length: 2,000 wds maximum. "Please send a query giving details of your proposal, together with clips (or URLs) and a short (4-line) bio." Do NOT want: Poetry, reprints, simultaneous submissions, multiple submissions, artwork, adult content. Payment and rights: "*This Way Up* will purchase First world-wide English language electronic rights, for a period of 8 months (4 months in the current issue, followed by 4 months in the *TWU* archive), after which the submission will be taken offline, and rights will revert to the author. Payment will be GBP Ł3 per 1,000 words (minimum payment GBP Ł3) for both fiction and nonfiction. Payment will be by sterling cheque, payable on publication. By arrangement with authors outside the UK, payment may be in the form of British postage stamps." E-mail submissions and queries OK.

Toon Talk the eZine—www.lynnsgallery.com

P.O. Box 1474, Alamo, CA 94595. Linda Tindall, Editor (ToonTalk@aol.com). "*Toon Talk* is for adults and teens who love animation and are interested in the voice talent." Frequency: Monthly. Format: Web magazine/zine. Est. May 1998. Circ. 3,500. Pays on publication. Kill fee: 100%. Rights: All rights. Byline given. Submit seasonal material 2 months in advance. Queries: E-mail. Reports in 1 week on queries. Reports in 1 week on mss. Lead time: 6 months. Mss published average of 2 months after acceptance. Sample: Free on Web site. Guidelines: On Web site. NONFICTION: Historical/nostalgic, how-to, humor, interview/profile, opinion, photo feature. Pays: $5. Mss bought/yr: 50. Length: 1,200-2,000 wds. How to submit: Query. Other: "I currently do all voice-actor interviews but I would be interested in interviews of other people in animation. Be sure you have signed releases before sending photos." TIPS: "The best way to start is to query about reviewing your favorite show or movie. I also look for reviews of books about the art of animation and voice-over. If you have an idea for a different type of article that you think I might be interested in, please e-mail me with the idea. I would like articles about writing animation scripts from knowledegable sources. Please note that I do not accept unsolicited articles."

Travelwise Magazine Online—www.travel-wise.com

Travelwise Publications, 6631 Albion Way, Delta, British Columbia. V4E 1J1 Canada. Vic Foster, Managing Editor (foster@ultranet.ca). "Most submissions are destination stories and experiences. Not only providing information on the destination, but in a personal experience style. Soft adventure welcome. Travel is fun, light-hearted, and personal is good. A 'brochure-ish' description is bad." Subject: General consumer leisure travel, neither age, gender, ability, or lifestyle specific. Frequency: Online magazine maintained daily. News items posted every few days. Stories posted weekly. Feature destinations posted monthly. Format: Web magazine/zine. Est. March 1993. Circ. Online "hits" averaging 3,500 visitors/day. 85% freelance written. Pays on publication. Kill fee: 50%. Rights: First-time electronic rights and second serial (reprint) electronic rights. Any pieces previously published anywhere in any media. Byline given. Accepts simultaneous submissions and previously published material. Submit seasonal material 3 months in advance. Queries: Post, e-mail, fax, phone. Reports in 4 weeks on queries. Reports in 4 weeks on mss. Lead time: 3 months. Sample: Free on Web site. Guidelines: E-mail foster@ultranet.ca. NONFICTION: Travel. Pays: $25 minimum for assigned or unsolicited articles. Mss bought/yr: 50. Length: 750-800 wds. How to submit: Query. Does NOT want: "We are not a forum for complaints, controversy, politics, special interest groups, and bad travel experiences." TIPS: "Travel writing is about informing, entertaining, and motivating readers. Your piece should make readers want to visit that particular destination . . . ask yourself what makes your experience of story different? How did it affect you? Be personal. Don't submit a 'brochure.' "

21st Century Adventures—www.21stcenturyadventures.com

10E Design, Inc., 265 Maple Dr., Hampton, GA 30228. Tel: (770)234-5861. Fax: (770)234-5861. Jennifer M. Tenney, Managing Editor (articles@21stcenturyadvent ures). "Our magazine is read by people who are active and have a love for nature. Articles should be geared toward exotic locations and/or adventure travel." Subject: Travel. Format: Web magazine/zine. Est. 1995. Pays on publication. Rights: First-time electronic rights. Byline given. Queries: E-mail. Reports in 4 weeks on queries. Reports in 4 weeks on mss. Sample: Free on Web site. NONFICTION: Personal experience, photo feature, travel. Contact: Editor (editorial@10e-design.com). Pays: $20-35. Length: "Length is not important, CONTENT is!" How to submit: Send complete ms.

Twilight Showcase—home.rica.net/gconn

New Talent in Horror Fiction. Strange Concepts, Ltd., 1436 Fifth St., Waynesboro, VA 22980. Gary W. Conner, Editor/Publisher (gconn@rica.net). "We are a publication strictly interested in the horror genre. We seek to advance the genre by bringing to light newer authors, as well as by providing opinions and, in some cases, illumination, about the genre." Subject: Horror fiction and nonfiction. Frequency: Monthly. Format: Web magazine/zine. Est. December 1998. Circ. Average 500 hits/month. 80% freelance written. Pays on publication. "We accept reprints, but do not require reprint rights from authors selling us a new piece." Rights: First-time electronic rights or second serial (reprint) electronic rights. Byline given. Accepts previously published material. Submit seasonal material 2 months in advance. Queries: Post, e-mail. Reports in 1 week on queries. Reports in 3 weeks on mss. Lead time: 2 months. Mss published average of 1 month after acceptance. Sample: Free on Web site. Guidelines: E-mail Gary W. Conner at gconn@rica.net or see home.rica.net/gconn/e-mail.htm. COLUMNS: Pays: $5-12.50. Mss bought/yr: 48-60. How to submit: Query. FICTION: Experimental, fantasy, horror, suspense. Pays: 1¢/wd regardless of length. Mss bought/yr: 48-60. Length: 250-2,500 wds. How to submit: Send complete ms. Does NOT want: "Vampire fiction, erotic fiction." NONFICTION: Essays, interview/profile, opinion. Pays: $5-12.50. Mss bought/yr: 48-60. Length: 250-2500 wds. How to submit: Query. Other: Book and movie reviews.

2-pop.com—www.2-pop.com

The Digital Filmmaker's Resource Site. Creative Planet.com, 4146 Lankershim Blvd., Suite #210, North Hollywood, CA 91604. Tel: (818)623-9260. Larry Jordan, Managing Editor (lj@2-pop.com); Tobias Nownes, Head Writer. "Interactive Resource and Community." Subject: Digital Video Film and Videomaking. Frequency: Daily. Format: Web magazine/zine online directory. Est. April 1999. Circ. 500,000 page views/month. 50% freelance written. Pays 14-30 days after submission of invoice. Rights: All rights. Byline given. Accepts simultaneous submissions. Queries: Post, e-mail, fax. Lead time: 1 month. Mss published average of 2-3 wks after acceptance. Sample: Free on Web site. Guidelines: E-mail: From tobias@creativeplanet.com. NONFICTION: How-to, interview/profile, opinion, personal experience, technical. Pays: $300-500 for assigned articles. Mss bought/yr: 40-50% of publication. Length: 1,200 wds minimum. How to submit: Send published clips. TIPS: "Digital Video Film and Videomaking tips and techniques and Specific software and hardware tutorials. Interviews with DV and Web Cinema Film/Videomakers. Perspectives on the DV world. Experiences in DV Film/Videomaking."

UPromote Marketer—www.upromote.com

UPromote, 1241 E. Deerfield Pkwy., Suite 204, Buffalo Grove, IL 60089. Tel: (847)537-6597. Fax: (847)537-6598. Brian D. Chmielewski, Editor (brianc@upromote.com). "We seek articles on Internet Marketing strategy, Web Promotion How-to's, Online Advertising Trends, and Technology updates, etc." Subject: Internet marketing and online Web site promotion strategy. Frequency: Monthly. Format: Web magazine, company Web site, newsletter. Est. August 1999. Circ. 100,000. 50% freelance written. Pays on acceptance. Rights: All rights. Byline given. Accepts simultaneous submissions. Submit seasonal material 2 months in advance. Queries: E-mail. Reports in 4 weeks on queries. Reports in 4 weeks on mss. Lead time: 2 weeks. Mss published average of 2-3 months after acceptance. Sample: Free by e-mail, on Web site. Guidelines: On Web site. NONFICTION: Exposé, general interest, historical/nostalgic, how-to, inspirational, interview/profile, new product, personal experience, technical. Pays: 10-20¢/wd maximum for assigned articles; 1-5¢/wd maximum for unsolicited articles. Mss bought/yr: 20 minimum. Length: 600-930 wds. How to submit: Send published clips, query. Does NOT want: "Sales pieces or advertorials for other clients."

UpsideToday—www.upsidetoday.com

Upside Media, 731 Market St., San Francisco, CA 94103. Tel: (415)489-5600. Kathleen Williams, Editor (kwilliams@upside.com). "*UpsideToday* seeks high-tech business news, opinion, and feature pieces written with a tongue-in-cheek attitude, or thorough reporting." Subject: High-tech business. Frequency: Daily. Format: Web magazine. Est. 1996. Circ. Unpublished. 60% freelance written. Pays on publication. Rights: Other. Byline given. Queries: E-mail. Reports in 2 weeks on queries. Mss published average of 1 week after acceptance. Sample: Free on Web site. Guidelines: On Web site. NONFICTION: Book excerpts, interview/profile, opinion. Length: 500-2,000 wds. How to submit: Query, send published clips.

Vicus.com—www.vicus.com

Vicus.com, Inc., 69844K Hwy. 111, Rancho Mirage, CA 92270. Tel: (760)770-7660. Fax: (760)770-3810. Mike Sturman, Editor (msturman@vicus.com); Mike Sturman, Editorial Contact (submissions). "Provide accurate, well-researched health information." Subject: Integrative health. Frequency: Monthly. Format: Informational Web site. Est. July 1999. 30% freelance written. Pays on acceptance. "Queries should include cover letter, resume, and clips that are topic specific to health/medical." Kill fee: 50%. Rights: All rights. Byline given. Queries: Post, e-mail, fax. Reports in 2 weeks on queries. Sample: Free on Web site. Guidelines: E-mail msturman@vicus.com. NONFICTION: Book excerpts, general interest, historical/nostalgic, how-to, humor, inspirational, interview/profile, technical, travel. Pays:

$300 for assigned articles. Mss bought/yr: No limit. Length: 500-700 wds. How to submit: Query. Does NOT want: "Essays, opinion pieces, single product pieces." Other: Integrative health feature articles, news, case studies, book reviews. TIPS: "We are looking for experienced health/medical writers who can write credible, well-sourced, and evidence-based copy. We are known for our well-referenced articles, each of which carries a number of citations."

Wcities.com—www.wcities.com

World's first global information and travel Web site. 1042 Howard St., San Francisco, CA 94117. Fraser Campbell, Editor (countryeditors@egroups.com). "Certain info is required (hours, location, prices, etc.) as well as a positive overall tone. If an establishment is mediocre, it is not good enough to include in our data base of reviews, as we like to focus on those places of interest to our target audience, i.e., the business traveler." Subject: Travel, full local information for business travelers in foreign cities. Frequency: Daily. Format: Web site. Est. May 1999. Circ. 3,000. 90% freelance written. Pays on acceptance. Rights: Exclusive electronic rights. Byline given. Submit seasonal material 1 month in advance. Queries: Post, e-mail. Reports in 2 weeks on queries. Reports in 1 week on mss. Lead time: 1 month. Sample: Free on Web site. Guidelines: Available after the writer is hired. NONFICTION: General interest, historical/nostalgic, opinion, personal experience, travel. Pays: Assigned articles. Unless writer is working on a special, longer project. Payment for longer guides runs approximately $500-1,500. Mss bought/yr: Thousands. Length: 70-120 wds. How to submit: Query. Does NOT want: "Negative reviews, anything not relevant to our site." Other: "Review places you know and enjoy."

WetFeet.com—www.wetfeet.com

609 Mission St., Suite 400, San Francisco, CA 94105. Fax: (415)284-7910. Frank Marquardt, Managing Editor (careers@wetfeet.com; put "Freelance Writer" in subject line). "Our Web site is devoted to connecting job seekers with companies. We look for information parsed by industry, job function, and, in some cases, region, as well as thoughtful pieces on other work and career-related issues." Subject: Careers. Frequency: Daily. Format: Web magazine/zine. Est. 1993. 20-30% freelance written. Pays prior to publication, but within a 4-week window of approving final manuscript and receiving invoice. "Byline given sometimes." Kill fee: 20%. Rights: Makes work-for-hire assignments. Byline given. Queries: E-mail, fax. Reports in 4 weeks on queries.

Reports in 4 weeks on mss. Mss published average of 1-6 months after acceptance. Sample: Free on Web site. COLUMNS: "We don't have columns per se. Presently we have several 'channels'; these include consulting, financial services, high-tech, and law. Writers should visit our site and identify the channel manager and submit to that person." Pays: $50-500. NONFICTION: Essays, general interest, interview/profile, opinion, personal experience. Pays: $100-1,000 for assigned articles; $50-500 for unsolicited articles. Mss bought/yr: Varies. Length: 200 wds minimum. How to submit: Send published clips, query. Does NOT want: "Anything not related to work and careers, we don't want to see it." TIPS: "Think carefully about what information we offer and what information you have to offer, and why it would complement our site. We don't have time-worn formal processes for dealing with freelancers, though we're always on the lookout for talented writers. Your best bet is to contact an editor with an e-mail—their names can typically be found on our site. If that doesn't work, fax in a letter with clips to Editorial at WetFeet.com."

WineToday.com—www.winetoday.com

New York Times Digital (affiliated with The New York Times Co.), 141 Stony Circle, Suite 235, Santa Rosa, CA 95404. Tel: (707)523-7933. Tim Fish, Editor (tfish@winetoday.com); Linda Murphy, Associate Editor (linda@winetoday.com). "We write seriously about wine but do it in a way that isn't precious or pretentious." Subject: Wine, with some emphasis on wine and food pairing and wine country travel. Frequency: Other. Format: Web magazine/zine. Est. 1998. Circ. 120,000 unique readers/month. 50% freelance written. Pays on publication. Rights: All rights. Byline given. Submit seasonal material 1 month in advance. Queries: Post, e-mail, phone. Lead time: Varies. Mss published average of 1 month after acceptance. Sample: Free on Web site. Guidelines: E-mail tfish@winetoday.com.

Wired News—www.wired.com

Wired Ventures, Inc., a Lycos Company, 660 Third St., 4th Floor, San Francisco, CA 94107. George Shirk, Editor-in-Chief (george@wired.com); Alison Macondray, Managing Editor (alisonm@wired.com). "No slant is necessary, but the reporter should be up on current events and trends in the tech world and be able to put news in context of that background. Also, we require strong reporting and newswriting skills." Subject: Technology news. Frequency: Daily. Format: News Web site. Circ. 4 million unique visitors/week. Pays on publication. "Technical news Web site. If the query letter is well written and the subject is pertinent and timely, we may respond the same day. We will not reply to poorly written queries or to those that do not fit our editorial profile." Kill fee: 25%. Rights: Exclusive electronic rights. Byline given. Submit seasonal material 1 month in advance. Queries: E-mail. Lead time: 1 day. Mss published average of 1 week after acceptance. Sample: Free on Web site. Guidelines: E-mail newsfeedback@wired.com. NONFICTION: Pays: 50¢/wd. Mss bought/yr: 3,600. Length is at editor's discretion. How to submit: Query, send published clips. Does NOT want: "First-person accounts, one-source stories, stories that read like ad or promo copy." TIPS: "If you haven't ever written a news story before, take a reporting and newswriting course, and read some good books on the subject."

Women's International Net Magazine (WIN)—www.winmagazine.org

301 E. 79th St., New York, NY 10021. Judith Colp Rubin, Publisher/Editor (editor@ winmagazine.org). "This is a magazine about women and women's issues world-wide." Subject: Women around the world. Frequency: Monthly. Format: Web magazine/zine. Est. 1997. Circ. 10,000 minimum. 100% freelance written. Pays on publication. Rights: One-time electronic rights. Byline given. Accepts previously published material. Queries: E-mail. Reports in 1 week on queries. Reports in 4 weeks on mss. Lead time: 1 month. Mss published average of 1 month after acceptance. Sample: Free on Web site or by e-mail. Guidelines: On Web site or e-mail editor@winmagazine.org. FICTION: Condensed novels, confession, ethnic, humorous, mainstream, novel excerpts, religious, slice-of-life vignettes. Contact: Helen Schary Motro, Fiction Editor (editor@winmagazine.org). Pays: $100. Length: 1,000-3,000 wds. How to submit: Query. NONFICTION: Book excerpts, essays, exposé, general interest, inspirational, interview/profile, opinion, personal experience. Contact: Judith Colp Rubin, Publisher/Editor (editor@winmagazine.org). Pays: $100-180 for assigned articles; $100 for unsolicited articles. Mss bought/yr: 60. Length: 1,000-3,000 wds. How to submit: Query. TIPS: "Read past issues to get a sense of the magazine, make sure your article idea has to do with women, and send a very detailed query. We like articles that give a sense of women in different countries and are of interest to women worldwide."

Working Writers Newsletter—www.freelancewriting.com

BSK Communications and Associates, P.O. Box 543, Oradell, NJ 07649. Tel: (201)

262-3277. Brian Konradt, Editor (webmaster@freelancewriting.zzn.com). "How to write for (break into) different types of editorial markets; how to write for Web sites and electronic media; how to freelance write for businesses and ad agencies; how to increase freelance work; where to find freelance work; how to establish relationships and rapport with editors and clients; how to increase the chances of securing work; how to write better copy; how to use new technology; how to write for magazines; how to promote your book; how to write for children; how to break into screenwriting; etc. Articles should be slanted toward the intermediate/advanced writer, instead of the beginner." Subject: The business and creative sides of freelance writing. Frequency: Biweekly. Format: E-mail newsletter. Est. 1999. Circ. 3,000. 100% freelance written. Pays on acceptance. Rights: First-time electronic rights and nonexclusive rights to reprint your work in "archival" issues of *Working Writers*, which are made available in their entirety at our Web site, FreelanceWriting.Com. After your article appears in *Working Writers Newsletter*, you are free to resell it. Byline given. Accepts simultaneous submissions and previously published material. Submit seasonal material 2 months in advance. Queries: E-mail. Reports in 2-4 weeks on queries. Reports in 4 weeks on mss. Lead time: 1-2 months. Mss published average of 1-2 months after acceptance. Sample: Free on Web site or by e-mail. Guidelines: On Web site or by e-mail. NONFICTION: Book excerpts, how-to, interview/profile, new product, technical. Pays: 5¢. Mss bought/yr: 60-75. Length: 200-1,000 wds. How to submit: Send published clips. Does NOT want: "Articles on how to handle rejections; how to set rates; how to write queries; how to work office equipment; how to do bookkeeping; reviews of office or productivity software and books; any topic on poetry; how to find online writers' markets; no fiction articles or theory-based articles." TIPS: "Since articles are bulleted, use short paragraphs of important information and focus on providing readers with essential how-to information instead of concentrating on proper writing style. Focus on short, solution-savvy, information-dense sentences. Always use specifics, solutions, step-by-steps, and experiences in your article. Do not give overviews or opinionated observations of the topic you're writing; rather, provide specific examples to get your point across."

The Write Markets Report—www.writersweekly.com/index-twmr.htm

Your Only Source of Markets Needing Writers TODAY. Deep South Publishing Co.,

900-G Brookside Dr., Andover, MA 01810. Tel: (978)738-0091. Fax: (978)738-1924. Angela Adair-Hoy, Publisher (aadair@writersweekly.com). "All articles must teach writers methods for making more money through freelance writing." Subject: Freelance writing. Frequency: Monthly. Format: Subscription-based, downloadable electronic magazine delivered in .pdf. Est. June 1997. Circ. 690. 30% freelance written. Pays on acceptance. Kill fee: 25%. Rights: First-time electronic rights. Byline given. Accepts previously published material. Submit seasonal material 2 months in advance. Queries: E-mail. Reports in 1 week on queries. Lead time: 2 months. Mss published average of 2 months after acceptance. Sample: Free on Web site. Guidelines: On Web site. NONFICTION: Book excerpts, interview/profile, how-to. Pays: $50 for assigned articles. Pays $30 for reprints. Mss bought/yr: 24. Length: 600-800 wds. How to submit: Query. Other: Articles that teach writers how to make more money writing, i.e., alternative forms of self-publishing (e-books, newsletters), writing for elusive markets (trade magazines), writing for newspapers, etc. TIPS: "Humor is always appreciated. Our readers want to work for themselves and be able to support their families with their writing. Most write for the magazine industry and are looking for other ways to supplement or enhance their writing careers. Past articles include ghostwriting, writing for the medical market, newsletter publishing, self-publish for profit, and unique ways to make money writing. We welcome ideas that expand on these or that lead writers to financial opportunities that they do not know exist. Marketing articles that deal with specific writing-related products and services are warmly welcomed. We will consider but not pay for poetry, cartoons, and jokes. We like tightly focused articles; bulleted or outlined queries; 'how to' produce this writing product (service) and 'how to' sell it. Don't tell us how to get into a type of writing business without telling us how to sell it, too."

Writer Online—www.novalearn.com/wol

Novation Learning Systems, Inc., 190 Mt. Vernon Ave., Rochester, NY 14620. Fax: (716)340-0193. Terry Boothman, Publisher; Cindy Mindell-Wong, Managing Editor (e-mail@novalearn.com); Clare Mann, Managing Editor (e-mail@novalearn.com). "*Writer Online* is a free newsletter/e-zine for writers of all kinds. Subscribers are English-speaking, educated, and literate. Many have been published already in one or more markets. Most readers are motivated by the desire to sell their writing."

Frequency: Biweekly. Format: Web magazine. Est. March 1997. Circ. 34,000. 100% freelance written. Pays on return of signed contract. Buys first electronic rights. We archive all material. Writers may resell published material 3 months after publication. Subject: Craft and marketing for writers. Sample: Free on Web site. Guidelines: E-mail support@novalearn.com. Reports in 1 month on queries and mss. Mss published an average of 1 month after acceptance. NONFICTION: Query first. We want well-written material that pertains in some way to the art, craft, and marketing of writing. Pays: 5-10¢/wd. Length: 800-1,200 wds. Mss bought/yr: 40-60. FICTION: Flash fiction 99 wds. Short fiction: All genres, including mainstream, 300-1,200 wds. Occasional feature: Short excerpts from novels in progress, by both published and unpublished writers. Pays: 5-10¢/wd for original ms; $20 for all reprints. Mss bought/yr: 45-60. COLUMNS: Guest Column: Wide variety of topics that don't fit in other columns, 1,000 wds; Writer's Advocate: Legal issues pertinent to the writer, 1,000 wds; M.O.: Mystery and Mayhem: On mystery writing, 1,000 wds; Screenwriting/Playwriting, 1,000 wds; Weblite (Humor), 1,000 wds. FILLERS: Short humor: On writing. Pays: $20. Mss bought/yr: 10-12. Length: 300-500 wds. How to submit: E-mail one of the 3 addresses above. FICTION: Send unsolicited fiction embedded in your e-mail. NONFICTION: "We prefer that you query first by e-mail. Send manuscripts embedded in your e-mail; we will return all unsolicited attachments unread."

The Writers' Guidelines Guide—www.writersdatabase.com

The Writers' Guidelines Database, 310 Salem Church Rd., St. Paul, MN 55118. Rachel E. Stassen-Berger, Editor (guidelines@mav.net); Dana Nourie, Managing Editor. "We feature advice-driven pieces that will help nonfiction writers in their careers." Subject: Nonfiction writing and marketing. Frequency: Monthly. Format: Web magazine/zine. Circ. 3,000. 70% freelance written. Pays on acceptance. Rights: We purchase one-time e-mail rights and an optional nonexclusive Web rights. Byline given. Accepts previously published material. Submit seasonal material 2 months in advance. Queries: Post, e-mail. Reports in 2 weeks on queries. Reports in 4 weeks on mss. Lead time: 2 months. Mss published average of 2 months after acceptance. Sample: Free on Web site. Guidelines: On Web site. NONFICTION: Essays, how-to, interview/profile, opinion, new product, personal experience. Contact: Rachel E. Stassen-Berger, Editor.

Writers Open Workshop—www.zyworld.com/voyagemag/WOW.htm

Global Markets Newsletter for writers, artists, and photographers. Regent Publications, 14 Honor Ave., Goldthorn Park, Wolverhampton WV4 5HH United Kingdom. Tel: (440)01902652999. Fax: (440)01902652999. John Dunne, Editor (Voyagema g@zyworld.com). "All features should be written with firsthand knowledge of the markets or techniques covered." Subject: Market information news and features for writers looking to sell their work to publications, companies, and exhibition venues worldwide. Frequency: Biweekly. Format: Web magazine/e-mail newsletter. Est. September 1999. Circ. 2,700. 100% freelance written. Pays on publication. Rights: One-time electronic rights. Byline given. Accepts simultaneous submissions. Submit seasonal material 6 months in advance. Queries: Post, e-mail, fax. Reports in 1 week on queries. Reports in 3 weeks on mss. Lead time: 1 month. Mss published average of 1-3 months after acceptance. Sample: Free by e-mail or on Web site. Guidelines: E-mail voyagemag@zyworld.com, subject "WOW_Guidelines". NONFICTION: Book excerpts, essays, how-to, humor, inspirational, interview/ profile. Pays: $10-150 for unsolicited articles. Mss bought/yr: 120. Length: 150 wds minimum for news items; 5,000 wds maximum for a major market segment report; 800-1,500 wds for standard one-off features. How to submit: Query, send complete ms. Does NOT want: "Basics of how to write." TIPS: "Studying the market carefully, obtain detailed guidelines and preferably obtain quotes from the editor, news editor, features editor, etc. If you have actually been published by the market, so much the better. Be concise, but be as detailed as possible and be accurate—we follow up on all market news submitted before publication."

WritersWeekly.com—www.writersweekly.com

Free weekly featuring freelance jobs and paying markets for writers. Deep South Publishing Co., 900-G Brookside Dr., Andover, MA 01810. Tel: (978)738-0091. Fax: (978)738-1924. Angela Adair-Hoy, Publisher (aadair@writersweekly.com). "All articles must teach writers how to make more money doing what they love. Past articles have included how to start a newsletter, how to make money writing for greeting card companies, how to write for weekly newspapers, how to self-publish booklets . . . a variety of ideas on alternative means of income utilizing your freelance writing talents." Subject: Freelance writing and self-publishing. Frequency: Weekly. Format: Web magazine/zine and e-mail newsletter. Est. December 1997. Circ.

34,000 minimum. 10% freelance written. Pays on acceptance. Kill fee: 25%. Rights: One-time electronic rights. Byline given. Accepts previously published material. Submit seasonal material 2 months in advance. Queries: E-mail. Reports in 1 week on queries. Lead time: 1 month. Mss published average of 1 month after acceptance. Sample: Free by e-mail or on Web site. Guidelines: On Web site. NONFICTION: Book excerpts, how-to, interview/profile. Pays: $20 for assigned articles, $10 for unsolicited articles and reprints. Mss bought/yr: 8-12. Length: 300-600 wds. How to submit: Query. Does NOT want: " 'How-to-write' articles." TIPS: "*WritersWeek ly.com* readers are primarily interested in obtaining freelance jobs (long-term) and landing freelance assignments. In addition, they want to quit their full-time jobs and be able to support their families with their writing. We're very interested in personal experience articles with the tone of 'I did this. You can, too!' that explain the steps required to achieve the same success, as well as marketing articles that deal with a specific writing-related product or service."

Writing for DOLLARS!—www.writingfordollars.com

AWOC.COM, PMB #225, 2436 S. I-35E, Suite 376, Denton, TX 76205. Fax: (940)591-9586. Dan Case, Editor (editor@writingfordollars.com). "*Writing for DOLLARS!* is about how writers can earn money. Feature articles cover new ways to make money as a writer, how to sell to specific markets, and interviews with successful writers." Subject: Writing. Frequency: Semimonthly. Format: E-mail newsletter. Est. December 1997. Circ. 18,500. 90% freelance written. Pays before publication. Rights: One-time electronic rights in newsletter and archived on Web site. Byline given. Submit seasonal material 6 months in advance. Queries: Post, e-mail. Reports in 1 week on queries. Reports in 1 week on mss. Lead time: 3 months. Mss published average of 3 months after acceptance. Guidelines: E-mail guidelines@writingfordollars.com. NONFIC-TION: Book excerpts, how-to, interview/profile, personal experience. Pays: $10 for reprints; $15 for original articles. Mss bought/yr: 30. Length: 500-1,000 wds. How to submit: Query. Other: Book excerpts: If the book is useful for a writer to make a buck. Interview/profile of successful writers. Personal experience: How I made that first sale. TIPS: "The best way to catch my eye is to send me a query letter (by e-mail) with an original idea, slanted for *Writing for DOLLARS!* Even if the idea is not right for us, I tend to give suggestions for article ideas to someone who is able to put together great query letters."

The Writing Parent, TWParent—www.klockepresents.com/TWParent.html

Klocke Publishing, 127 Bishop Rd. NW, Cartersville, GA 30121. Tel: (770)607-9086. Fax: (530)323-8867. Angela Giles Klocke, Publisher/Editor (TWParent@klockepresents.com). "Articles should address the needs of those trying to become writers themselves while caring for children, but any on writing are accepted if they are relevant and helpful." Subject: *TWParent* is especially geared toward writers who are caring for children while striving for a career in the writing field. Frequency: Weekly. Format: E-mail newsletter. Est. July 1999. Circ. 550 online subscribers minimum. 50% freelance written. Pays on publication. Rights: First-time and reprint rights. Byline given. Accepts previously published material. Queries: Post, e-mail, fax. Reports in 2 weeks on queries. Reports in 1 month on mss. Mss published average of 1-2 months after acceptance. Sample: Free by e-mail. Guidelines: E-mail TheWritingParent@sendfree.com. NONFICTION: Book excerpts, essays, how-to, humor, inspirational, interview/profile, personal experience. Pays: $20 for original works. Mss bought/yr: 50-60. Length: 250-1000 wds. How to submit: Send complete ms. Does NOT want: "Pieces based on parenting alone. *The Writing Parent* is NOT a parenting publication." Other: How to find time to write with children; ideas and tips, etc. POETRY: Avant-garde, free verse, light verse, tradial. Pays: $8. Mss bought/yr: 10-15. Maximum poems/submission: 5. Does NOT want: "Poetry not related to writing." TIPS: "New writers are encouraged. Read the magazine; too many assume that the publication is a parenting newsletter."

ZD Journals Publications—www.zdjournals.com

"ZD Journals is the leading provider of computer technology journals and information products" (28 journals, see Web site). Subject: Computer technology. Frequency: Monthly. Byline given. Queries: E-mail. Guidelines: www.zdjournals.com/contrib.htm. TIPS: "We're interested in articles that save our readers time and provide techniques they can immediately put to use in their work. *ZD Journals* prefers queries, sent via e-mail to appropriate editor, describing your proposed topic (see www.zdjournals.com/contrib.htm#editors for e-mail contact info): *Inside the Internet, The MacAuthority, Inside Microsoft Office 2000, Inside Microsoft Office 97, Inside Microsoft Access, Inside Microsoft Excel, Inside Microsoft PowerPoint, Inside Microsoft Word, Inside Microsoft Windows 98, Inside Microsoft Windows 95, Inside Corel WordPerfect Suite, Inside NetWare, Exploring Oracle, Inside Solaris, SQL Server*

Solutions, Windows Professional, Exploring Windows NT, Windows NT Professional, Active Server Developer's Journal, Inside AutoCAD, Inside Microsoft FrontPage, Inside the Internet, Inside Visual Basic, Inside Illustrator, Inside PageMaker, Inside Photoshop, Inside QuarkXpress, The MacAuthority. Our writing style is casual first person, so you'll notice we use contractions and pronouns, such as 'you' and 'we.' In addition, we write in direct, active voice. For instance, we'd use 'After you place the control on the form' rather than 'After the control is placed on the form.' If your article uses figures, please reference them in the text ('As shown in Figure A . . .') and include a figure caption ('Figure A: In this dialog box, you can . . .') after the referring paragraph. Please do NOT embed figures in the article file; send them as separate files. If possible, capture figures in a 256-color TIFF format. If necessary, you can send bitmaps instead. If the topic of your article involves programming code, please create a separate listing for any code that exceeds 10 lines, and reference the listing in the article text, as you would a figure. When applicable, please send a sample application that demonstrates your technique. We use these samples to test your technique, and we upload them to the publication's FTP site for readers to download. When you submit an article, be sure to include your mailing and e-mail addresses, phone and fax numbers, and a brief bio (less than 75 words). Please see online guidelines for an article template and general style guidelines."

Alternative Markets

The following are examples of markets or "showcases" that pay authors in methods other than cash up front. Be sure to check the guidelines and terms of service carefully before submitting material, and pay special attention to what rights you are giving away. Be sure to read the "Cautions for Writers" on page 45 for more information.

Author "showcases"

In theory, an author posts a manuscript or a profile in an author showcase. In theory, editors, publishers, and agents will browse the showcase and find the writers or articles they need. Some questions to ask before placing your work with such a service:

1. Is the site content of high enough quality or organized so that editors, publishers, and agents would actually use it?

2. What rights am I giving up by posting my work with this service? Can I withdraw the piece anytime, for example, if I find a market for it?

3. Would I be better off trying to sell this piece on my own?

CreativeWrites—www.creativewrites.com

> Writers create online profiles of themselves in a searchable database, outlining skills and experience. Profile-matching, peer reviews of and by editors and writers. Company deducts a commission from each sale.

GoodStory.com—www.goodstory.com

> Conceived by a former executive at Creative Artists Agency, this site was still in beta-testing mode at the time this book was being written. For a fee, writers can post brief descriptions of their work. For a fee paid to the writer, users can purchase and then download the work(s).

RoseDog—www.rosedog.com

> Showcases author manuscripts. No fee. Authors can revise work after it has been posted.

Pay per view

Epinions.com—www.writers.epinions.com

> Writers are paid a fee each time their product reviews are read.

Mind's Eye Fiction—www.tale.com

> Visitors to the site can read the beginning of any story for free. To read the rest, they can either pay a small fee or agree to view banner advertising. Due to a corporate reorganization, Mind's Eye Fiction was temporarily closed to new submissions during the writing of this book.

PennyaPage—www.pennyapage.com

> 50% royalties. *PennyaPage* buys exclusive rights for a minimum of 90 days. Seeks fiction, nonfiction, art. Visitors can view some free pieces on the site, pay "a penny a page" for others.

Themestream—www.themestream.com

> Visitors can read (and rate) articles on a wide variety of topics for free. Authors receive a small payment every time their articles are viewed.

Royalty paying

MightyWords—www.mightywords.com

> Writers can upload their original content. MightyWords secures those files in an encrypted Adobe PDF format. Writers set the prices of their work and receive a royalty for each sale made. Minimal listing fee.

Other payment methods:

The Southerner—www.southerner.net

> A Magazine Online. The Southerner Corp., 1221 Laurel Ave., #5, Knoxville, TN 37916. Pays for articles and fiction in stock.

YourTravelNews.com—www.yourtravelnews.com

> Pays for travel articles and columns according to their ratings by the site's readership. Fee range: $0-100. For more info, click on the Travel Writers section of the navigation bar.

Commercial E-publishers

The following is a partial list of royalty-paying commercial e-publishers who publish book-length manuscripts and do not charge authors fees. For tips on how to choose a commercial e-publisher, please see Jamie Engle's article in this book. Also see Karen Wiesner's book *ElectronicPublishing: The Definitive Guide* (Petals of Life Publishing, Avid Press, www.avidpress.com).

Guidelines change frequently, so be sure to carefully check submission guidelines on the publisher Web site before submitting. No erotica or simsubs (simultaneous submissions) unless otherwise stated. No unnecessary gore and violence.

Antelope Publishing—www.antelope-ebooks.com

> 1382 NE Tenth, Hillsboro, OR 97124-2505. John Rutis, editor. E-mail: editor@antelope-ebooks.com. Est. 1996. 58 titles. Releases 1 title minimum/month. Receives 50 submissions minimum/month. Responds within 1 week. Simsubs OK. Query first. Submission format: Text or URL. Guidelines: www.antelope-ebooks.com/submissions.html. Royalties: 15-35% depending on form of mss and form of finished book. Contract term: Negotiable. Provides editing, cover art, book design, and layout. Marketing and advertising all online. File format: HTML. Delivery

options: CD-ROM to be viewed on personal offline Web browser. MATERIAL SOUGHT: Fiction: "Children's picture books, juvenile, fantasy, mystery, romance, science fiction, young adult." Fiction: "Anything that helps lift the spirits, teaches important skills, or furthers physical, spiritual, or emotional development is considered." TIPS: "We are a very family-oriented e-publisher. No sexually explicit material is published. No books with obscene language or excessive violence will be accepted."

Avid Press, LLC—www.avidpress.com

5470 Red Fox Dr., Brighton, MI 48114-9079. Fax: (503)510-6765. Submissions: Colleen Schulte, Kate Gleason. E-mail: cgs@avidpress.com, kate@avidpress.com. Est. March 1999. 15 titles. 100 minimum submissions per month. Average acceptance rate: 1%. Turnaround time on submissions: 45 days. Simsubs OK. Send proposal first. Submission format: Word or WordPerfect as e-mail attachments. Guidelines: www.avidpress.com/authorsub.htm. Time between acceptance and publish date: 6-12 months. Royalties: 30% of download price for electronic books; 10% of net for print books. Contract term: 12 months, renewable. Sample contract: www.avidpress.com/authorcontract.htm. Provides complete editing, cover art, book design, and layout. File formats: PDF, HTML, RTF, RocketEditions. Delivery options: E-mail attachment, diskette, mass market paperback. MATERIAL SOUGHT: Romance, suspense/thriller, historical romance, mystery, paranormal.

Awe-Struck E-Books—www.awe-struck.net

2458 Cherry St., Dubuque, IA 52001. Kathryn D. Struck, Co-Publisher, President, and CEO. Dick Claassen, Co-Publisher. E-mail: kdstruck@home.com. Est. November 1999. 42 titles. Releases 2-3 titles/month. Receives 40-70 submissions/month. Average acceptance rate: 20% maximum. Average turnaround time on submissions: 2-5 weeks on excerpts. Simsubs OK. Also accepts submissions for incomplete mss—send a synopsis and first two chapters. For complete mss, send query cover letter, attached synopsis, and two chapters. Proposals are not preferred. File format preferred: Word98. Guidelines: www.awe-struck.net/asubmit/authsub. html. Time between acceptance and publish date: 4-12 months. PAYS: 40% of selling price on our site; other rates by contract agreement with distributors. Info available to authors at request. Contract term: 2 yrs, negotiable and renewable. Provides editing, basic cover art, book design, and layout. File formats available:

HTML, HTML for RocketReader, RTF, PDF, RocketBook, and Print on Demand. Delivery options: Downloads and diskettes in the mail, print versions. MATERIAL SOUGHT: Fiction genres/subgenres: "Romance—SF romance, historical romance, contemporary romance, romantic suspense, paranormal romance, Regency, teen reader, and inspirational; SF adventures; 2 novellas marketed as 1 electronic volume—usually a romance or a SF—we call it a DoubleTake; fiction with a disabled person as a central character." Nonfiction: Self-help/inspirational; some mainstream.

Bibliobytes—www.bb.com

71 Hauxhurst Ave., Weehawken, NJ 07087-6803. Tel: (201)601-0300. Acquisitions: Glenn Hauman. E-mail: comment@bb.com. Incorporated March 1993. 400 titles. Simsubs OK. Submissions: Query, proposal, or full mss. Submission format: "RTF, or our own HTML standards." Guidelines: www.bb.com/howtosubmit.cfm, www.bb.com/WriterGuidelines.cfm. Royalties: "Up to 35% of all revenues generated." Contract term: "Varies. Usually can be terminated with 90 days notice." Sample contract: www.bb.com/WriterGuidelines.cfm. Rarely provides editing and cover art. Provides book design and layout if necessary, to their formats: "The authors are invited to do it themselves to shorten time from acceptance to publication." Distribution: "Mainly www.bb.com, some syndication to other Web sites." File formats available: HTML. Seeks wide variety of material.

Book-On-Disc.com—www.book-on-disc.com

P.O. Box 6028, Palm Harbor, FL 34684-0628. Tel: (727)785-2217. Acquisitions: William R. Brennan, Publisher. E-mail: Brennan@book-on-disc.com. Est. March 1999. 16 titles. Releases 1-3 titles/month (on CD-ROM, diskette, file transfer). Receives 20 submissions/month. Acceptance rate: 5%. Average turnaround time on submissions: 3 months if invited to submit, 6 months if unrequested submission. Query first. File format for submissions: "Word for Windows 95 and up, or Rich Text." Guidelines: www.book-on-disc.com/submiss.htm. Time between acceptance and publish date: 6-12 months. Pays: Varies, depending on publishing medium. Contract term: 2 yrs, "with renewals based on mutual agreement." Sample contract: www.book-on-disc.com/author's1.htm. Provides cover art, book design and layout, formatting in various types of e-book files. File formats available: "Adobe PDF, Internet HTML, RTF, and other file formats if requested." Delivery options:

CD-ROM and file transfer. MATERIAL SOUGHT: Fiction: All genres for new imprint. Nonfiction: "Depends on the subject matter, but open to most nonfiction material." Is reviewing books for publication in new imprint, with shorter turn-around time and more titles published.

Booklocker—www.booklocker.com

Booklocker.com, 900-G Brookside Dr., Andover, MA 01810. Fax: (978)738-1924. Acquisitions: Angela Adair-Hoy. E-mail: angela@booklocker.com. Purchased by Deep South Publishing September 1999. 700 titles minimum. Releases 40 titles/month. Receives 150 submissions/month. Average acceptance rate: 40%. Average turnaround time on submissions: 2-4 weeks. Has author submission tracking system. Simsubs OK. Accepts queries, proposals, full manuscripts. File format preferred: PDF. Guidelines: www.booklocker.com/getpublished/published.html. Time between acceptance and publish date: 2-4 weeks. Pays: 70% on list price. Contract term: Nonexclusive. Sample contract: www.booklocker.com/contract.html. Distribution through Web site. File formats available: PDF. Delivery options: Download and CD-ROM. MATERIAL SOUGHT: "All genres: Fiction and nonfiction. However, authors should know that nonfiction how-to books are the best-sellers at Booklocker.com."

Bookmice—www.bookmice.com

Bookmice.com, Inc., PMB 257, 4291 Meridian St., Bellingham, WA 98226. Acquisitions: Aliske Webb. E-mail: Editor@Bookmice.com. Est. August 1999. 100 titles. Titles include *Sound the Ram's Horn* by S. Joan Popek, *Striking Back From Down Under* by Dr. Bob Rich. Average turnaround time on submissions: 6-8 weeks. Accepts simultaneous submissions. Submissions: Send synopsis with full ms. Submission format: PDF, HTML, PalmPilot, and on CD-ROM and Rocket. Guidelines: On Web site. Royalties: 50%. Contract term: 3 yrs, exclusive. Sample contract: www.bookmice.com/asamplecontract.htm. Provides free editing, book design, and layout for contracted books; paid editing available for $20/hour. File formats available: PDF and HTML. Delivery options: E-mail attachment. MATERIAL SOUGHT: Fiction genres/subgenres: Contemporary fiction, romance, SF/fantasy/paranormal (no gore or vampires), historical/western, children, teen, poetry. Nonfiction: Humor, self-help, philosophy, psychology/insight, biography/memoir, cookbooks, health/lifestyle. TIPS: "We look for quality writing, something fresh or a new slant on an old chestnut, and works of particular interest to women in all their various roles as workers, lovers, healers, mothers, daughters, spouses, adventurers, thinkers, entrepreneurs, wild women . . . you get the idea."

C&M Online Media—www.cmonline.com

3905 Meadow Field Lane, Raleigh, NC 27606. Imprint: Boson Books. Nancy McAllister, President. Submission e-mail: cm@cmonline.com. Est. 1994. 60 titles. Receives 15-30 submissions/month. Average turnaround time on submissions: 3-4 wks. Query with a well-organized and tightly composed synopsis in Rich Text Format (RTF). Guidelines: www.cmonline.com/boson/information/information.html. Time between acceptance and publish date: "Typically 3-5 months. This varies quite substantially, depending upon the number of submissions and other work that must be done." Royalties: 20%. Provides cover art, book design, layout. File formats available: PDF, RocketBook, SoftBook, Librius. Delivery options: Download, direct mail. MATERIAL SOUGHT: All genres considered. Boson publishes fiction, nonfiction, drama, and poetry. Provide a well-organized, tightly composed synopsis.

Crossroads Publishing Company—www.crossroadspub.com

806 N. Black St., Silver City, NM 88061. Sharon L Reddy, CEO (no period behind L, please). Kenneth A. Sheets, President. Leslie Chowlowsky, Head Editor. Cindy Penn, Children's Division. Gladys Fackler, Acquisition Editor. E-mail: acquisitions @crossroadspub.com. Nick Adams, Media Contact. Tracey Laird, Art Director. Steve Lazarowitz, Author Development Specialist. Est. March 1999. 120 titles. Average 10 releases/month, 85 submissions/month. Acceptance rate: 15% unsolicited; 85% referral. Turnaround time on submissions: 3 months. No simsubs. Response time on submissions: 2 weeks. To submit: Query with brief description, target audience, and 3 chapters or 10,000 wds. Submission format: RTF or Word 97. Guidelines: www.crossroadspub.com/Manu.htm. Time between acceptance and publish date: 3 months. Pays: 50%, 60% on well-edited previously published mss. Contract term: 1 yr from publication or 15 months from signing, automatically renewed. Standard contract: www.crossroadspub.com/contrac.htm. Provides story and copyedit, creation of cover with full participation of author, book design, and layout. File formats available: HTML designed for fault-free conversion to all other formats, RocketEdition; Print-on-demand available through association with

Sprout. MATERIAL SOUGHT: "Good books of all types, particularly unique books; cross-genre and experimental styles that are consistent and well written."

DiskUs Publishing—www.diskuspublishing.com

P.O. Box 43, Albany, IN 47320. Acquisitions: Marilyn Nesbitt. E-mail: DiskUsMail@aol.com or editor@diskuspublishing.com. Est. January 1996. 35 titles. 2-3 new releases/month. 100-150 submissions/month. Average acceptance rates: 5% maximum. Response time on submissions: 6-8 months. Submission tracking system available (see link on main page). Surface mail submissions only (no e-mail). "We want the entire manuscript on disk, a printout of the synopsis, and the first chapter." Submission format preferred: MS Word, WordPerfect, or RTF. Guidelines: www.diskuspublishing.com/submission.htm. Time between acceptance and publish date: 4-6 months. Royalties: 40% royalty on the US cost of downloads. Contract term: 1 yr, with a renewing contract available if both author and publisher agree. Sample contract: www.diskuspublishing.com/Contract.html. File formats available: PDF, HTML, PRC (Palm Pilot), RocketBook, SoftBook, Windows CE. Delivery options: Download, CD-ROM, disk, and e-mail attachment. MATERIAL SOUGHT: Nonfiction plus every fiction category except for erotica. DiskUs is also going to have books available in print format.

DLSIJ Press—dlsijpress.com

1717 E. Calumet St., PMB 188, Appleton, WI 54915. Acquistions: Ms. Sidney Jameson, sidney@dlsijpress.com. Est. November 1998. Releases 1 new title/month. 15-20 submissions/month. Average acceptance rate: 10%. Average turnaround time on submissions: 1-2 months. Simsubs OK. Prefers query plus sample. Submission format preferred: MS Word. Guidelines: dlsijpress.com/authors. Time between acceptance and publish date: 1-2 months. Royalties: 45%. Contract term: 3 yrs, electronic rights only. Sample contract: Available on request. Provides complete in-house editing involving author in process, cover art, book design, and layout. Distribution outlets: Several online e-bookstores: Barnes & Noble, Powell's, and e-campus distribute our RocketEditions. File formats available: PDF, Braille Printer-Friendly, RocketEdition; beginning to offer paperback. Delivery options: Download. Open to all types of work written by women.

Dreams Unlimited—www.dreams-unlimited.com

P.O. Box 543, 90 Village St., Northford, CT 06472. Tel: (203)484-9245. Fax:

(203)234-7824. Imprints: Daylight Dreams. Acquisitions: Bonnee Pierson. E-mail: editor@dreams-unlimited.com. Est. February 1998. 25 titles. Releases 1-4 titles/month. Receives 20-30 submissions/month. Average acceptance rate: 5-10%. Average turnaround time on submissions: 3 months. Provides submission tracking system for authors. Simsubs OK. Accepts proposals from authors who have already published with them; prefers complete manuscripts from new authors. On initial contact, prefers a query with synopsis. Submission format: Prefers RTF. Guidelines: www.dreams-unlimited.com/writers_guidelines.htm. Time between acceptance and publish date: 4-6 months. "Sometimes sooner, but we prefer to schedule out so we can generate reviews to coincide with the release of the book." Royalties: 30-40%. Pays an advance. Contract Term: Initial, 6 months; second contract is optional for 6-12 months. After the first yr, renewal is annual. Sample contract: www.dreams-unlimited.com/contract.htm. Provides full service on editing, cover art, book design, and layout. Distribution: "Our books are carried by three online bookstores, and we receive a number of orders through physical bookstores like Borders, B&N, and Amazon.com." File formats available: PDF, RTF upon special request and we've signed a contract with Librius, Inc. for formatting for palm readers. Delivery options: E-mail attachment or diskette. MATERIAL SOUGHT: Futuristic, fantasy, paranormal and gay/lesbian and erotic romances. To be developed is a line of contemporary and historical romances. No nonfiction.

Erotic-Ebooks.com—www.erotic-ebooks.com

P.O. Box 912, Andover, MA 01810. Acquisitions: Justine Solei. E-mail: webmistress@erotic-ebooks.com. Est. April 1999. 10 titles. Releases 2 titles/month. Receives 8 submissions/month. Average acceptance rate: 60%. Average turnaround time on submissions: 1-2 weeks. Simsubs OK. Send book proposal with writing sample. Submission format: PDF. Guidelines: www.erotic-ebooks.com/publisher.html. Our submission guidelines walk writers through the submission process and show them where to convert their books to PDF for free. Time between acceptance and publish date: 1-2 weeks. Royalties: 50%. Contract term: Nonexclusive. Sample contract: www.erotic-ebooks.com/publisher.html. Provides editing, cover art, book design, and layout. File format preferred: PDF. Delivery options: Download and e-mail. MATERIAL SOUGHT: Fiction: "Currently in need of romance novels with heavier love scenes than is the norm. However, our site attracts readers who want more than just romance in mind."

Nonfiction: Especially interested in how-to books of a sexual nature. TIPS: "Please read our guidelines for specific details as to what we need at the time you are reading this. As of this writing, we are seeking romance novels with graphic erotic scenes and books that teach readers how to explore their sexuality in a . . . recreational way. There are many sexual activities that people are curious about but are afraid to ask. We want to provide a category of how-to sex books that are not available anywhere else. Very open to suggestions for this category!"

The Fiction Works—www.fictionworks.com

P.O. Box 1066, Corvallis, OR 97339-1066. Tel: (541)953-8803, Fax: (541)752-0996. Imprint: Serious Business (nonfiction business titles). Ray Hoy, Publisher. E-mail: thefictionworks@home.com. Est. 1995. 200 titles minimum. Releases 10 titles/month. Receives 90-125 submissions/month. Average acceptance rate: 10%. Average turnaround time on submissions: 30-60 days. Author submission tracking system. Send full manuscript via e-mail attachment (only). Submission format: "E-mail attachments (only), in any format (PC, Mac, Word, WordPerfect, etc.—we can open anything)." Guidelines: www.fictionworks.com/guidelines.htm. Time between acceptance and publish date: 90 days. Royalties: 30% of retail for any title sold from our Web site (download or display case); split net profit with author for any download title sold through a major distributor; 15% of cover price for any display case title sold through a major. Contract term: 3 yrs. Sample contract: www.fictionworks.com/ebookagreemen t.htm. Provides basic editing, cover art, book design, and layout. File formats available: HTML, RocketBook, SoftBook. Delivery options: Download as well as display versions (floppy disk, 4-color cover, plastic case). MATERIAL SOUGHT: Fiction: All genres. Nonfiction: Self-improvement, reference works, business titles.

GLB—www.glbpubs.com

P.O. Box 78212, San Francisco, CA 94107. Tel: (415)621-8307. Contact: W.L. (Bill) Warner. E-mail: glbpubs@mindspring.com. Submission guidelines: www.glbpubs .com/ebookinfo.html. Est. 1989. 28 print books and 10 e-books plus novellas, short stories, plays, etc. 3-6 submissions/month. Average acceptance rate: 50%. Turnaround time on submissions: 3 weeks. No simsubs. Query first. Royalty rate: 50%. Contract term: 1 yr with automatic renewal. Provides general editing, book design, and layout. Author must pay part of cover art charge. File formats available: PDF, HTML, RTF, text, Rocket (RB), Word, and WordPerfect. Delivery options:

E-mail attachment. MATERIAL SOUGHT: Fiction genres: Gay, lesbian, bisexual, literate erotica OK, no outright porno; novels, novellas, short stories/collections, plays. Nonfiction: Essays, historical, political/lifestyles. Also poetry.

Hard Shell Word Factory—www.hardshell.com

P.O. Box 161, 8946 Loberg Rd., Amherst Junction, WI 54407. Fax: (715)824-3875. Contact: Mary Z. Wolf, Publisher and Editor-in-Chief. E-mail: submit@hardshell .com (submissions), books@hardshell.com (general). Est. November 1, 1996. 160 titles. 6-12 new titles/month. Receives 100 submissions/month. Average acceptance rate: 5-7%. Average turnaround time on submissions: 6-10 months. Submission tracking system for authors. Accepts simsubs if informed. Accepts submissions for incomplete mss, "if the author has at least a rough draft of the whole book." How to submit: "Proposal from authors not previously published in book length; proposal or cover letter and full manuscript from previously published authors." Submissions format: "Electronic: Either on disk or sent as an e-mail attachment. Proposals may come as hard copy, but complete and final submissions must be electronic." Guidelines: www.hardshell.com/guide.html. Time between acceptance and publish date: "3-8 months depending on genre (romance is the most booked out)." Royalties: "30% of retail download price for sales from our site; sales from bookstores and e-book distributors: 50% of net after deducting store or distributor's commission." Contract term: 1 yr with option for annual renewals on mutual agreement. Sample contract: www.hardshell.com/contract.html. Provides editing, cover, book design, and layout. File formats available: "HTML, PDF, RTF, Rocket, SoftBook, Librius, NetBooks, Peanut Press (Palm OS) WebTV at special request (book broken into smaller parts)." Delivery options: Disk, e-mail attachment, direct download, CD-ROM. MATERIAL SOUGHT: Fiction: Mystery/thriller/suspense, SF, fantasy, horror, historical, western, action/adventure, paranormal, romance (all subgenres except gay), humor/comedy, young adult and children's, literary, poetry collections, short-story collections, anthologies, and comic (illustrated) books." Nonfiction: "Self-help and health, true crime, business, computer, cooking, current events and political, travel, young adult and children's." TIPS: "Don't submit anything you don't think 'will make it' with a large publisher (unless it's a case of not fitting a particular marketing niche). Our standards are very high. Don't worry about your character's age, race, career, or the period or setting of the story. We have no 'rules' about these. If you write a great book we will publish it, and we especially like those stories that fall between the cracks of the NY publisher 'rules.' DON'T submit at this time: Sports books; highly specialized, technical works; plus, gay fiction or nonfiction, pornography."

Ltdbooks—www.ltdbooks.com

200 N. Service Rd. W., Unit 1, Suite 301, Oakville, Ontario L6M 2Y1 Canada. Acquisitions: Laura Adlam. E-mail: editor@ltdbooks.com. Est. November 1999. Releases 4 titles/month. 10-20 submissions/month. Average acceptance rate: 5%. Average turnaround time on submissions: 2-3 wks. Accepts simsubs if informed. Prefers query with synopsis and first 3 chapters. Submission format: Word or RTF. Guidelines: www.ltdbooks.com/Submission_Guidelines/submission_guidelines.html. Time between acceptance and publish date: 3 months. Royalties: 30%. Contract term: 2 yrs. Sample contract: www.ltdbooks.com/Sample_Contract/sample_contract.html. Provides editing and copyediting, full cover art by professional graphic artist, book design, and layout. File formats available: "Currently PDF, HTML (used in voice synthesis and other programs), and Rocket eBook Reader format. We plan to introduce Palm Pilot versions at the site as soon as possible." Delivery options: "Currently, we offer books as a download or on disk." MATERIAL SOUGHT: Fiction: All genres except erotica. Nonfiction: None. TIPS: "Please follow the submission guidelines at the site. We want the query, synopsis and first 3 chapters in either Word or RTF. Please don't send it in another format . . . we probably won't be able to open it and therefore cannot read it."

New Concepts—www.newconceptspublishing.com

New Concepts Publishing. Imprints: Category Duets: Nostalgia; Romantique: Long series romance. 4729 Humphreys Rd., Lake Park, GA 31636. Contact: Andrea DePasture, Senior Editor. Acquisitions: Margaret Wright. E-mail: ncp@newconceptspublishing.com (no e-mail submissions). Est. October 1996. 95 titles. 4-6 releases/month. Receives 50 submissions/month. Average acceptance rate: 5%. Average turnaround time on submissions: 4-6 months. Accepts simultaneous submissions if informed. Prefers full ms. Submission format preferred: "Hardcopy printout unless the book is coming from overseas, in which case we prefer Word or RTF on disk." Time between acceptance and publish date: "Varies. No more than 1 yr." Pays: $1/sale direct; 50¢/retail. Contract term: 1-4 yrs. Provides editing, cover art, book design, and layout. Distribution outlets: Via the Internet: Retail through Baker & Taylor distributors. File formats available: HTML, RTF, RocketEditions, Word. Delivery options: Disk and attachment. MATERIAL SOUGHT: Fiction. TIPS: "We want genre fiction that stretches the boundaries. We're always looking for really fresh story lines."

Online Originals—www.onlineoriginals.com

6th Floor, Charter House, 2 Farringdon Rd., London EC1M 3HP. Imprints: Online Originals "Editions," "Proofs." E-mail: editor@onlineoriginals.com. Est. December 1995. 100 titles. Releases 6-10 titles/month. Average submissions/month: 300-500. Average acceptance rate: 10-12/month. Average turnaround time on submissions: 3 months. Submission format preferred: MS Word saved as text only. Guidelines: www.onlineoriginals.com/submissions.html. Time between acceptance and publish date: 1-3 months. Royalties: 50%. Contract term: Full term of copyright with renegotiation possible. Provides full professional editing (including line editing and proofreading), professional typographic design and layout. File formats available: PDF, 3Com Palm (and Handspring Visor), text-only (for visually impaired), Rocket eBook, WinCE. MATERIAL SOUGHT: Fiction: "Most types of fiction, including novels for younger readers. Must be book length." Nonfiction: "Intellectual works proposing an idea and supporting it with research or rhetoric." TIPS: "We are most interested in the literary and intellectual end of the market."

Orpheus Romance—www.OrpheusRomance.com

Pinegrove P.O. Box 64004, Oakville, Ontario L6K 2C0 Canada. Tel: (905)337-2188. Fax: (905)337-0999. Imprints: Orpheus Romance, Greater Love Stories, Ozone. Dorothy Doiron, Editor. E-mail: editor@orpheusromance.com. Est. Fall 1995. 40 titles. Release 3 titles/month minimum. Receives 80 submissions/month. Average acceptance rate: 5%. Average turnaround time on submissions: 3 months. To submit material: Query with sample chapters, or complete story for shorts and novellas. Submission format: MS Word or RTF. Guidelines: www .OrpheusRomance.com/guidelines. Time between acceptance and publish date: 3 months. Royalties: 25%. Offers advance. Contract term: 5 yrs. Sample contract: www.OrpheusRomance.com/contract. Provides editing, cover art, book design, and layout, all by subcontracted professionals. File formats available: PDF, RocketEdition (plusHTML for short stories and some novellas). Delivery options:

"E-mail attachment or disk; download available soon (shorts and novellas are online at www.iReadRomance.com)." MATERIAL SOUGHT: Romance and sensual romance (erotica). TIPS: "We are looking for original stories, with rich settings, superiorly crafted."

Pagefree Publishing—www.booksonscreen.com

733 Howard St., Otsego, MI 49078. Tel: (616)692-3386. Fax: (616)692-3926. Imprints: Books OnScreen. Kim D. Blagg, President and Editor. E-mail: editor@books onscreen.com. Est. May 1999. 110 titles. Approximately 7 new releases each month. Publishes out-of-print titles. 20 submissions/month. Average acceptance rate: 75%. Average turnaround time on submission: 2 months. Simsubs OK. Query first for incomplete mss, or send full ms. Prefers rich-text format. Guidelines: submissions@ booksonscreen.com. Time between acceptance and publish date approximately 3 months. Royalties: 10-12% of Books OnScreen site price (average royalty is $2.47/ book sold). Contract term: 2-6 yrs. Sample contract: www.booksonscreen.com/ authorssite.html. Provides minimal editing, cover design and art, book design and layout. File formats available: PDF. Delivery options: CD-ROM and downloads within 2 months. MATERIAL SOUGHT: "Any but pornography, erotica, illegal, or tasteless topics."

Renaissance E-Books:—www.renebooks.com

P.O. Box 494, Clemmons, NC 27102-0494. Acquisitions: David O. Dyer Sr. E-mail: submissions@renebooks.com. Est. September 1999. 40 titles. Releases 0-5 titles/ month. Receives 30 submissions/month. Average acceptance rate: 50%. Average turnaround time on submissions: 1 week for rejections; 1 month for acceptances." Prefers full ms, but "authors may initially submit the first chapter if they prefer." Submission format preferred: MS Word 6.0 or higher, or RTF. Please note: E-mail submissions ONLY. Guidelines: renebooks.com/Guidelines.html. Time between acceptance and publish date: "Roughly 1 month. We publish within days of receipt of a signed contract from the author." Pays: "40% of the retail price of the e-book. Exceptions are spelled out in the contract." Contract term: 12 months, extended by mutual agreement. Provides limited editing, cover art, book design, and layout. Formats: PDF, Rocket eBook (RB), HTML, and RTF; other formats soon. Delivery options: E-mail attachment. MATERIAL SOUGHT: Fiction genres/subgenres: "We publish multigenre novels and short story collections with splashes of erotica.

Our lovers rarely disappear behind closed bedroom doors. Obviously, our books are for mature audiences." Does not publish nonfiction. TIPS: "We do not have the time or staff to rewrite manuscripts. We offer limited editing only. To date, all rejections have been based on poor sentence structure and punctuation. Read one or more of our titles or at least the excerpts on our Web site, and edit, edit, and edit some more before submitting."

SelfHelpBooks.com—www.SelfHelpBooks.com

A division of the Wellness Institute, Inc. 1007 Whitney Ave., Gretna, LA 70056. Tel: (504)361-1845. Fax: (504)365-0114. Acquisitions: Mindy Asby. E-mail: publisher @selfhelpbooksnow.com. Est. 1976. 60 titles minimum. Releases 5-7 books/month. Publishes out-of-print titles. Receives 15 submissions/month. Average acceptance rate: 70%. Average turnaround time on submissions: 3-4 weeks. Prefers full ms. Submission format: "Electronic—WordPerfect or Microsoft Word. Would also like a hard copy. Please send stamped, self-addressed envelope." Guidelines: www.SelfH elpBooks.com/submission.htm. Time between acceptance and publish date: 2-3 months. Royalty: 20%. Contract term: "All rights for as long we publish the book." Provides editing, cover art, book design, and layout. File formats: PDF. Delivery options: Download. MATERIAL SOUGHT: Fiction: "Fiction will be considered if it focuses on successful coping with adversity." Nonfiction: Self-help—"We publish problem-focused self-help books (*Freedom From Fear*, *Weight Control From Inside Out*, *How to Treat Depression*) and personal success stories of people who have triumphed over adversity (*Living With John—Dealing With Alzheimer's Disease in a Loved One*; *The Road to Hell and Back—How I Conquered Panic Fear and Drugs*; *Between Marriage and Divorce*; *Single Again and Surviving*)."

Word Wrangler—www.wordwrangler.com

Word Wrangler Publishing, Inc., 332 Tobin Creek Rd., Livingston, MT 59047. Tel: (406)686-4230. Fax: (406)686-4230. Acquisitions: Barbara Quanbeck. E-mail: WrdWranglr@aol.com. Est. August 1999. 15 titles. Release 2-6 titles/month. Receives 30 submissions/month. Average acceptance rate: 10%. Average turnaround time on submissions: 2-3 months. Accepts simultaneous submissions and submissions for incomplete mss. Prefers full mss. Submission format: TXT, WPS, RTF, DOC. Guidelines: www.wordwrangler.com/authorinfo.html. Time between acceptance and publish date: Approximately 60 days. Royalties: 50%. Contract term: 1

yr. Sample contract: www.wordwrangler.com/wwpcontractp.html. Provides editing, cover art, book design, and layout. File formats available: HTML (Win3.1/95/98 and Mac). Seeks wide variety of material.

Wordbeams—www.wordbeams.com

P.O. Box 23415, Portland, OR 97281-3415. Est. November 1999. Acquisitions: Susan Bodendorfer. E-mail: books@wordbeams.com. 48 titles. Releases 2-4 titles/month. Est. November 1999. Receives approximately 100 submissions/month. Average acceptance rate: 10%. Simsubs OK if informed. Mss must be fully completed before queries are accepted. Initial contact should include a cover letter; 3 to 5-page (double-spaced) synopsis; and entire ms. Submission format preferred: MS Word (any version) or RTF. Guidelines: www.wordbeams.com/guidelines.html. Time between acceptance and publish date: At least 2 months (to allow time for reviews). Has author submission tracking system. Pays: 35% of the US retail download price on all sales of their book sold through the publisher site. Contract term: 1 yr, renewed by mutual consent. Sample contract: www.wordbeams.com/contract.html. Provides editing, cover, book design and layout. Active marketing. File formats available: PDF, HTML, RocketEditions. Delivery options: E-mail, diskettes. MATERIAL SOUGHT: Fiction: "Commercial fiction including, mainstream fiction, women's fiction, romance novels, and all other genre and subgenre fiction, children's fiction, middle grade fiction, young adult fiction, short stories (which are grouped and published as anthologies)." Nonfiction: "Humor, humorous diet books, new age/metaphysical, meditation/visualization, self-help/self-healing, how-to books, inspirational, motivational, etc.; poetry (must be enough to fill a book—do not send single poems)." No textbooks. TIPS: In addition to reading guidelines, read FAQs (www.wordbeams.com/writer-faq.html) and page about rejection (www.wordbeams.com/rejection.html). Offers monthly newsletter.

Zeus Publications—www.zeus-publications.com

P.O. Box 2554, Burleigh MDC 4220 Qld. Australia. Tel: +61 7 55 755 141. Fax: +61 7 55 755 142. Contact: Bruce Rogers. E-mail: zeus@omcs.com.au. Est. August 1999. 90 titles. Releases 7-8 titles/month. Receives 15 submissions/month. Average acceptance rate: 30%. Average turnaround on submissions: 5-6 wks. Accepts simultaneous submissions. Accepts queries, proposals, and full mss. Submission format: Word, RTF, Text, Works, HTML. Guidelines: www.zeus-publications.com/new.ht

ml. Time between acceptance and publish date: 6-8 weeks. Royalties: 30%. Contract term: 12 months. Provides basic editing (charges only apply to rewrites and major editing jobs), cover art, book layout organization. Marketing: "We market titles on the Internet and submit to newspapers and magazines for review, based on advice from the author." Advertising: Online and at book fairs. File formats available: HTML, Word97, Text, RTF, Rocket. Delivery options: "Floppy disk, e-mail attachment." MATERIAL SOUGHT: All genres considered.

APPENDIX A

Further Reading

Allen, Moira. *Writing.com: Creative Internet Strategies to Advance Your Writing Career.* New York: Allworth Press, 1999.

Kilian, Crawford. *Writing for the Web.* North Vancouver: International Self-Counsel Press, 2000.

Tedesco, Anthony. *Online Markets for Writers: How to Make Money by Selling Your Writing on the Internet.* New York: Owl Books/Henry Holt & Co., 2000.

Author Bios

Many thanks to the hundreds of authors and editors who answered my survey about writing for the online marketplace. The following is a list of some of those I've mentioned specifically in my book.

Adair-Hoy, Angela. Self-published Internet writer, publisher of *The Write Markets Report* (writersweekly.com).

Alcorn, Pete. Pete Alcorn is the CEO of NetRead (www.netread.com), an online marketplace and resource for the book publishing community.

Allen, Mary Emma. Journalist, children's author, columnist, and editor.

Allen, Moira. Freelance writer, author of *Writing.com: Creative Internet Strategies to Advance Your Writing Career* (Allworth Press).

Appel, Cindy. Weekly online humor columnist at the Fort Worth *Star-Telegram* online, freelance writer, struggling novelist, wife, mother, and woman (not necessarily in that order).

Asp, Karen. Health and fitness writer whose credits include *Shape, Walking, Fit Pregnancy,* and *Fitness.*

Becker, Sabina. Author of several short stories and poems, and editor of e-zine *after/shock/thoughts.* (www.crosswinds.net/~thescholary).

Bickford, Carolyn J. Author of *Daft Musings* online newsletter; freelance writer for *Productopia.com, MacUser, Desktop Journal,* and other magazines.

Bracken, Michael. Author of *Deadly Campaign* (Books in Motion), *Even Roses Bleed* (Books in Motion), *Just In Time for Love* (Hard Shell Word Factory), *Psi Cops* (Books in Motion), and nearly seven hundred short stories, essays, and poems.

Burton, Elizabeth. Freelance writer.

Calvert, Pam. Freelance author for adult and children's magazines with over thirty articles/stories sold (www.50megs.com/pamcalvert/writersheaven.html).

Casanova, Mary. Author whose books continue to appear on state reading award lists around the country. She lives on the Minnesota-Canadian border (www.marycasanova.com).

Childers, Leta Nolan. Author of the number one best-selling e-book in 1999, *The Best Laid Plans*, (www.diskuspublishing.com), co-owns site that provides services to authors and publishers (www.pubpromos.com).

Cooper-Posey, Tracy. National award-winning, best-selling author (www.sashaproductions.com).

Dorner, Jane. Author of eighteen books including *The Internet: A Writer's Guide* (A&C BLack), is also involved with Web publishing. She became involved in the new tools for authors when writing a report for the British Library called "Authors and Information Technology."

Dunham, Alison. Author and relationship expert (users.rcn.com/adunham).

Ehmann, Lain Chroust. Freelance writer.

Engle, Jamie. Freelance writer and editor of eBook Connections (eBookConnections.com).

Enos, Lori. Author of *The Portable Coach* (Hard Shell Word Factory), co-creator of the site Cyberlife: Your Guide to Life Online.

Estigarribia, Diana. Freelance writer.

Feldcamp, John. CEO of Xlibris, a print-on-demand publishing service (www.xlibris.com).

Gahran, Amy. Content consultant Amy Gahran (gahran.com) is the editor of *Contentious* (contentious.com). She also co-edits the online newsletter *Content Spotlight*, and is VP of Content Exchange (content-exchange.com).

Gilks, Magee. Freelance writer.

Gollnick, Kim Swenson. Freelance writer.

Graham, Bob. Freelance writer.

Guran, Paula. Teacher, critic, and editor of a newsletter for Writers on the Net (www.writers.com) *DarkEcho*, a weekly newsletter for horror writers (www.dark echo.com).

Gustafsson, Katie. Freelance writer.

Guth, Tracy. Freelance editor-writer—books, magazines, online.

Harrington, Cheryl Cooke. Author of three hardcover romances with Avalon Books before testing the e-waters with a short romantic suspense, best-selling *One for Sorrow, Two for Joy* (Hard Shell Word Factory). (www3.symptico.ca/harrington).

Hewitt, John. Editor and author, maintains Writer's Resource Center (www.poewar.com).

Hopkins, Brian. Author of more than sixty stories in a variety of professional and semiprofessional magazines and anthologies (www.sff.net/people/brian_a_hopkins).

Jenks, Ken. Online editor and publisher.

Kilian, Crawford. Author of twenty books, most recently *Writing for the Web* (International Self-Counsel Press). (www.capcollege.bc.ca/magic/cmns/crofpers.html).

Klocke, Angela Giles. Publisher of several free online newsletters, including those that help writers (www.klockepresents.com).

Ladouceur, Lisa. Freelance music journalist who has sold over forty music reviews, news pieces, artist interviews, and features online.

Lay, Kathryn. Author of "The Healing Truth," short fiction that is included in Bruce Coville's anthology, *A Glory of Unicorns* (Scholastic Press).

Ledford, Jerri. Freelance writer with more than 250 publications credits.

Lowe, Tasha. Author of dozens of published articles and the comics series Raggedy Man, President of Friends of Lulu (FoL).

McQuillin, Kristen. Freelance writer living in Japan (www.lm.com/~kristen).

Nesbitt, Marilyn. CEO of DiskUs Publishing.

Nourie, Dana. Freelance writer, maintains Writers' Guidelines Database (www.writersdatabase.com) and *Freelance Success* (www.freelancesuccess.com).

Oriah Mountain Dreamer. Poet, author of *The Invitation* (HarperSanFrancisco).

Outing, Steve. Journalist and Internet entrepreneur, CEO and founder of Content Exchange (www.content-exchange.com). He also writes a column, "Stop the Presses!" about interactive media for *Editor & Publisher Interactive*, and is recognized internationally as an expert on online journalism.

Pirillo, Chris. Author of *Poor Richard's E-mail Publishing* (Verulam Publishing). Writes and publishes a daily e-mail newsletter called *Lockergnome* (www.lockergnome.com).

Price, Nancy. Editor and co-owner of *Myria* (myria.com), *Interactive Parent* (interactiveparent.com), *SheKnows* (sheknows.com), and *ePregnancy* (epregnancy.com). She and Managing Editor Betsy Gartrell-Judd use freelancers for all but *SheKnows.com*. Price has been a freelance writer since her teens.

Reynaga, Christopher. Novelist, editor of *The Write Market*. (www.WriteMarket.com).

Rose, M.J. Author of *Lip Service* (Pocket Books), coauthor of *The Secrets of Our Success* (Deep South Publishing), an e-book about how to self-publish and self-promote on the web. (mjrose.com).

Sagert, Kelly Boyer. Author of *'Bout Boomerangs, America's Silent Sport* (Plant Speak Products and Publications) and managing editor of *Over the Back Fence* magazine (www.backfence.com).

Saperstein, David. Author, screenwriter, director. One of his novels, *Cocoon* (Jove), was turned into a movie by director Ron Howard and ended up winning two Academy Awards. (www.darkagain.com).

Saundby, Kate. Author. Two of her science fiction fantasy titles are coming out in Starlight Writer Publications' new Starfarer line, and Crossroads Publishing is reissuing her popular Nublis series.

Schick, Charlie. Editor for the Hello Direct Information Network, columnist, and author of numerous scientific publications. (www.edubba.com).

Sharples, Diane. Co-editor of *Electric Wine*, an online magazine of science fiction, fantasy, and horror (www.electricwine.com).

Sheldon, Howard. Freelance writer.

Shelley, Susan Jean. Author of *Dance With the Demons* true-crime series, poet, and cartoonist.

Soon Lee, Mary. Speculative fiction author (www.cs.cmu.edu/~mslee/mag.html).

Terhune, Margaret. Music reviewer, FamilyWonder.com.

Thomaston, Carmel. Writer. Published in nonfiction and book-length fiction. She publishes *The Rock* magazine and owns Paintedrock.com writers colony.

Tibbetts, Peggy. Novelist, editor. Her stories and articles have appeared in *Wee Wisdom, I Love Cats, The Writer*, and *Cross Country Skier*, among others.

Towse, Sal. Freelance writer and online researcher, working for a Silicon Valley dot-com startup.

Walton-Porter, Bev. Freelance writer-editor whose work has appeared in many well-known writer's publications.

Wardlaw, Lee. Award-winning children's book author. Titles include *101 Ways to Bug Your Parents* (Dial Books for Young Readers) and *Hector's Hiccups* (Random House) (www.leewardlaw.com).

Wright, Richard. Author of *Cuckoo* (Hard Shell Word Factor) and *Apocalypse Year: The Book of Days* (Blindside Publishing). (darkterrains.cjb.net).

Yudkin, Marcia. Author of *Writing Articles About the World Around You* (Writer's Digest Books) and other books and magazine articles (www.yudkin.com/publish.htm.).

Zukowski, John. Author of *John Zukowski's Definitive Guide to Swing for Java 2* (A Press) and the Focus on Java guide at About.com (www.zukowski.net/~jaz.).

Index

Get Published Online
and Everywhere Else With
Writer's Digest Books!

The Writer's Market Companion—Complementing the "where-to" information in *Writer's Online Marketplace*, this "how-to" guide features an easy-to-reference format you can quickly browse to find solutions and guidelines for all kinds of writing issues. *#10653/$19.99/352 pages/paperback*

Guerrilla Marketing for Writers—Packed with proven insights and techniques, this practical manual shows you 100 no-cost, low-cost ways to sell your books, before and after they're published. Written by the master of Guerrilla Marketing, Jay Conrad Levinson! *#10667/$14.99/224 pages/paperback*

Get Organized, Get Published—In this lively, inspirational, browsable book, you'll find a plethora of easy-to-find, easy-to-use tips for organizing and managing the writing life and for staying motivated. *#10689/$18.99/256 pages/hardcover*

Insider's Guide to Getting an Agent—This book simplifies the publishing industry, explaining exactly what literary agents do and what you should and should not expect from them. You'll learn how to research and contact agents, plus write agent queries, proposals, synopses, outlines, cover letters and follow up correspondence. *#10630/$16.99/240 pages/paperback*

Your Novel Proposal From Creation to Contract—The only guide of its kind created just for fiction writers. Drawing upon the insights of experienced authors, editors and agents, it provides you with the crucial information you need to get published in today's rapidly changing fiction industry. *#10628/$18.99/256 pages/hardcover*

Jump Start Your Book Sales—Here is the information you need to generate thousands of additional sales—fantastic ideas for booking author events, signings, TV appearances and radio interviews, and promoting on the Web. *#10623/$19.95/320 pages/paperback*

Writer's Digest Handbook of Making Money Freelance Writing—A collection of articles by top writers, editors and agents, this manual helps part-time and full-time freelancers find income-producing opportunities and make the most of them. *#10501/$19.99/320 pages/hardcover*

Formatting & Submitting Your Manuscript—Throughout this easy-to-use guide, dozens of charts, lists, models and sidebars show you everything you need to know to submit your work correctly and enhance your chances of being published. *#10618/$18.99/208 pages/paperback*

How to Write Irresistible Query Letters—This popular book shows writers how to increase their chances of a sale by pre-selling the idea via a query letter that's too good to turn down. It's the most indispensable tool and companion that an author can have. *#10146/$12.99/144 pages/paperback*

Writing the Novel From Plot to Print—Lawrence Block, recently named Grand Master of Mystery Writing, covers every step of the novel writing and selling process to help you to deliver a salable manuscript to the right editor's desk. *#2747/$14.99/218 pages/paperback*

How to Write & Sell Your First Novel—The proven, definitive resource for first novelists. Newly revised and updated, this guide reveals the keys to writing and publishing a successful novel in today's complicated market. *#10530/$16.99/272 pages/paperback*

The Writer's Digest Flip Dictionary—You know what you want to say but can't think of the word. This book provides the answer, offering cues and clue words to lead you to the exact phrase or specific term you need. It's an indispensable desk reference, as necessary as a dictionary or thesaurus, but a whole lot more fun. *#10690/$24.99/704 pages/hardcover*

How to Write Attention-Grabbing Query & Cover Letters—Use the secrets John Wood reveals to write perfectly tailored queries that are too good to turn down. If you want to make yourself stand out from the pack and receive a quick response, you must have this book! *#10707/$14.99/208 pages/paperback*

Facts in a Flash—Take the frustration out of research projects with this unique reference—an exceptional mix of humor, data and savvy research techniques. From libraries, newspapers and the Internet to scholars, experts and directories, you'll learn how to access hundreds of viable resources for virtually every subject. *#10632/$24.99/432 pages/hardcover*

Roget's Superthesaurus, Second Edition—With more than 400,000 words, including 2,000+ new and expanded entries, *Roget's Superthesaurus* offers you more features than any other word reference on the market. Also features a timesaving "reverse dictionary" and sample sentences. *#10541/$19.99/672 pages/paperback*